Critical Acclaim for *The Past i*

"Faith Gibson's wide-ranging and impeccably researched book links theory and practice relating to reminiscence work in a way that is accessible, informative, and inspiring. This book is exactly what care workers, their managers, family members, and older people themselves will want to read and read again. This is the definitive text for practitioners who are looking for ways to enhance the lives of the people they work with through recall of the past. Using research-based evidence as well as her own observations and experience she demonstrates the rewards of reminiscence work for older and younger people and her treatment of reminiscence approaches is all the more engaging given her ability to deal convincingly with debates and controversies in the field."

—Professor Joanna Bornat,
coeditor Oral History

"Those working with reminiscence have long needed such a comprehensive guide to good practice. Faith Gibson writes with the authority and wisdom derived from long experience as a pioneer in the field. This book deserves a place in every health and social welfare centre serving older people."

—Professor Peter G. Coleman,
President, International Institute
for Reminiscence and Life Review

"This book is a valuable contribution to understanding the processes of reminiscence and their benefits for use with older adults. The author's impressive experience with the use of reminiscence will convince the reader of the advantages of the constructive use of the recall of life-long memories. The constructive use of memories is the basic theme of the book. The author describes how recalling the past can contribute to helping older persons get in touch with their past lives. They integrate their lives and move toward achieving a higher quality of life. She describes different settings and different audiences from the healthy to those with limitations, including dementia, in which reminiscence and the recounting of life stories can be helpful.

The book is well grounded in contemporary knowledge about the processes of memory and how they can be focused on helping individuals find meaning in their lives. Reconciling the past as lived in the context of present life can be a difficult task. The author shows ways that it can be helped in group processes oriented to the recalling of life stories with their many events.

The reader is provided with an impressive review of the relevant literature. Research on memory and evaluations of practice methods with reminiscence have an expanding future. We have much to learn, but Faith Gibson encourages us to use what has already been learned about reminiscence processes employed with many populations and in many settings. Reminiscence can be therapeutic for older persons when guided by informed and skillful leaders using the principles described in this book."

—James E. Birren, Ph.D.,
Associate Director,
UCLA Center on Aging

The Past *in* the Present

The PAST *in* the PRESENT

USING REMINISCENCE
in Health and Social Care

by

FAITH GIBSON, M.A.

HEALTH
PROFESSIONS
PRESS

Baltimore • London • Winnipeg • Sydney

Health Professions Press
Post Office Box 10624
Baltimore, Maryland 21285-0624

www.healthpropress.com

Typeset by Barton Matheson Willse & Worthington, Baltimore, Maryland.
Manufactured in the United States of America by
Versa Press, East Peoria, Illinois.

The cases that appear in this book are based on actual cases. Fictitious names
have been used in some of these cases, and permission has been granted for the
cases in which real names are used.

Library of Congress Cataloging-in-Publication Data

Gibson, Faith.
    The past in the present: using reminiscence in health and social care / by Faith Gibson.
      p.   cm
    Includes bibliographical references and index.
    ISBN 1-878812-87-4
      1. Reminiscence in old age—Therapeutic use. 2. Reminiscing—Therapeutic use.
    3. Dementia—Patients—Rehabilitation. I. Title.

    RC451.4.A5G53 2004
    155.67—dc22   2003067639

British Library Cataloguing in Publication data are available from the British Library

To Benjamin, Robert, Rebecca, and James, our grandchildren...

May you each accept the past, enjoy the present, and look forward to the future.

CONTENTS

ABOUT THE AUTHOR

Faith Gibson, M.A., is Emeritus Professor of Social Work in the University of Ulster, Northern Ireland. She holds degrees in psychology, education, and social work and is a graduate of the Universities of Sydney, Queensland, and Chicago. While a student in the School of Social Service Administration at the University of Chicago, she received awards from the University of Chicago and the American Association of University Women as well as a Fulbright travel award.

While her earlier social work career was in the child care field, Faith Gibson has been interested in social work practice, policy, research, and teaching concerned with aging for more than thirty years. She is widely known for her writing concerned with social work, social gerontology, dementia care, and reminiscence theory and practice.

FOREWORD

This is a great book, and I am honored to write this foreword at a time when telling one's story is the linchpin not only for conducting reminiscing and life review sessions but for using many varied therapies and oral history techniques. Accounts of the use of reminiscence have been ongoing since the times of Aristotle and Socrates, but today the method has come into its own as an important and self-preserving process. Once the domain of older people, reminiscing and life review are now seen as important developmental tools used throughout a lifetime, starting in childhood when one is old enough to have memories. We are at the threshold of an interesting renaissance in the decade of the brain, and the use of memory plays an important part in that renaissance. Reminiscence and life review may surface as the most important pathways to a peaceful existence with our past and thus a hopeful future.

Since the 1990s, there have been many literary contributions to the field of reminiscence but never one that explains the processes so clearly and definitively as this book does. This book is truly the work of an expert practitioner who can share her knowledge in a helpful format for all to use the modalities in practice. A practitioner, who is also a gifted writer, Faith Gibson has added to our expertise in this field of storytelling. Starting with her beliefs in the processes after decades of personal use for her clients, Gibson discusses the interactive process of memory, open to constant editing and based on life experiences, as a pathway to deriving comfort and self-knowledge as one grows older. She defines reminiscence, recall, review, and partial reconstruction as the building blocks of memory work and simplifies the work of the brain to be more understandable to readers of every level.

In Chapter 3 she explores reminiscence as a tool for staff development, something not done in other books, and uses her extensive teaching experience to lay out a format for the reader. Particularly helpful are the figures that summarize and explain the content. These figures can help administrators incorporate reminiscing modalities into their institutions—something needed to humanize what is often a sterile environment.

Parts II and III offer practical guidance to those who wish to follow in Gibson's footsteps. Gibson shines in her discussion of reminiscing with people who have dementia. She generously shares her lifetime experiences and knowledge base with clarity and conciseness. Gibson continues to take giant steps in her discussion of the promotion of social inclusion through reminiscence, using the Troubles in Belfast as one of several examples. These examples can easily be translated to the southern United States where many have undergone similar injustices due to segregation, or they can be translated to Europe to the Jews who suffered during the Holocaust. Perhaps these memories can also be used to teach the rest of us that we are not unique but a part of the injustice that pervades the world and thereby endowed with a responsibility to challenge it.

"Thank you" is the only way to end this foreword. Thank you, Faith Gibson, for sharing a lifetime of insightful thinking that will serve the younger generations as they carry the old knowledge forward and meld it with new discoveries. This book is truly a gift to the reminiscers of the future.

Barbara K. Haight, Dr.P.H., R.N., FAAN
Professor Emeritus
College of Nursing
Medical University of South Carolina

INTRODUCTION

The Past in the Present is based on the conviction that although each of us is unique, our singular identity and personhood can only be fully experienced in loving relationship and communication with other people. Whatever the present holds for each of us we can only live comfortably with it—and dare to be hopeful about the future—if we have come to understand and accept our personal past. If we are to reach such understanding we need to dare to tell our stories, first to ourselves and then to others. It is through this process of storytelling and being assured that our stories have been heard that we come to understand who we are and what our lives might mean.

When thinking about the modern reminiscence and life review movement, several characteristics are apparent. The theory and practice of reminiscence and life review straddle many boundaries. Although multidimensional, multiprofessional, multidisciplinary, and multicultural, reminiscence is also intergenerational and international. It embraces a range of approaches and activities with individuals, couples, small groups, and communities both of interest and of place. It embraces intellectual, emotional, physical, creative, and spiritual aspects of life. Paradoxically reminiscence is both intrapersonal and interpersonal; it encourages introspection and private reflection yet promotes sociability and engagement with others. Much reminiscing takes place in the company of others and may be purposely organized; it also occurs in private, with or without special preparation. Although not regarded as entertainment, reminiscence is frequently lighthearted and entertaining; it can also be sad and distressing. Although not a therapy, it is usually therapeutic.

Although reminiscence is not restricted to old age, the growing number of people living to advanced old age means that interest in reminiscence and life review is increasing. More and more people are using reminiscence to assist them to reflect upon their past lives, now largely lost except to memory or preserved in more tangible reminders of the times through which they have lived. A growing interest in spirituality or a search for meaning in late life parallels this considerable interest in reminiscence. Psychology, philosophy, history, religion, and the creative arts intersect in the experience of many older people who pursue their quest for meaning making down many and varied paths, including reminiscence and life review.

Reminiscence can be thought of as re-membering again what has been forgotten without needing to relearn it (Erdelyi, 1996). The past that was can never be recaptured except through the processes of remembering, recall, review and partial reconstruction in the imagination. Each subsequent re-visiting or recalling of the past inevitably involves reconstructing it, and in this process we reconstruct ourselves. All re-membering seems to involve a process of over-writing rather than obliterating the previously remembered version. In our imaginations we construct our stories, and by telling our stories to other people we consolidate our sense of personal identity. The recall and recording in one form or another of past memories and the stories that they nourish has become for many people an important part of making sense of their life's journey. The stories told about that journey are not assets to be stripped or plundered; they are a gift, and those to whom they are entrusted should guard them well.

Butler, whose 1963 article is widely regarded as the inspirational foundation of the contemporary reminiscence movement, more recently suggested,

> While it is useful to develop objective, quantitative, psychological, and psychosocial measures of reminiscence and life review, perhaps their strength lies ultimately in the qualitative realm—reflecting a kind of meditation on an individual's vanished world, that is, one's own life and the anticipated loss of self as one grows older and experiences the rising expectation of death. The life review may help guide individuals during the final stage and help organize a sense of one's own life purpose. (Butler, 1999, p. 36)

Reminiscence and life review serve many different functions for diverse people and different functions for the same person at different times. Reminiscence does not have a discrete body of theory but draws from many disciplines and is nurtured by many sources. Reflecting this diversity, many professions use it in many varied contexts. In some ways reminiscence is regarded as a normal, everyday, straightforward part of life, something that we all know about and most of us engage in from time to time. Yet its complexity and diversity has attracted the interest and attention of researchers and practitioners from many different academic and professional backgrounds. Reminiscence work is still evolving and developing. As it simultaneously draws ideas from autobiographical memory, oral history, and the creative arts, it deepens its theoretical and therapeutic base while extending and broadening its myriad applications; herein lies its attractiveness, dynamic strength, rewards, and challenges.

Memory plays a central part in forming our subjective understanding of our individual selves throughout our lives and our collective identities as citizens of nation states and increasingly of the world at large, for we are all captives of our personal and collective memories. Because memory is a dynamic, not a static, source of ideas and imagination whose meanings are open to change, interpretation, and to some extent reconstruction, each time we recall them, we all retain an ability to re-make our lives and contribute toward the re-making of our fractured communities.

In reminiscence work we are seeking to explore where we started and where we have arrived, and through the partial reconstruction of our memories, to paraphrase T.S. Eliot, we come to know the place as if for the first time or in a different way. Understanding these processes of how memories are acquired, recovered, and reconstructed challenges the most learned brain scientists. Yet these same processes bring immense pleasure to people of all ages who meanwhile understand almost nothing of the neuroscience, biochemistry, and physiology of the complex neural processes involved. Nonetheless we all have available to us almost limitless possibilities for enlarging our understanding of the past and using this understanding for enriching our lives in the present.

Increasingly reminiscence is being used in conjunction with other therapies and artistic activities or as a bridge or pathway into them. Reminiscence is particularly valuable if used in this way because reminiscence is usually an acceptable and easy way to establish initial contact and to convey genuine interest in and empathy for others. Consequently reminiscence deepens relationships and demonstrates respect for and appreciation of other people and the life each has lived. It can be used on its own or in association with other approaches with individuals, couples, or small groups. It fits well with multidisciplinary and multiprofessional approaches based on mutual respect and under circumstances in which knowledge, skills, and experience complement each other and are grounded in a common value base.

Although the scope of this book goes beyond the realm of older people, its major emphasis is on older people. The values, knowledge, and skills that it seeks to explain are founded on the conviction that whatever we do, we need to do something in terms of making an effort to communicate with and relate to other people, regardless of age. The worst mistake we can make as members of families and communities—and whether we are artists, teachers, health and welfare professionals, museum and library staff, or community workers—is to assume that we and those who we encounter day-by-day are self-sufficient and independent. Because each one of us is bound together with others in inter-dependent relationships, we all have a responsibility to attempt to reach out to others, for none of us is self-sufficient. As the capacity and opportunity for people to make this effort diminishes for whatever personal or contextual reason, our responsibility to reach out becomes all the greater.

> Controversy often erupts over who should be doing group work with older people. Professionals tend to guard their territory zealously and to feel that nonprofessionals doing group work will unleash strong feelings and emotions with which they cannot deal. This attitude sells older individuals short: They are a tough lot. The danger is not in the practice of group work with older adults: the real danger is in not conducting groups and thereby fostering the still-prevalent attitude of "therapeutic nihilism." It is better to take a risk than to sit by and watch apathy, fear, sensory deprivation, loneliness, and helplessness continue in older adults. (Burnside, 1984, p. iv)

Burnside's position, although especially applicable to older people, is equally relevant to many other people contending with diminished life chances, poverty, disabilities, and problems in living. Her focus on group work also embraces individuals and her call to responsible, concerned action, even in the face of incomplete knowledge and rudimentary skills, is as relevant to this century as to the last. Despite much progress, too little has changed in the human service professions; much still remains to be done.

A life span developmental perspective informs this book, and I hope that professional people from many different backgrounds will find it relevant. Regardless of particular professional allegiances, we all need to take responsibility for making it possible for any person who wants to tell his or her life story to have access to a person who is willing, able, and prepared to listen. It has been said that we lose our souls when someone else takes it upon him- or herself to tell our story. This reaction is not inevitable, and there will be some people who, because of disabilities or special circumstances, may need assistance in telling their story and being heard. It is important that skilled help is available to those who need it so that they can tell their own story, in their own way, and in doing so feel enriched rather than diminished.

Much reminiscence and life review work has traditionally taken place in health and welfare facilities, but increasingly it is also occurring in many different community settings. Whatever the context and whatever sponsoring agency is involved, if high standards are to be achieved senior staff must endorse and support the process. It is essential that all reminiscence facilitators—whether they are staff members, volunteers, or independent practitioners—be interested in reminiscence, equipped to undertake it, and supported in their efforts. Good practice requires that all reminiscence sessions whether with individuals, couples, or small groups are well planned, well resourced, and regularly evaluated.

There are both technical and artistic aspects to reminiscence work. "If technique without feeling is ineffectual, feeling without technique is inefficient. If technical competence without compassion is sterile, compassion without competence is an exercise in futility" (Kadushin, 1978, p. 4). For reminiscence work is still both art and science, a confluence of the imaginative and the therapeutic, requiring both feeling responses and technical skill. One without the other, or concentration on one at the expense of the other, will fail to achieve the varied possibilities for people of all ages inherent in using recall of the past to enrich the present and give courage for the future. The justification for using art, if justification is needed in this increasingly technology-ridden world, is well summed up by an unknown author:

> Art gives hope—a hope that transcends the immediate world of experience. Creative activity provides a counterbalance to all that is restrictive, pedestrian, ordinary, and limiting in our lives as we age, becoming almost imperceptibly but inevitably the captives of diminishing physical health, reduced energy, and shrinking social circles. Feeding the world of the imagination is as essential as nourishing the physical body. And if we attend to one and not the other, we hasten dreariness and death.

The term *reminiscence therapy* is commonly but inaccurately used regardless of who is undertaking it, for what purpose, and within what service context. Bluck and Levine (1998) preferred the term *technique.* I prefer the term *reminiscence work.* Only when professionals who hold a recognized therapy qualification use particular types of reminiscence for specific purposes in clinical settings might the term reminiscence therapy sometimes be appropriate. Therapy suggests illness or malfunction with intervention by an expert who is employed to assess, diagnose, and treat in order to remedy a disease, defect, or malfunction. People alone can be regarded as experts in terms of recalling and recounting their own personal life experience, and they need to be affirmed as such. They are not necessarily ill or suffering from an identified condition (although some may be) that can be cured by prescribed reminiscence therapy.

The term *therapy* also conveys a misleading precision, a spurious exactness, and sits uncomfortably with the free flowing creativity and diversity so characteristic of most reminiscence exchanges. The term *work* on the other hand suggests serious mutual engagement in a shared enterprise. Therapy suggests an imbalance of power, status, knowledge, and authority. It elevates the professional healer or superior leader and conflicts with the egalitarian mutuality of most reminiscence work. Many reminiscence workers or facilitators may not hold recognized health qualifications and there is no widely recognized specific qualification in reminiscence and life review work, as far as I am aware. Although training and preparation are necessary and supervision highly desirable, to use the terms *therapy* and *therapist* in this connection is misleading and may create false expectations.

The term *work*, rather than *therapy*, reflects a strengths perspective and a person-centered approach. It stresses the importance of interpersonal relationships, mutual interdependency, and active participation. It rejects negative stereotyping and emphasizes empowerment, citizenship, and development throughout the entire life course. It recognizes each person as the authority on his or her own life. Much reminiscence practice occurs in contexts unrelated to health and social welfare. It is well established in schools, colleges, museums, libraries, arts organizations, community clubs, and groups of many kinds. Such organizations would describe their mission more in educational, artistic, citizenship, recreational, or community service terms. The idea of these organizations delivering therapy would be inappropriate, misleading, and probably unacceptable. They are likely to have other objectives and legitimately seek other outcomes from reminiscence work.

Discussion about the meaning of memory, remembering, imagination, and creativity is found in the literature of many disciplines, including neuroscience, biology, physiology, psychology, artificial intelligence, philosophy, history, literature, art, and many clinical or therapeutic human service professions. This book does not attempt to encompass this vast range of learning and practice expertise yet in many different direct and indirect ways it draws from all of these rich streams. I hope that it will inform the practice of professionals and also encourage volunteers and family caregivers to use reminiscence and to reminisce themselves. I have tried to provide sufficient relevant background theory to interest, inform, and justify the practical applied suggestions that are aimed at contributing to the well being and life satisfaction of people of diverse ages and varied life circumstances.

To do this is a tall order, and where my understanding of the theoretical ideas is incomplete or fails adequately to represent their complexity, or where the practice interventions appear to be confused, simplistic, or irrelevant, I alone must bear responsibility. It would be easy to ignore the literature of contributing disciplines and to write a simple how-to-do-it kind of reminiscence cookbook. Alternately, it would be easy to become so overwhelmed by the extent and erudition of writing about memory that stretches back over many centuries to decide the task is impossible and should be abandoned. It seems to me, having spent many years researching, practicing, teaching, and thinking about memory and reminiscence work, that either response is inadequate. So despite my acute awareness of all the pitfalls, I hope that readers will be intrigued about memory and will explore for themselves some of the implications of remembering in order to nourish their own and other people's lives. For although I have made strenuous efforts not to over-state the case for reminiscing, I hope that its exciting possibilities and numerous benefits are made clear so that we come to appreciate how reminiscence helps us to enjoy life but even more profoundly to endure it with hope.

The book has three parts. Part I considers memory, aging, and values, the why and what of reminiscence and the ways in which staff who use reminiscence may benefit. Part II gives guidance about planned reminiscence and life review with individuals, couples, and small groups, shows how to capture personal and collective memories in tangible ways, and shows how it might assist marginalized communities. These chapters seek to answer the how-to-do-it questions. Part III considers aspects of memory, dementia, and creativity and concentrates specifically on adapting reminiscence practice for people who have dementia and involving families, volunteers, adult day services, and residential staff in using it to encourage communication and preserve relationships.

ACKNOWLEDGMENTS

I am indebted to many people who have reminisced with me and helped me to understand something about the processes involved. Without doubt, my best teachers have been the many children, adolescents, and adults of various ages and circumstances who have shared their life stories and their life experiences with me. My husband has patiently survived my preoccupation with reminiscence over many years, and colleagues and friends in the European, Northern Ireland, and United Kingdom Reminiscence Networks have been a wonderful source of ideas, constructive criticism, and encouragement. I thank them all. I am especially grateful to Barbara Haight for writing the foreword for this book, Sue Ballinger, Michael Bender, Sue Benson, and Joanna Bornat for permission to reproduce material, and the staff of Health Professions Press for all of their publishing expertise and assistance. I would also like to thank the individuals and organizations that contributed photographs.

PART I

REMINISCENCE THEORY AND VALUES

Part I aims to provide a theoretical framework within which to locate the other two applied parts of this book. Different types of memory are outlined in order to help practitioners deepen their understanding of how to stimulate memories and assist people to reflect constructively on recalled memories. Present knowledge about how memory actually works is very incomplete and the relationship between mind and brain remains obscure. Some of the major definitions of reminiscence and life review will be examined and particular attention paid to formulations of the various functions or purposes reminiscence and life review serve for those who engage in it. The values that underlie and inform reminiscence practice in different contexts are explored, and this discussion then leads to examining how reminiscence work affects staff members who undertake it and the ways in which staff members may benefit personally and professionally from involvement in reminiscence work.

Chapter 1

Reminiscence, Age, and Memory

Reminiscence is regarded as part of autobiographical memory and life review as a special kind of reminiscence. Stafford described the process: "Memory is made as a quilt is made. From the frayed cloth of time, frayed scraps of sensation are pulled apart and pieced together in a pattern that has a name when memory rekindles the past" (cited in McConkey, 1996, p. 82). Our memories are not fixed and unchangeable, deposited in one big vault or filing cabinet in spatially segregated parts of the brain; rather, "memories are dynamic and dispersed, located in different ways in different parts of the brain" (Rose, 1992, p. 316).

This chapter examines current understanding about the nature of reminiscence, memory, and how and what people of different ages at different stages of the life span tend to remember. It considers how long- and short-term memory influence reminiscence and recall. Many reminiscence workers pay meager attention to what is known about different kinds of memory and how we call on our memories to provide the basic bricks for constructing and reconstructing our life stories that represent our unique identity. Memory making is considered to be at least in part a reconstructive process, whereby personal meanings, pervaded by emotions, inform the stories we recount from the memories we recall.

The idea that memory is dynamic and reconstructive in nature has replaced earlier views of memory as a filing cabinet, with more recent memories stored in the top drawers and memories relating to more distant times stored in the less accessible, rarely opened, recesses of the bottom drawer. This earlier view suggested that memory was a fixed static repos-

Photograph courtesy of Elders Share the Arts, New York, New York.

itory of slowly decaying, disconnected independent items. The bottom drawer was occasionally opened and an item retrieved, dusted off, and re-examined before being returned once more to its original place in much the same state as before. Contemporary brain science suggests a more interactive dynamic system in which retrieved memories are open to retrospective editing in order to offer alternative views of past experience and to keep the newer versions alive in a more readily accessible form.

This contemporary viewpoint raises interesting questions about the reliability and veracity or accuracy of memories. Kotre (1995) suggested that instead of asking "Can I trust my memories?" we should be asking, "In what setting and for what end can I trust my memory?" He maintained that our earliest memories change as we use a series of stories that we tell ourselves and other people to underwrite our present identity. People's earliest memories are actually about the present and the past that leads to it. He argued that we create our own myths over a lifetime to account for how we are today. Young people are more likely to create myths concerned with visions of the future. Older people are more likely to create myths about their parents and to dream about the past as a way of deriving comfort in the face of a lifetime of loss and present failing powers. Our memories provide us with a resource as we seek continuity as well as change and long for satisfying personal relationships in the present.

DEFINITIONS OF REMINISCENCE

The following discussion demonstrates that there is no agreed standard definition of reminiscence used in an expanding international literature concerned with reminiscence and life review theory, research, practice methods, and applications. The most quoted definition comes from Butler, who referred to "reminiscence—the act or process of recalling the past" (1963, p. 66). Webster defined *reminiscence* as "the recalling of memories from one's personal past" (1997, p. 137), whereas Spector, Orrell, Davies, and Woods defined *reminiscence therapy* as "vocal or silent recall of events in a person's life, either alone, or with another person or group of people" (2000, p. 1).

Because different writers define *reminiscence* in different ways, the task of comparing outcomes is extremely difficult. Webster (1993) and Parker (1995) stressed the process by which memories are evoked, selected, and reconstructed. Others, such as Wong and Watt (1991), stressed content and referred to personal memories of a distant past. Webster and Cappeliez (1993) suggested that autobiographical memory and reminiscence are closely related as both concern personal memories, a position that is supported by Bluck and Levine (1998). Rubin, Wetzler, and Nebes (1986) stressed both the process and function of reminiscence and used the term to refer to conscious recollections retrieved for their own purpose rather than recollections that are requested by someone else (as happens in laboratory-based memory experiments) or used to retrieve specific information. This book does not attempt to address complex and contested issues concerning the recovery of unconscious memories (Erdelyi, 1996).

Everyone's memories are reconstructed, at least in part, which means they are not strictly accurate records of original events (Conway, 1996; Funder, Parke, Tomlinson-Keasey, & Widerman, 1993). Memories are affected by the interweaving of personality, cumulative life history, life satisfaction, and life circumstances. Instead of talking about reminiscence and recall, it is probably more accurate—but more unwieldy—to refer to reminiscence, recall, review, and partial reconstruction as the four essential components of memory. Reminiscence does not refer to one single phenomenon as different types of reminiscence have been identified. Private, internal thinking or talking to oneself, for example, is distinguished from the kind of reminiscence that involves communicating with other people in a social context, whereas life review seeks to evaluate and integrate personal memories.

Private recall may happen spontaneously; it can be and frequently is involuntary, which means its cause cannot be readily identified. Personal memories frequently become conscious without any particular effort being made. They may arise because of surroundings, prior thoughts, emotions, moods, present problems, or other factors such as exposure to particular sensory stimuli (e.g., music, smells, sights, sounds). Social reminiscence—that is, reminiscence occurring in the presence of others that usually involves some verbal or nonverbal exchange of memories—is likely to be prompted by conversation, questions, or activities shared with other people. So our past and our present are inextricably bound together. In reminiscence and recall we are engaged in two-way traffic. McConkey put it another way:

> We are always what we were; we know ourselves—to the degree that knowledge of the self is possible—through our ever-growing past . . . memory gives us a double perspective . . . not only does the past inform the present but the present informs the past. In other words, the understanding of our present selves that memory provides us is capable of returning the gift, enabling us to know our earlier selves in a manner that eluded us then. (1996, p. 311)

Reminiscence and *recall* are terms often used loosely and sometimes interchangeably to refer to the retrieval and reconstruction of various types of memories. *Life review* is also used to refer to the process in which memories are recalled for the express purpose of surveying, examining, taking stock, or appraising them. Life review as a formal, structured intervention is described in detail in Chapter 5. Although life review may occasionally occur spontaneously and be a partial rather than a systematic survey of the whole of one's past life, it is usually thought to be more deliberate and more systematic than simple reminiscence. It may be triggered by a growing awareness of advancing age or by a serious illness, a period of bereavement, or other major life transition. It can occur at any age, such as in a young person whose parents divorce or die; however, it is more commonly associated with later life (Merriam, 1993).

Coleman (1974) described four different types of reminiscence:

1. Simple reminiscence: remembering that is nondirected and relatively automatic

2. Narrative reminiscence: recollection of past experiences as in day-dreaming

3. Informative reminiscence: recollection concerned with teaching or entertaining others

4. Life review: remembering involving analysis and evaluation

Lo Gerfo (1980) identified three types of reminiscence: 1) informative; 2) obsessive, which is concerned with recollections of guilt and failure; and 3) life review. Gibson (1994), in reference to planned reminiscence practice interventions, distinguished four categories involving the focus of work, whether it is general or specific, and the number of people engaged, whether an individual or a group. The contributors to Haight and Webster (1995), Hendricks (1995), and Webster and Haight (2002) illustrated the variety of definitions used in reminiscence, life review, life story work, narrative, and biographical writing.

Watt and Wong (1990) and Wong and Watt (1991) identified six types of reminiscence, but here type and function overlap:

1. Integrative reminiscence resembles life review as it seeks to achieve or enhance self-esteem and self-understanding. Wong and Watt suggested it differs in some ways from life review because it may include negative memories. Other writers agree because although life review tends to concentrate on positive memories, it also provides opportunities for the integration of disturbing memories, including those relating to loss and grief (Beecham, Anthony, & Kurtz, 1998).

2. Instrumental reminiscence is concerned with the achievement of goals and problem solving.

3. Transmissive reminiscence refers to the passing on of personal and cultural knowledge and values.

4. Escapist reminiscence is defensive because it permits escape from present difficulties and retreat into past happier times.

5. Obsessive reminiscence concentrates on recalling bitter, painful past memories.

6. Narrative or storytelling reminiscence seeks to entertain.

WHAT IS MEMORY AND HOW DO PEOPLE REMEMBER?

Although reminiscence is an everyday occurrence for most people, remembering and what it is we remember is a complex process. Memory is a central aspect of our being: "Nothing in biology in general, or in our human life in particular, makes sense except in the context of memory, of history" (Rose, 1992, quoted by McConkey, 1996, p. 58). Chamberlain outlined some of these complexities:

> What we remember and recall is not random. . . . Memory and narrative are shaped by social categories, by language and priorities, by experience and tense, by choice and context. They are shaped also by imagination, by dreams and nightmares, hopes and fantasies which, however private they may feel, are molded by culture. We recall past events through present time, and the present always anticipates the future, what might have been and what may yet be. . . . Memory not only recounts events, but offers also the attitudes and emotions that surrounded events, then and now. (1997, p. 10)

How memories are stored is much less important than how memories are laid down and then subsequently retrieved. Recall is crucial because we can only know what we remember by being able to bring past memory into present awareness, whether we are conscious of the memories recalled or not. As Rose suggested, "It is 'to bring to mind', to think of again, to recollect—to suggest a reconnecting, an assembling, a bringing together of things in relation to one another" (1992, p. 319).

Memory is closely identified with creativity or imagination. Warnock (1987, quoted in McConkey, 1996, p. 124) argued that it is quite impossible to separate the two. Whether we are imagining or recalling, we are thinking of something that is not before our eyes or ears, of something that has meaning for us and may be imbued with strong emotions. We could say that in recalling something, we employ imagination; in imagining something (exploring it imaginatively), we use memory.

Memory does not ever replicate the exact original event or relationship recalled. Because memory and imagination are so intertwined, imagination modifies or colors the memory while memory feeds our imagination in such a way as to make us able to live with our recollections. Memory and imagination working effectively together illuminate the dark places and help us to work toward achieving harmony or synthesis, a coherent whole story with which we can live. Intuitive and analytical processes dismantle memories and reassemble them in fresh ways so that a new wholeness or completeness is achieved, at least for the time being.

This process of seeking wholeness or harmony seems very like Erikson's (1982) view of the developmental task of late life, the struggle to achieve integrity rather than despair. Each time we remember our lives as they have been, we are coming to accept ourselves as we are now and are becoming. This dynamic process comes about not just from the exercise of mind and memory, but also from the interplay of memory and imagination. Each time we recall the past, we are rewriting the story, which effectively means that we are rewriting the self through a process of recall, selection, amplification, and interpretation. "The past that was, is no longer," said Freeman (1993, p. 89), and the images that we bring to mind are only imaginings because as conscious beings, we bring to mind images of what is no longer present and cannot be present.

Some common myths about old age affect discussions about memory and reminiscence. Three such myths claim that older people live in the past, that people reminisce more as they grow older, and that older people reminisce more about their earlier life than about more recent times. The relationship between age and reminiscence is much more complex than these general statements suggest. Researching questions about the frequency of different types of reminiscence and whether the frequency of these types varies with age, gender, ethnicity, personality, clinical conditions, or life circumstances is not straightforward (Randall, 1999). Nor is it easy to be sure whether different periods of the life span or different circumstances produce different types of reminiscence.

Webster (1993, 1997) made the most systematic attempt to explore how people of various ages use reminiscence. He established that people of all ages reminisce and developed a Reminiscence Functions Scale (RFS; see Chapter 2 for an in-depth description). The RFS is founded on the self-report of informants and includes both their private and public reminiscence. In constructing the RFS, however, it is possible that bias may have distorted the results because informants may have withheld information about the frequency of negative reminiscences, and generalization from an artificial investigation to naturally occurring reminiscence may not be valid.

It is now generally agreed that frequency of simple reminiscence is not directly correlated with age, although there are some associations in that younger and older people reminisce more than middle-age people. Webster (1997) stated that frequency is more related to gender and personality than to age. A number of studies show that the type of reminiscence varies with age, although the results on this point are not consistent. Differences in personality, lifestyle, and present circumstances, regardless of age and gender, also need to be considered as possible explanations for the inconsistent results between studies (Rubin, 1986, 1996; Rubin, Wetzler, & Nebes, 1986).

Butler (1963) argued that life review was universal and undertaken by all older people, and he inferred that it functioned as preparation for death. Merriam (1980, 1993) and Wink and Schiff (2002) did not believe that it occurs universally. Lieberman and Falk (1971) suggested that middle-age people use reminiscence and life review for problem solving, looking for present solutions from past experiences, whereas older people do more restructuring and comprehensive life reviewing. De Vries and Watt (1996) found differences in the kind of life events recounted by young, middle-age, and older adults and also differences between men and women. Cohen and Taylor (1998) found that older adults spent more time reminiscing about children, friends, and partners—functions similar to intimacy maintenance. Webster (1997) studied the full age range and found some age-related variations, with older informants scoring higher on death preparation than younger or middle-age people. Older people also scored higher on intimacy maintenance and on teach and inform functions. Younger people scored higher for boredom reduction, identity problems, and bitterness revival.

There is also interest in knowing which period of the life span is most often recalled, as it is frequently suggested that memory fades with time. If this were true it would mean that more recent memories are recalled than are more distant or remote ones. A reminiscence bump or cluster of memories from the age range of approximately 10–30 years has been suggested, whereas there seem to be few memories recalled from infancy up to approximately 7 years of age. One possible explanation for this bump may be that the majority of people experience their most personally significant life events between the ages of 10 and 30—through late childhood, adolescence, and young adult life (Habermas & Bluck, 2000). This explanation suggests that if equally significant events were to occur at other ages, they too would be equally well remembered. It may, however, be a cluster of significant events rather than an isolated event that contributes to survival of the memory.

Present life circumstances and emotional states seem to exert considerable influence on the content of recall. Older people living in their own homes, for example, recall as many recent memories as younger people do. People residing in hospitals, nursing homes, or other institutional facilities seem to recall many more remote memories, perhaps because they have little control over their present daily lives and little motivation to think about recent events. Possibly, they prefer to escape in memory to more interesting and significant times because they experience the present as so bleak. Present experience has to be sufficiently rich to be worth storing in memory for future remembering. If contemporary experience is not stored, then it will be lost irretrievably, even if a person later wishes to remember. Older people living active, autonomous lives think more about the recent past than the distant past. This suggests that lifestyle and the retention of personal control rather than chronological age may be more important in laying down and recalling memories (Holland & Rabbitt, 1991).

People of all ages, including children, are involved in prospective thinking and planning. Old age is not necessarily preoccupied with thinking about the past. Women tend to reminisce more about friends and relationships than men do, but most people, regardless of gender, tend to want to make peace with themselves and with others as they grow older. To be able to see the past as the past and to accept one's own part in it is a desirable goal and a developmental challenge.

It is very easy to ignore the importance of reminiscence in the lives of children and young people because much of the original reminiscence writing concentrated on older people; interest in reminiscence applications with younger age groups, however, is steadily developing. Even very young children reminisce, and there is interest in linking childhood attachment behavior and maternal reminiscing talk with subsequent personality, happiness, and styles and types of reminiscing in adulthood (Fivush & Reese, 2002; Molinari, Cully, & Kendjelic, 2001; Webster, 1998). Long-term influences on self-esteem and the maintenance of identity have also been claimed for reminiscence. McConkey (1996) suggested that memory is responsible for our identity by enabling us to make connections between the past and present that assist us to make sense of our lives and our circumstances. It may be that if the past has been satisfying, then there are likely to be positive gains from reminiscing about it, at whatever age. If past life has been unhappy, then common sense suggests it might well be better not to dwell too much on it. Again this is not easy to research by means of quantitative studies that rely on randomized controlled trials. There are also immense problems in expecting people to disclose negative memories in research situations, whereas they may be willing to do so within therapeutic clinical relationships. Similarly, social or group reminiscence is unlikely to yield many unhappy disclosures, and private reminiscence is by its very nature virtually inaccessible.

The functions or purposes performed by reminiscence differ according to age, personality, life history, lifestyle, and present circumstances. Bored people will reminisce to keep boredom at bay; grandparents may reminisce to maintain intimacy within families and to bequeath their personal history to their descendants. People of any age who are confronted with problems or challenges will call on their past to assist them in coping with the present. Life review may occur at all ages in the face of life-threatening or life-shrinking circumstances. People facing terminal illness or emergent dementia may wish to review and evaluate their lives and integrate troubling memories while they still retain the physical or cognitive capacity to do so. Many different intertwining factors help to account for who reminiscences about what, how frequently, at what age, and for what purposes. Reminiscence may seem an everyday process, and at one level it is. Beneath its simple ordinariness, however, lurks immense complexity and innumerable possibilities of interpretation. Much more research is needed before any predictions can be safely made about the likely outcomes of particular types of reminiscence and life review that are undertaken by specific individuals in defined circumstances and at different stages or times in their lives.

MAKING MEMORIES

We mostly think about memory as being retrospective, but it can also be prospective when used to anticipate something still to come, such as remembering to do something in the future. We use memory to muse, to meditate, or to call something either particular or general to mind. Memory can have both negative and positive outcomes if used to honor and celebrate or to blame and denigrate. It can be a means for calling ourselves or others to account or to promote reconciliation. The memories we recall and then use to construct our life stories are constantly being modified. One memory comes into focus while another recedes into the background, only to reemerge at another time, subtly changed, or maybe never to emerge at all or not for many years. We do not always manage to remember the source or the origin of a memory, although we may remember the content in considerable detail, especially if a present actual or imagined association replicates similar circumstances, surroundings, or associations.

Recall is cumulative in the sense that the recall of one memory recruits similar memories so that memories, although originating at different times, become grouped together by means of rehearsing, retelling, and incorporating new information. In the company of other people, one person's recollection can provide sufficient stimulus for an entire group to begin recalling related memories that have remained dormant for long periods. In these circumstances, each person becomes a resource to others. Separate memories cluster together, linked by emotions to emerge as coherent themes. Each memory recovered is likely to produce a succession of associated memories as their owners continue to reflect, probably in private and perhaps hours or days after the collective recall experience. This cumulative reconstructive process of recall cannot easily be corralled or contained. It is as if the door of a long locked repository is opened with its treasures becoming available for endless exploration and rearrangement. Some memories will remain undisturbed; others will be taken out, dusted down, partially reconstructed, and possibly enjoyed for a short time before being returned for further storage and future recall or neglect. We understand very little about why this is so or why some memories become constant companions on a present journey, bringing pleasure to their owners and fresh hope for the future, whereas other memories continue to give pain or are consigned to oblivion or only occasional revival.

Two sisters, now in their seventies, had not seen each other for years. When they met each other again at a family wedding, they spontaneously began to reminisce about various family events. One recalled a childhood memory of going on a picnic where their father had killed a snake. The other sister remembered the picnic, the food, the names of other children and adults who were present, and even what many wore but had no recollection of the snake incident. She even suggested her sister was making up a good story about something that never actually occurred. As the sisters talked together, each recalled many general and specific details associated with this and other picnics, although for one sister the snake incident remained beyond recall.

This forgetting suggests several possible explanations and illustrates the complexity of memory processes. Did the woman actually miss the specific snake event because she was elsewhere? Were the ensuing excitement and other people's accounts at the time insufficient to fix the event in her memory? Was the incident too frightening to remember and therefore repressed? Was it distorted or confused with memories of other aspects of the picnic? Was it submerged over time by more personally significant life events? Was the memory obliterated because it had not been recalled and rehearsed in the intervening years? Had the incident occurred elsewhere and become erroneously attached to the picnic in the other sister's memory? Or was it a figment of the sister's imagination?

Reminiscence workers value the cumulative nature of reminiscence and recall. Once begun, each memory seems to activate other memories. At first, the process may seem slow, even laborious, but then the mind often seems to take off and memories crowd one on the other in quick succession, demanding attention. Later, other memories may intrude as if unbidden yet probably stimulated by the earlier recall. People often report that events not thought about since they occurred emerge in conscious memory many years later. It is impossible to know how accurate such statements are. This is because earlier memories, once recalled, become more available for future recall, although they may seemingly be forgotten until again reactivated in response to some particular present stimulus. So although memory and recalling memories is familiar to us all (unless we suffer from some form of amnesia), it is a process that is only partially under our conscious control and only partially understood.

Although there is very little understanding about how memory actually works, we now know that it is much more complex than can be explained in terms of the biochemical and electrical functioning of specific neurons and their connections in particular areas of the brain. Memory involves the whole of the brain, even the whole of the organism (Rose, 1992). Forgetting is as important as remembering, for to remember everything would be an unimaginable burden, perhaps only eclipsed by an inability to sleep. Although the value to be gained from remembering is usually emphasized, we should also appreciate the protection afforded by forgetting. Brain scientists are making impressive progress in unraveling the molecular, biochemical, and cellular structures that underlie memory, and psychologists like to stress the importance of the dynamic multiple functions memory performs, but good memory is not everything (Qualls & Abelas, 2000). Moody (1995) suggested that good judgment, wisdom, and an enduring capacity for love are to be more prized than good memory. These characteristics may endure longer, but as with memory, they too can disappear because "the art of losing isn't hard to master" (Bishop, 1991, p. 183).

Diverse processes, most of which happen spontaneously and without our knowledge, lay down memories. Except when we are purposely trying to learn something to ensure that it will be available to be retrieved, reorganized, and used at some future time, as in formal learning situations, we usually do not consciously know when we are laying down memories. Throughout life—except perhaps in childhood, when memory is probably more accurately described as a constructive rather than a reconstructive process—rehearsing, retelling, and processing new inputs are continuously transforming our memories. Memory is laid down within social situations as well as in isolation. It is influenced by suggestion, errors of inference or misunderstanding, variability over time, emotional states, and relationships with others (Ballinger, 2001). Memories can be fallible because they suffered distortion or inaccuracy when originally laid down in addition to the myriad influences that inevitably operate in the process of recall. For memories to exist, new information has to be acquired by learning, and memory refers to the persistence of this learning in a form that allows it to be retrieved at a later time. The learned material has to be first encoded, meaning that it is translated or transformed into mental representations or images that persist in a form that can be stored until a later time, when the images are retrieved by bringing them into conscious awareness in a knowable form.

Types of Memory

Different types of memory are depicted in Figure 1.1 (Ballinger, 2001). The diagram and the descriptions that follow, although an oversimplification of very complex processes and interconnections, should help to clarify the meaning of the various terms in common use and provide some guidance about the type of memories more readily retrieved in reminiscence work.

Memory is described as short term or long term. Short-term memory lasts from seconds to 1 or 2 minutes. It is divided into temporary short-term memory, in which the information is subject to the passive process of either being encoded within a few minutes, or else forgotten, and working memory, which stores incoming information in an active complicated way more or less indefinitely.

Long-term memory is subdivided into implicit, or procedural, memory and explicit, or declarative, memory. Implicit or procedural memory, largely unconscious, refers to memory for habits or actions such as riding a bike, swimming, or driving a car. Procedural memories seem not to be forgotten. Other body systems, for example muscles and sinews, appear to be involved in the learning and recall of these memories. Procedural memories that involve physical actions are relatively easy to recall and reenact.

Explicit or *declarative memory* refers to remembering items that are learned facts or general knowledge, such as is used in tasks such as writing an exam. Many explicit or declarative memories are forgotten over time or become difficult to recall because they are integrated into other memories or schema or may be distorted by the person's emotions at the time of recall.

Explicit memory is further subdivided into semantic memory and episodic memory. *Semantic memory* refers to meaningful general knowledge and concepts (traditional school learning) about the world in general that are independent of personal experience (e.g., Washington, D.C., is the federal capital of the United States). *Episodic memory* consists of information about specific contexts and experiences concerned with events such as special occasions.

Autobiographical memory is a particular kind of episodic memory that refers to memory for events, information, emotions, and experiences related to one's personal past—for example, a person's wedding day or the birth of one's first child. Reminiscence is one way in which these memo-

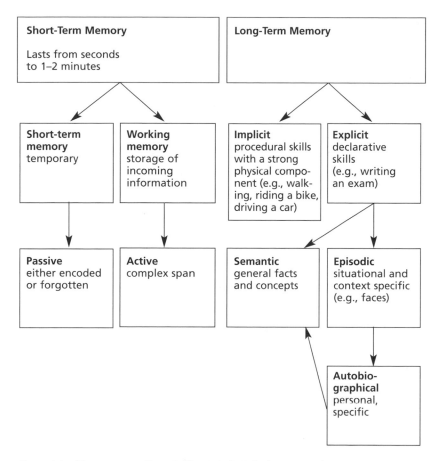

Figure 1.1. Memory types. (From Ballinger, S. [2001]. *The recovered memory debate.* Australian Psychological Society, unpublished conference paper; adapted by permission.)

ries can be retrieved. Autobiographical memories are usually thought to be stored in episodic memory. On the contrary, Badderley, Wilson, and Watts (1995) suggested that some autobiographical memories are retrieved so frequently that they become *crystallized*. This means that some often-rehearsed memories become a part of an individual's general knowledge store. They are stored as semantic rather than autobiographical memory and remain relatively intact well into advanced old age. This implies that it is highly desirable to recall significant personal memories frequently, as rehearsal of these memories aids their preservation and increases their potential as an available resource for people as they grow older.

Prospective memory concerns remembering to do something in the future.

There are three other types of memory. *Meta memory* refers to knowledge about one's own memory and how it works—for example, knowing how to rehearse something to be able to remember it in the future. *Remote memory* refers to nonautobiographical memories about nonpersonal events occurring within a person's lifetime. *Traumatic memories* seem to result in extremes of either remembering or forgetting. Some writers suggest that these extremes are due to high emotions aroused at the time of the traumatic experience interfering with the processing of the memory.

Stability, Development, and Change over Time

Human beings are distinguished by consciousness, memory, and intentionality, which is why writers as different as the neurobiologist Rose (1992) and the novelist Morrison (1984) both used the term *re-membering* as a way of stressing that memory is an active, not a passive, process. When Morrison remembers a person, she experiences "a whole galaxy of emotions" before she recaptures a facial image. She first feels the emotions and only then recalls the associated image. Rose explained the part played by nature and nurture, or inherited and environmental influences in our lives, by suggesting that all living organisms possess two contradictory properties. One is stability or specificity that remains throughout a lifetime of development. The other is plasticity, the ability to adapt and modify in the face of the repeated experience of acquiring new learning.

Some scientists now believe that it is an individual's genes, actively expressed throughout his or her entire lifetime development, which permit a person (or other organism) to be influenced by both plasticity and specificity. Our genes produce a brain capable of learning by experience or possessing plasticity of which memory is a major component. Our genes also give us specificity that enables us to resist the constant changes to which we are exposed during development so that we retain a continuing core to our being. If we are to understand the mechanisms of memory, of plasticity, then we also must understand the mechanisms of specificity, for each interacting with the other is essential for change as well as stability throughout the entire life cycle (McConkey, 1996).

Personal Coherence and Collective Memory

Rose (1992) suggested that humans have explicit, declarative, or verbal memory, unlike animals that are dominated by procedural memory. Humans can transfer their memories into speech or commit them to paper or other formats in order to preserve, share, or transmit them to other people. Because of this ability to use artificial memory in the form of various types of records made by people, it is no longer necessary for humans to remember vast amounts of information. This capacity for creating records by using artificial memory enables each of us to contribute to the creation of collective memory. Each individual experiences the world uniquely but, gaining access to the memories of others, can reconstruct or modify individual memories. By these means, a mass consensus or collective memory about what is to be remembered and how it is to be remembered emerges in different groups and societies. Through these individual and shared processes, interpretations of history are created and used to assist in making sense of the present.

Memory helps us to compose our separate memories in ways that make us feel reasonably comfortable with the life stories or life scripts that we construct from them. This is a dynamic process involving plasticity and specificity that permits growth, change, and development throughout life. It also permits continuity and relative stability of a core self represented in a reasonably consistent and coherent story over time (Parker, 1999). Thomson referred to some of the tensions inherent in this ongoing process:

> We seek composure, an alignment of our past, present, and future lives. . . . Our memories are risky and painful if they do not conform to the public norms or versions of the past. We compose our memories so that they will fit with what is publicly acceptable, or, if we have been excluded from general public acceptance, we seek our particular publics that affirm our identities and the way we want to remember our lives. (1998, p. 301)

Bluck and Levine believed that "the self is largely constant over time but subject to revision through selectively accessing and modifying memories" (1998, p. 198). This accounts for both consistency and change in our stories over time. These are newer versions of older stories presenting different facets of the self rather than entirely new stories about a completely different person. Augmenting the recall of memories by writing them down may help achieve a sense of continuity and composure, especially if a sympathetic listener is unavailable. Writing is like talking to oneself but in a socially acceptable way; it also brings a certain distance to the process. It is as if one part of the self is observing and reflecting on another part of the self from the dual vantage points of distance and familiarity. Perlman noted,

> Recall may offer review; perhaps from that, some re-vision of ourselves and of others, some greater self-knowledge, some expanded capacity for empathy with other human beings, some greater sense of self-possession, which is the essential condition for inner freedom and consciously determined self-management. (1989, p. 187)

Julius, age 85, had spent his adult life hiding from his memories until in the reminiscence group he began writing about the breakup of his marriage 50 years ago, when his wife left him for another man:
"I got into my car. I started to drive east, quite away from Toledo, practically numb, when it started to dawn on me what had happened. It finally dawned on me what had happened TO ME, who was so anxious to have a family and keep it together in any kind of condition. It was lost so easy, with a single easy deception" (De Medeiros, 2002, A14).

It is important to realize that the composition of an acceptable life script or story achieved through a process of recall, reflection, and review is always a work in progress. It can never be fully comprehensive because of all we fail to remember, and it is impossible to say at any point in time that a life review has been completed. Until the point of unconsciousness or death, there will always be the possibility of further learning and new experience, leading to further remembering and, consequently, further additions or modifications. As people age, most continue to explore in their own idiosyncratic way questions concerned with understanding the meaning of life at the personal, communal, and cosmic levels (Moody, 1986; Moody, 2002; Moody & Carroll, 1997). The more aware a person becomes of his or her own impending death, the more open that person may be to searching for ultimate meaning (Moberg, 2001). Life review and meaning making is thus an ongoing process, although sometimes the erroneous impression may be created that life review is a product capable of being encapsulated in formats such as a life storybook, video diary, or autobiography. These tangible outcomes represent a life review only up to a particular point in time, not a completed review. Such formats also contain hidden limitations, as noted by Rose: "A videotape, a written record do more than just reinforce memory: they freeze it, and in imposing a fixed, linear sequence on it, they simultaneously preserve it and prevent it from evolving and transforming itself with time" (1992, p. 61). Any reminiscence worker who is encouraging people undertaking life review and life story work to make tangible representations of their memories needs to appreciate this potential limitation and to convey a sense of incompleteness, of work in progress, to any person who is embarking on such a journey of self-exploration. The practice implications of these issues are considered further in Chapter 6.

Kotre (1995) and Thomson (1998) were not alone in suggesting that we employ remembering to provide us with a storyline that reconciles past and present. We construe the present in ways that emphasize familiarity and acceptability. This then reinforces our conviction that because we have coped in the past, and we perceive the present as resembling the past, so we dare to hope that we will be able to cope in the future. This is not meant to suggest that such a process is either consciously deliberate or necessarily neat and tidy. Kotre saw memory more as a collage that assists the dynamic process of mingling changing accounts of past experience to construct the most probable, or the most symbolically meaningful, story to satisfy our desire for continuity in the face of uncertainty. Pear (1922) saw memory not as a collage or a photograph, but as a painting—a painting subject to many different representations and interpretations, ever changing according to the variations of present mood and circumstance.

CONCLUSION

Reminiscence and life review mean different things to different people. Before introducing reminiscence work into a health or social care facility, a museum, a library, or an education or community agency, it is important to agree with staff colleagues on an acceptable working definition. Staff will develop a growing understanding about the layers of complexity underlying this simple, seemingly straightforward idea as their practice experience grows.

This chapter has suggested that reminiscence and life review are a part of autobiographical memory. It has considered some seminal definitions of reminiscence, examined various explanations of the nature of memory, and explained how we lay down memories and then "re-member" and partially reconstruct them. It has described conventionally understood types of memory and stressed the dynamic nature of memory throughout the life span while also briefly examining differences in recall linked to age, gender, life experience, and present social circumstances. Remembering and verbalizing memories as reminiscences is viewed as an act or process that takes place in the present; although about the past, it is a here-and-now experience.

By means of cumulative recall, life stories can be shared with other people but also influenced by them directly and indirectly. Through creating and using written, visual, or other forms of records, we become open to collective memory and to historical understandings and distortions. Memory retrieved through imagination, reminiscence, and recall becomes a vehicle for developing awareness of our unique personal identity and for developing a sense of coherence or wholeness and of how we wish to represent ourselves to other people. The processes of reminiscence and life review, through which a person seeks to get in touch with his or her personal past and make sense of it, also contain the potential for connecting each person with others, a theme that is developed in Chapters 4 and 5.

Chapter 2

Why Encourage Reminiscence?

Theologians, philosophers, novelists, and poets have all speculated about the nature and influence of memory and the place of memories in people's lives for hundreds of years—long before psychologists, clinicians, and brain scientists became interested. Since the 1960s, many different academic and clinical writers have tried to answer the questions "Why encourage reminiscence?" and "What functions or purposes does reminiscence serve?" Various answers have been suggested by many different writers who have contributed to the ongoing debate about the purposes served by reminiscence and life review (Butler, 1963; Haight & Webster, 1995; Lewis, 1971; Merriam, 1980; Molinari & Reichlin, 1985; Moody, 1988; Romaniuk & Romaniuk, 1981; Thornton & Brotchie, 1987; Webster, 1993, 1997; Webster & Haight, 1995, 2002; Webster & McCall, 1999; Wong & Watt, 1991).

Some people wonder if it is necessary to provide a reason for encouraging reminiscence. However, to be responsible practitioners and to accumulate evidence about the effectiveness of reminiscence, we need to know why we are encouraging people to reminisce. People being invited to engage in reminiscence work need to understand—in simple terms—what they are being invited to do and for what reason. These reasons will not be the same for all people or for the same person on all occasions. If people are invited to reminisce jointly in a group, then they must share sufficient common objectives to make possible a coherent program that potentially will provide a satisfying experience for each group member and for the group as a whole. If undertaking evaluative research in reminiscence, then

Photograph courtesy of The Turner Writing Group, Ann Arbor, Michigan.

there must be clarity about terminology, objectives or intentions, and methods of work and some standardization of the characteristics of participants.

This chapter summarizes the views of various writers about the purposes or functions of reminiscence. It raises the most commonly voiced reservations about reminiscence work and identifies possible risks that may be associated with reminiscing for some people. It also explores the major similarities and differences between reminiscence work and oral history. Many interdependent factors or circumstances determine the reason or justification for undertaking reminiscence with any individual, couple, or group at any particular time. These include the needs and characteristics of the people involved, the place or practice context in which the work is to be done, and the underlying guiding philosophy and values of the organization responsible for the practice context. All of these facets are likely to vary over time and between locations. The broad general principles are described here, and the more specific aspects and practical applications are covered in Part II.

WEBSTER'S TAXONOMY

Webster (1993, 1997) and Webster and McCall (1999) identified eight separate reminiscence functions by administering questionnaires to males and females of various ages and diverse educational, cultural, and ethnic backgrounds. From a factor analysis of these results, Webster produced a robust 43-item Reminiscence Functions Scale (RFS) organized according to eight functions defined below that apply across all age groups, from young adulthood to late life (Webster, 1997, p. 140):

1. Boredom Reduction: having something to do
   "Our propensity to reminisce when our environment is understimulating and we lack engagement in goal-directed activities."

2. Death Preparation: valuing the life lived and becoming less fearful of death
   "The way we use our past when thoughts of our own mortality are salient and may contribute to a sense of closure and calmness."

3. Identity: discovering and better understanding a sense of who we are
   "How we use our past in an existential manner to discover, clarify, and crystallize important dimensions of our sense of who we are."

4. Problem Solving: drawing on strengths and experience from the past for coping in the present
   "How we employ reminiscence as a constructive coping mechanism whereby the remembrance of past problem-solving strategies may be used again in the present."

5. Conversation: rediscovering common bonds among old and new friends
   "Our natural inclination to invoke the past as a means of connecting or reconnecting with others in an informal way."

6. Intimacy Maintenance: remembering personally significant people
   "Cognitive and emotional representations of important persons in our lives are resurrected in lieu of the remembered person's physical presence."

7. Bitterness Revival: sustaining memories of old hurts and justifying negative thoughts and emotions
   "The extent to which memories are used to affectively charge recalled episodes in which the reminiscer perceives themselves as having been unjustly treated."

8. Teach/Inform: teaching younger people, including family members about values and history

    "The ways in which we use reminiscence to relay to others important information about life (e.g., a moral lesson). It is an instructional type of narrative."

Webster provided a useful, relatively brief and comprehensive, valid, and reliable measure of the uses of reminiscence by adults of all ages. The eight categories of the RFS can be applied in both clinical and experimental contexts. Although some reminiscence practitioners do not believe that the richness and variety of behavior associated with reminiscence, life review, and autobiographical narrative can easily fit into these eight precise categories, there is no doubt that Webster provided the most comprehensive, rigorous, and empirically based classification of reminiscence functions so far available. As work continues on refining the theoretical understanding of reminiscence functions, processes, and outcomes, using the RFS to guide practice and research would bring greater coherence to a very imprecise collection of ideas and disparate formulations.

OTHER FORMULATIONS OF THE FUNCTIONS OF REMINISCENCE

There are other more speculative formulations of the various purposes served by reminiscence. These largely arise from direct clinical experience and are found in a growing international literature that includes a small number of comparative cross-national studies (Bender, Baukham, & Norris 1999; Bornat, 1994; Bruce & Gibson, 1998; Gibson, 1998a, 2000a; Haight & Hendrix, 1995; Nomura, 1998; Ohta & Agari, 1999; Webster & Haight, 2002). A composite formulation derived from these various sources is described in the following section. Again, depending on where reminiscence is undertaken and the people involved, the purpose will vary over time and multiple functions may be served simultaneously for some participants.

Reminiscence Provides a Sense of Coherence and Continuity

A sense of wholeness or integrity about the whole of life seems very important to many people, especially those who are facing particular challenges or changes. These challenges come in many forms. They may be a single crisis event or more drawn-out states that may last for days, weeks, months, or even years. The challenge may arise from illness (acute or chronic), encroaching disability, divorce, bereavement, joblessness, bankruptcy, or other transitions or major life changes. Children may lose parents through death, divorce, or separation. They may face major changes in living arrangements, schooling, and friendships. Young adults face leaving home, starting college or work, and developing and losing significant relationships. People in mid-life are likely to experience many changes concerned with family life, employment, death of parents, health, and the departure of children. Nobody will reach late life without experiencing multiple losses, grief, numerous transitions, and manifold threats to well-being.

When faced with such events, people naturally seek safety in the past. This is not to be viewed as retreat or escapism but rather as a spontaneous security-seeking mechanism that is closely linked to problem solving. Recalling episodes in the past when one managed to cope with threatening events can give confidence for coping in the present and even optimism about coping in the future. Past experience is drawn on as a present resource; old learning is revived and used to reduce present and imagined or anticipated future threat. If a person's past coping skills have not proved satisfactory, then any present threat may arouse considerable anxiety, pessimism about the present, and deep uncertainty about the future. A problematic past coupled with restricted learning opportunities for developing new coping mechanisms in the present usually indicates that caution should be exercised before encouraging such a person to embark on reminiscence. Unless there are persuasive indications that the person is well motivated to learn more effective ways of managing present and possible future problems and that he or she can be well supported through effective cognitive counseling while doing so, reminiscence and life review should not be encouraged. Reminiscence does not suit everyone and is not a panacea for all ills. People who are excessively private; have psychotic ideas; are very hostile toward others; or are hyperactive, habitually fearful, or obsessive are unlikely to be suitable for group reminiscence. For most people facing present difficulties, however, recalling and reviewing the past can illuminate the present and provide hope for the future.

Reminiscence Encourages
Sociability and Opens Up New Relationships

Sharing memories about past experience with others helps people to discover common ground. It can give courage to risk venturing into new relationships, often at a time in life when problems may be occurring. Reminiscence has proved particularly valuable for people who, through role losses associated with ill health or disability, are facing social transitions such as attending an adult day center or moving to a retirement community or a long-term care facility.

It is not always easy to reach out to strangers, initiate new social contacts, embark on new friendships, or begin new activities. At a stage in life when social networks—meaning the significant people to whom we are connected—are probably shrinking or unraveling because of death or changes in living circumstances, reminiscence can help people make new friends or rediscover old friends. Inviting newcomers to join group reminiscence and sensitively introducing them to others who are probably feeling much as they do is an effective means for lessening isolation, reducing anxiety, and stimulating new relationships.

Even people who are surrounded by others in care facilities or hospitals—perhaps sharing a dining room, sitting room, or bedroom—may find it overwhelmingly difficult to initiate worthwhile conversation (Haight, Michel, & Hendrix, 1998). Some manage to do so; others feel isolated, lonely, and unhappy. They may be grieving for lost places, lost people, and lost independence. They may be struggling with coming to terms with how to lead private lives in public places. Caregivers need to be able to assist residents to reconcile their need for personal privacy with their need for having significant relationships. Both needs are legitimate, and both must be respected.

Some residents will find that joining a small reminiscence group may help solve this dilemma. Here they can share those aspects of their lives that they choose to talk about. They remain in control of what they say about themselves, and the group provides opportunities for them to talk in their own way and in their own time. No particular expertise is demanded of the members in such a group, and emotional warmth develops as group members converse about common experiences. They may discover that they have lived in the same town, attended the same school or college, worked in similar jobs, served in the military, shared the same interests, or now are facing similar challenges. Although focused on the past, reminiscence is a present activity that assists a person to locate or situate him- or herself in relation to both his or her past and present lives (Buchanan & Middleton, 1995). Shared talk about the past can lead naturally to talk about the present, which can help people to discover new resources in others and in themselves as they anticipate the future.

Althea, age 65, agreed to enter a nursing home after her neighbors complained that she was living in unhygienic conditions, was unable or unwilling to care for herself, and had become a liability they were no longer willing to undertake. When the social worker visited, she found Althea living in squalor and physically frail, breathless, malnourished, looking generally neglected, disheveled, and scarcely able to communicate coherently.

The long-time neighbors in the adjoining apartment indicated that for more than 3 years Althea had slept in a chair rather than a bed because she feared burglars, although apparently she had never been attacked or molested in any way. She now seldom left her small apartment but increasingly relied on neighbors to keep her supplied with basic food and other necessities. As far as they knew, she was unmarried, seemed to have no living relatives, and subsisted on a modest inherited income. The social worker referred her for a physical assessment that indicated serious malnourishment, chronic heart failure, and high blood pressure. The social history prepared for nursing home admission concluded that Althea probably had a paranoid personality, was incapable of caring for herself, and likely suffered from a lifelong learning disability that was exacerbated by advancing age.

Following admission, Althea remained aloof, solitary, and disinterested in activities but appreciative of regular meals, assistance with personal care, and the security provided by the structured regime of the home. She now slept in a bed and never referred to burglars. After 3 months, Althea was persuaded to join a small reminiscence group that met for eight weekly sessions with the objectives of promoting socialization and integration and providing detailed life history information to assist staff to develop more individually focused care plans.

At the first reminiscence group meeting, Althea was immediately excited when shown enlarged photographs of the town in bygone days, especially the river and men and boys fishing from small boats. Without hesitation she told how she always fished with her father, who had taught her to row, handle a boat, and catch fish. She described in detail the type of lines and bait they used and the fish they caught. Her animation was infectious, and soon the entire group was recalling and sharing their experience of the river and what it had meant to them. In subsequent meetings, Althea described her school days and how, having no brothers or sisters, her parents encouraged her to stay at home and not take a job. As the weeks passed, she grew increasingly confident and coherent in telling stories about her earlier adult life and appreciative of other people's stories. In between group meetings, she sought out two members and began to spend time talking with them in the dining room after lunch.

A more socially confident, articulate, well-educated woman began to emerge who now felt sufficiently energetic and secure in her present environment to engage in new relationships, despite her continuing physical problems. The social worker followed up the group sessions with further discussions and concluded that her initial assessment had been inaccurate. She now saw Althea's gradual decline in health, her ensuing self-neglect, and her over-reliance on the neighbors as a process that had revived old feelings of dependency that had been encouraged by her parents and, in older adulthood, had led to increasing insecurity and anxiety. Reminiscence had provided an opportunity for Althea to reassess her past, including her past competencies, and to feel appreciated in the here and now. Her reappraisal of herself and her contemporary needs enabled her to feel sufficiently secure to reengage with others within the protected structured environment provided by the nursing home.

Reminiscence Confirms Personal Identity and Encourages Feelings of Self-Worth

People only gradually develop a sense of identity and awareness of their own personal uniqueness; adolescence is regarded as a particularly important formative time. This sense of self is further developed and consolidated throughout adult life but is prone to various internal and external assaults as people face life crises or grow old. Being old in contemporary Western society usually means frequent exposure to discrimination based on ageism and a tendency in younger people to regard all older people as the same.

Adolescents, who are still establishing a sense of their own unique identity and the personal confidence that this bestows, may experience similar stereotyping. This can erode self-esteem, as it is all too easy to accept the evaluations made by other people and consequently to perceive oneself as being of less value. Regardless of age and circumstances, if one does not feel valued by others, it is difficult to value oneself. People can be reminded of their unique identity and value by recalling details of their past achievements and the esteem in which they were once held. Whether peoples' lives have been long or short, recalling their personal life stories reminds them and others around them of each person's singular identity and value as an individual. It helps them to continue to value themselves, to retain control at a stage in life when events, opinions, circumstances, and other people may be eroding their independence and paying them less respect. By reminding themselves of who they used to be, they may retain a stronger sense of self in the present. As Warnock explained:

> Proust (1981) wrote, "The true self, that is the self which is continuous throughout life, is revealed only at the moment of experiencing two fragments of time together, the present with the past." Memory and identity are inextricably linked, and each person's sense of identity provides a sense of continuity through time. Who we presently perceive ourselves to be is indisputably connected with a sense of who we perceive ourselves to have been in the past and will be in the future. Although we realize there have been changes over time, we are still the person we always were in core ways and will be hereafter, for change and continuity go hand in hand. (1987, p. 100)

Fry and Barker (2002) ran "Tell Us Your Story Groups" in which young female survivors of domestic violence used reminiscence to alleviate depression and enhance self-esteem. These storytelling groups met regularly over 6 months and illustrated the value of telling one's story in the presence of empathetic, affirmative listeners who had endured similar experiences. Such groups also encourage participants to identify past coping successes and serve as a means for recovering threatened self-esteem. The objectives of this work resemble that of Mere (1995), who used reminiscence with people who were hospitalized for various psychiatric conditions. There are also similarities to the confidence-building approach of

Atkinson (1994). She assisted people with learning disabilities who had spent many years in institutions and were coping with being resettled in small houses in the community to write their stories as a means of valuing themselves and their achievements.

Reminiscence Assists the Process of Life Review

As people face major life transitions, particularly in later life, many like to take stock and review their lives while trying to come to terms with life as it has turned out, for good or ill (Butler, 1963, 1995; Erikson, 1950). This kind of reminiscence contains both evaluative and integrative elements. Sometimes the process may be distressing or depressing, especially if it brings to light earlier disappointments, mistakes, or failures. Awareness of past wrongs, either inflicted or endured, may be revived. If seeking forgiveness, achieving reconciliation, or making restitution is no longer possible, then people may feel miserably burdened. Some find release in telling their stories, which can lead to other ways of making amends (Coleman, 1999; Coleman, Hautamaki, & Podolskij, 2002). Others find that the process of reviewing or evaluating the past assists in making sense of it and helps them to integrate these painful experiences into their life story (Kimble, McFadden, Ellor, & Seeber, 1995; McKinlay, 2001; Moody, 1988, 1995, 2002). Reminiscence brings a sense of coherence or completeness that equips the person to face the final developmental challenge of life, namely preparation for death. Most people may only partially achieve this aspiration to wholeness or integrity although many do strive to achieve spirituality in late life. Moody defined *spirituality* as "that which lies at the core of one's being—what the individual attaches most meaning to in their lives" (1995, p. 76). In this search for spirituality, he counsels us to be sensitive to cultural, ethnic, and religious differences, for "in a multicultural society it is understandable that there will be many different ways of weaving and painting the meaning canvass of life" (p. 120).

Memory enables people to sift the significant from the ordinary (Birren, 1993). As they review their lives, most people probably attach a greater emotional intensity to the recalled memory than the original experience possessed because as McConkey stated, "memory searches for connections among present and past experiences in its desire to know, to evaluate, to make sense of life" (1996, p. 447). The term *life review* has so far been used loosely rather than technically to refer to the almost inevitable evaluative component that accompanies most reminiscence, regardless of the other functions or purposes it is serving. The combined term *reminiscence and life review* is also very common, and many writers tend to use the two as alternatives for each other. Some writers use *life review* more technically. Haight, Coleman, and Lord (1995), for example, identified it as a short-term, planned, and structured intervention. This kind of reminiscence differs from simple and informative reminiscence, although each type may overlap by containing some element of general review or stock-taking (Coleman, 1974; Lo Gerfo, 1980). A detailed account of systematic life review is given in Chapter 5.

Reminiscence Changes the Nature of Caring Relationships and Contributes to Staff Development

Knowledge of the past often sheds light on why people of various ages talk and behave as they do in the present. Others, especially caregivers, come to appreciate the life experience of older adults, people with disabilities, and those with problem behavior, thereby seeing these individuals differently and understanding them better. Past pain can leak into the present and influence actions, mood, and morale that may be impossible to understand without detailed knowledge of a person's past experience.

Involvement in reminiscence work can assist staff to develop confidence. It can enhance communication skills and aid ability to individualize and empathize with people whose ages, cultural backgrounds, values, and personal life experiences may differ greatly from their own. It assists staff to develop new knowledge, skills, and attitudes in congenial, informal, stimulating, and personally satisfying ways. When staff and residents in care facilities share in the social experience of reminiscing, understanding is enhanced, attitudes are changed, relationships become less formal, and the distribution of power among staff and residents may radically change. This function of reminiscence is explored further in Chapter 3, which discusses using reminiscence as a staff training and development tool.

Reminiscence Aids Assessment of Present Functioning and Informs Managed Care Plans

Only considering how a person is in the present is like taking a single snapshot instead of looking through a whole photograph album. It is not possible to fully understand someone without knowing what he or she used to be like, used to be able to do, and liked to do. Life stories, either oral or written, reveal how people think about their own lives and what they wish for themselves in their present circumstances. A clinical history is usually constructed by consulting a number of informants, not necessarily the subject person, and is usually written by a professional. Often a clinical history has a negative or problem focus rather than a strengths focus (Fast & Chapin, 2000; Kivnick & Murray, 2001).

Life stories are constructed by individuals themselves and thus are more authentic. Life stories show how the person wishes to represent him- or herself and portray core values and past and present desires and priorities. A life story can be used to assist and inform the preparation of an initial assessment and care plan. Some people may need assistance in voicing their wishes, but even people with mild or moderate dementia, given sufficient time and a skilled listener, are capable of articulating their present desires as well as accounting for their past.

If professional caregivers are to accurately assess present functional and cognitive capacity, interests, values, aspirations, and hopes, then reminiscence is a relaxed, accessible approach for gathering and collating information and preparing current plans for managing care. Life stories are increasingly being used as the basis for encouraging people to express their views about how they wish to be occupied, treated, and cared for in the future if a time comes when they are no longer capable of expressing a view. McAdams summarized this idea when he said, "If you want to know me, then you must know my story, for my story defines who I am. And if I want to know myself then I too must understand my story" (1993, p. 11).

Although living wills or advanced directives concerning physical care and medical treatment are familiar, advanced psychological directives are slowly increasing in popularity. People prepare their own account of who they are and what values and hopes have underpinned their lives. They may record anything of personal significance, including details such as what they like to be called and preferences and aversions concerning food, music, clothing, hobbies, interests, care arrangements, and companions. Such a document can then become an authentic passport, traveling with the person if his or her living arrangements change and health or independence become compromised (Moody & Small, 2002).

Reminiscence Helps to Transmit
Knowledge, Values, and Wisdom and to Bear Witness

Words are used to convey either information or atmosphere. If oral history conveys information, then reminiscence conveys both information and atmosphere. Those who have lived history are its best teachers. They become active contributors to members of the younger generation, who become the beneficiaries of their knowledge. Although the knowledge of older people may be less relevant now than in the past because of the speed of technological change and their wisdom may be less regarded than it used to be, distilled life experience or wisdom can still contribute to the lives of younger people. Just as Hongo's (1995) grandfather chose him to be the bearer of his stories, so Basting's grandmother chose her: "I knew why she told them to me, and she knew I knew. I had been chosen as the one most likely to pass them on" (2001, p. 3).

One dimension of being entrusted with these stories is the obligation of bearing witness to specific personal, family, or public events. This can be enormously important to many survivors of past catastrophes who feel they owe a debt to those who did not survive and an obligation to record for posterity the evidence of past suffering. Holocaust survivors have demonstrated the importance of contributing to the private and public preservation of memory for the sake of their own and succeeding generations. Bearing witness becomes a duty. Wiesel said, "For a Jew, nothing is more important than memory. He is bound to his origins by memory. These wounds exist; it is therefore forbidden and unhealthy to pretend that they don't" (1992, p. 71). Survivors of the Armenian genocide have similarly spoken of how denial of this crime against humanity has deprived them of opportunities for healing. For Coleman et al., "Memory, trauma, healing, generativity, reconciliation—these are key themes for the future of all our societies . . . the first aim of memory is to bear witness to truth. Without the search for truth, healing and reconciliation are impossible" (2002, p. 231).

Survivors of September 11, 2001, have also demonstrated the overwhelming need to bear witness. This event has shaped many lives worldwide and become a defining focus for personal and collective memory, reminiscence, and recall for generations to come. The Oral History Research Office of Columbia University has been awarded funds by the National Science Foundation for the purpose of undertaking an extensive oral history project on the events of that day. Over a 2-year period, volunteer researchers will gather life stories from people who were affected either directly or indirectly by the attacks in New York, Washington, and Pennsylvania. Interviews were carried out in the immediate aftermath of the attacks and 6 months later. These recordings will be followed up again after 2 years to see the extent to which individual life stories have been shaped by the events of September 11. These recordings will become a memorial of immense significance because there are no graves through which the dead may be remembered:

> As oral historians, we know that people make sense of their experiences through stories. We want to give people affected by this tragedy the opportunity to offer their own interpretations of this historical event. Through doing so, we will provide the public and generations of future scholars and researchers, a record that represents, to the fullest extent possible, the uniqueness and diversity of responses to this tragedy. (Clark, 2002, p. 26)

Through reminiscing the voice of so-called ordinary people is heard concerning both everyday events as well as great public occasions that they have witnessed, either directly or indirectly. Most people do not normally contribute to the making of public or official historical records, so oral testimony provides opportunities not otherwise available. Through the vivid oral accounts of eyewitnesses, history is made from the bottom up, and a rich vein of experience has the possibility of being preserved for posterity with an immediacy and conviction that more formal public history mostly lacks.

It is not only stories of public events that are worth preserving. At a personal and family level, oral testimony preserves and transmits family history as well as linking families with the wider cultural heritage. Those with sufficient foresight to make sure that family stories are heard and preserved are to be envied. Each time an older person dies, it has been said, history dies with them; a book is lost. Close family members feel this loss most acutely. Encouraging families to discover and preserve their family history before it is too late can lead to great mutual excitement and shared pleasure among the generations. If we learn to listen to people remembering and to remember ourselves, then we capture the past. If we share our recollections by telling someone else or making a record in some other way, then aspects of culture and history are preserved and transmitted. Reminiscence gives a voice to people within their families and possibly further afield within their own communities. Historical knowledge gleaned through life experience can be a valuable gift to future generations.

Reminiscence and Related Activities Are Accessible and Enjoyed by Most People

For those people who are interested in recalling the past, reminiscence can provide enjoyable social exchange. It can readily become a springboard for many other related recreational, diversional, developmental, and creative activities. Reminiscence promotes communication, develops relationships, and provides intellectual stimulation. Stressing the pleasurable characteristics of reminiscence in no way denies the emergence of sad, unhappy, or angry memories. These too are a part of life, and speaking about them to warm, empathetic listeners may bring relief and release. Not everyone wants to speak of past times, however, and this reticence must be respected. Some people can keep a painful past from intruding destructively into the present only by ignoring it. Others may be so occupied with living in the present and perhaps thinking about the future that they have neither time nor desire to think about the past (Burnside & Schmidt, 1994; Coleman, 1986). The vast majority of people of all ages, however, get enormous pleasure from recalling the past, sharing memories, and exploring the meanings attached to them with appreciative listeners.

At the very least, reminiscence and recall can provide a simple diversion, a means for reducing boredom and for passing the time. As care facility residents Bridget Friel and Mary Jackson said, "It's a change from looking at people sleeping. It's something to come to. It passes the day." Nor should such purposes be lightly dismissed. Time hangs heavily for people whose present life circumstances may provide few sources of satisfaction and opportunities for personal fulfillment. Because everyone has a past, long or short, and each person is the authority concerning it, reminiscing is a constructive occupation that can enrich and transform the present. Reminiscence provides a way for the past to be used creatively in the present.

Reminiscence Work Contributes to Social Inclusion and Community Development

Many contemporary neighborhoods and communities lack a sense of social cohesion with different groups experiencing isolation, dislocation, discrimination, and alienation from mainstream society. Reminiscence and oral history can provide a vehicle for bringing marginalized people together and for extending understanding of their needs, desires, and aspirations in some situations (Perlstein, 1995). Reminiscence can serve as a link between isolated minorities and become a force for promoting social inclusion and community solidarity. Chapter 7 explores these aspects through descriptions of various projects undertaken to achieve communal objectives such as these.

COMPARISONS BETWEEN REMINISCENCE WORK AND ORAL HISTORY

Although reminiscence and oral history frequently share overlapping objectives, methods, processes, and outcomes, it may be helpful to identify major similarities and differences between the two. In the United Kingdom, reminiscence work is undertaken largely in health and social care contexts and has had a central place in the oral history movement, partly because of historical origins, institutional developments, academic traditions, and the contribution of particular key individuals. In the United States, oral history has been less incorporated into health and social care work, but, with its strong academic base, has been much concerned with developing collective history. Kaminsky (1988), in his pioneering living history workshop in the South Bronx, combined many aspects of oral history and therapeutic reminiscence when he encouraged Holocaust survivors to recount and preserve their personal stories. The workshop created opportunities for these survivors to contribute to the public record and also to partially resolve their private pain while bearing witness to world events and ensuring personal and family continuities.

Greenspan (1999), in his oral history work with Holocaust survivors, distinguished between retelling and recounting. For him, when people engage in retelling, they put together a coherent story in which all the pieces are available to the teller and the listener; they tell a structured story with a beginning, middle, and end. In recounting, however, the account is incomplete; much is left unsaid because the story is fragmented and parts are only fleetingly visible or not fully accessible. He suggested that it is important to learn about people's lives before, during, and after the Holocaust and to provide repeated opportunities for being heard. Only then will it be possible to comprehend how past suffering is also reflected in the ways in which people live their current lives: "To understand the meaning of life surrounded by death during the Holocaust, we must also examine how that death remains in the midst of current life" (p. 17). He wrote that although repeated dialogue is necessary to enable "the pattern of the separate mosaic pieces to begin to emerge" (p. 17) for an individual, it is also important to listen to multiple accounts from various people if a public understanding of history is ever to be achieved.

It is exceedingly difficult for people to satisfy the need to tell their story and contribute to both the private and public record if other people are indifferent and fail to show interest. Members of an attentive, sympathetic reminiscence group can help to validate an individual's story, but some find that another wider audience is also necessary. This consists of "outsiders" who have not endured the same experiences and may not share the same views yet are implicated in various ways. This happened, for example, with the members of a reminiscence group for Russian immigrants attending a day center whose stories failed to conform to the prevailing view of America as a land of opportunity; "Coming to America represented an end for them rather than a new beginning" (Feinberg, 1996, pp. 42–43). An 82-year-old former teacher said, "I was raised in the Ukraine; my parents are buried there. Memories of playing are there. My grandchildren never ask (about this). Ah, I so miss the countryside." Another group member Isaac, an 81-year-old engineer and prison camp survivor expressed a similar sadness: "When I boarded the plane to leave Russia 8 years ago, my life ended. Once I was on the plane, it could have landed anywhere. I didn't care."

The process of preserving an identity forged in one place and threatened by transition to another in later life is enormously complex in the best of circumstances. If this transition revives earlier traumatic experiences and if people feel disregarded in the present, then their lives may become exceedingly problematic. Opportunities to relate one's story to appreciative listeners and to contribute to creating public, collective accounts seem central to preserving identity in times of threat and are a means for achieving some measure of satisfaction from a new phase of life in a new location.

Bornat (2001, 2002) suggested that although reminiscence resembles oral history, the approaches differ in three ways. The first concerns aims or purposes, the second refers to methods or techniques, and the third refers to the relative importance placed on process and outcomes. Reminiscence work also shares some common attributes with reality orientation and validation therapy yet differs from both in important ways. These two approaches are described in Chapter 5, which addresses reminiscing with individuals and small groups. At the risk of gross oversimplification, Figure 2.1 draws on Bornat's work summarizes the major similarities and differences between oral history and reminiscence work.

TYPES OF REMINISCENCE AND SPECIAL APPLICATIONS

Having considered various ways in which the functions or purposes of reminiscence have been classified, it is important to understand that some of these purposes are more relevant than others for people with certain problems or disabilities. This is particularly true, for example, for people with dementia, for whom social and intellectual stimulation and the maintenance of self-esteem, continued communication, and being able to preserve relationships and have fun must be preeminent. For people with depression (an epidemic of late life), issues of identity, self-esteem, problem solving, bitterness revival, conversation, and intimacy maintenance may be important; although for people with a terminal illness, meaning making, death preparation, and issues of reconciliation may be urgent. The work of Cappeliez (1999, 2002); Haight and Hendrix (1998); Haight, Michael, and Hendrix (1998, 2000); Watt and Cappeliez (2000); and Wong and Watt (1991) is particularly relevant concerning reminiscence and life review with people who are depressed.

Taking forward the earlier work that identified six types of reminiscence (listed in Chapter 1), Watt and Cappeliez (2000) stressed the importance of integrative and instrumental reminiscence and life review. They showed that when reminiscence is linked with a cognitive therapy approach to group work, significant improvement in coping, adaptation, and mood is achieved in depressed older people. They suggested that integrative reminiscence assists depressed people to perceive their past as significant and worthwhile. This is achieved when past negative experiences

Oral History	Reminiscence Work
Instrumental purpose: to preserve and transmit knowledge	Instrumental purpose: to benefit the individual in specific ways
Predominant interest is in content and product outcome	Predominant interest is likely to be in process and relationship building and only sometimes in creating a product
Style is mainly interrogative, structured, designed to seek material relevant to prepared hypotheses or to seek answers to prepared questions	Interactive, less interrogative, less structured, more responsive and open ended
Relates to the academic desciplines of history, sociology, and politics	Relates to the academic disciplines of history and psychology and to human service professional training
Undertaken by oral historians, volunteers, and school and college students	Undertaken by many different health, social care, and community professionals, arts workers, volunteers, and family members
Usually undertaken with individual informants on a one-to-one basis, but sometimes group interviews are used	Undertaken with either individuals, couples, or most frequently in small groups
Ownership usually passes to the interviewer	Ownership is negotiated and agreed
Power is vested with the interviewer	Power is vested in participants
Interviewer sets the agenda and controls the session	Agenda or program mutually agreed among informant and worker who acts as facilitator or enabler
Takes place in various contexts	Takes place in various contexts
Growing awareness of ethical issues with an emphasis on individual rights	Considerable awareness of and sensitivity to ethical issues
Legitimizes telling of personal stories and seeks out connections between individual accounts and collective history	Celebrates personal stories and is usually, although not always, less concerned to locate individual accounts within their public historic contexts
Uses triangualtion of various oral and documentary sources to check veracity and reliability of accounts	Less concerned with truth telling and historical accuracy—more tuned to the social contruction of reality and views memory making as a process of partial reconstruction, transformation, and interpretation
Habitually uses audio or video recording and note taking	Does not habitually use audio or video recording but usually makes some written records of content and process

Figure 2.1.   Similarities and differences in oral history and reminiscence work.

are integrated with the present and present reality is reconciled with the ideal. To achieve this integration and sense of coherence, significant experiences are recalled and reviewed, and in this process, people learn to reattribute responsibility; challenge negative thoughts about self and others; and reconnect with ideas, values, and sources for promoting self-worth. This links with instrumental reminiscence that involves recalling past plans, goal-directed activities, and achievements in overcoming past difficulties as a basis for solving present problems. This process leads to the reduction of problem avoidance. By using strategies that are perceived as having worked successfully in the past, feelings of control and increased ability to represent oneself as competent in the present emerge.

If a sense of coherence is to be achieved, then remembering must embrace coming to terms with what did not happen as well as with what did happen (i.e., the lived life). This involves remembering and integrating hopes that were never attained but may remain forever alive in memory, casting a long shadow over subsequent experience.

Regret and disappointment over paths missed or opportunities lost can intrude into reminiscence and will require perceptive exploration. It is impossible to know how life might have been; we can only know how it has been, and integration and integrity lie in acceptance of how it has turned out. If people are to feel satisfied with life in the present and to experience a sense of aging successfully, then they will be well served by reminiscence and life review. Rewarding interactions with other people, achieving a sense of purpose in life, maintaining personal autonomy (at least over some aspects of life), accepting the need for interdependence (not independence), working at personal growth and acceptance of the self and others are all possible functions served by various approaches to reminiscence (Fisher, 1995).

RESERVATIONS ABOUT REMINISCENCE WORK

Having considered the many positive reasons for undertaking reminiscence work with individuals, couples, and small groups, and its wide acceptability to most people of all ages, it is also important to consider the reservations that are sometimes expressed about its use.

Reminiscence Encourages People to Live in the Past

This view used to be common but has attracted little support since the 1960s. No longer is conversation about things past thought to be either a sign of mental illness or evidence of escapism. New understanding and liberation was experienced by Dobrof when she reflected on the way Butler's (1963) writing had influenced so many health care professionals:

> I remember well being taught by our consulting psychiatrists and the senior social work staff about the tendency of our residents to talk about childhood in the shtetls of East Europe or arrival at Ellis Island or early years on the Lower East Side of New York. At best, this tendency was seen as an understandable, although not entirely healthy preoccupation with happier times, understandable because these old and infirm people walked daily in the shadow of death. At worst "living in the past" was viewed as pathology—regression to the dependency of the child, denial of the passage of time and the reality of the present, or evidence of organic impairment of the intellect. It was even said that "remembrance of things past" could cause or deepen depression amongst our residents and God forgive us, we were to divert the old from reminiscing through activities such as bingo and arts and crafts. And then the Butler paper came out and was read and talked about and our world changed. The life review became not only a normal activity . . . it was seen as a therapeutic tool. . . . (1984, p. xvii)

This sense of liberation and understanding is the common experience of people in many different human service occupations when they learn to listen to the stories told by older men and women when speaking of their personal past.

Reminiscence Does Harm by Reviving Sad Memories

Some workers, particularly those new to reminiscence practice, fear they may do harm by encouraging conversation about painful past events and from arousing distressing emotions associated with these memories. Often, this anxiety is triggered as much by a fear that workers will find themselves confronted with intense emotions, especially tears and sadness, that they personally find disturbing and with which they feel ill equipped to cope. Practice experience indicates that powerful emotions associated with positive and negative, happy and sad memories can be aroused and expressed in reminiscence sessions. Stories of past pain and hardship may well be recounted, sometimes for the very first time, although the original event may have occurred many years before. Very seldom is such an experience of sharing painful memories reported as having negative outcomes, providing that the person feels the story is listened to, that he or she has actually been heard, and that his or her experience has been validated. Other group members and workers too are likely to be emotionally affected by hearing and sharing another person's pain. This is the nature of empathy, of feeling with others, as if walking in their shoes or sitting in their chair. It is important to retain this "as if" quality to avoid becoming overwhelmed by or lost in the other person's pain. In this connection, the humanistic nondirective counseling principles of honesty, congruence, and genuineness are very relevant. Also important are opportunities for debriefing after a reminiscence session and supervision or consultation to enable workers to reflect on how the work they are doing is affecting them. These issues are explored further in Chapter 3, which addresses staff training and development.

All human service professionals risk doing harm as well as doing good. Learning "how to do good well," to borrow a phrase from Robert Frost, is the challenge. Responsible, ethical practice requires the worker to weigh the relative possibilities of doing good or doing harm before encouraging any person to join a reminiscence group or undertake life review or life story work. Clearly the individual's preferences must be respected at all times (McCormack, 2003). Although members of the human service professions, especially those in health and social care contexts, need to weigh the risks of incurring harm by their actions, they also must consider the risks associated with their inaction (Burnside, 1984).

In caring for frail or older people and those with disabilities, particularly those living in long-term care establishments, the biggest risk is exposure to the negativism of professionals, because this carries tremendous potential for causing harm. The attractions of reminiscence work are its genuinely wide but not universal acceptability, its relative ease of implementation, and its low cost compared with many other psychosocial interventions. Doing nothing—meaning the absence of effort to provide sensitive, relevant, and acceptable social and intellectual stimulation and human companionship—is morally reprehensible. Doing reminiscence is risky (someone might get upset, someone might recall a disturbing memory, someone might even cry) but this is less risky for the majority of people than doing nothing. Responsible practice requires that arrangements should be in place to provide appropriate skilled psychotherapeutic help on the very rare but concerning occasions when an individual becomes so distressed by reminiscence that referral to a clinician is necessary.

Reminiscence May Provoke Family Opposition

Some staff fear encountering opposition or arousing antagonism from family members who may oppose their relative's involvement in reminiscence. This may arise from fears that long-kept family secrets may be exposed, memories may be inaccurately recalled, people's emotional equilibrium may be disturbed, or present placement arrangements may be upset. Frank explanations about the work intended, its nature, and its purpose usually allay such fears. Exploration of the underlying causes of the resistance may be ill advised, but an invitation to the family member to see what is being proposed or to join in may provide reassurance and achieve cooperation. To proceed without the agreement of the responsible family caregiver is probably unwise, even if it is not legally required. To do so invites difficulties for all concerned and might worsen relationships within the family or between the family and the staff of the facility. It is usually preferable to offer alternative activities that family members perceive as less threatening if it is not possible to secure their cooperation.

Reminiscence Requires Considerable Skill

"Fools rush in where angels fear to tread." Some managers may fear that staff will require too much support and supervision if they are to undertake reminiscence work. Some staff members are natural listeners and revel in hearing about the past; others are less interested and may be better described as doers. Everyone, given encouragement, time, and training can enhance their intrinsic interpersonal skills and extend their capacity for empathic listening. They can learn to become more comfortable in hearing and sharing other people's pain and more able to face their own past and present life experience, thereby reducing anxiety about their own aging and mortality.

Reminiscence Encourages Dishonesty and Distortion

Because a person's story changes from one telling to another, some people may wish to dismiss the changing accounts as inaccurate, dishonest, irrelevant, not worth telling, and not worthy of being heard. Not everyone accepts the idea that memories are partial reconstructions rather than exact replicas of original experience. They may find it hard to accept that everyone practices selective remembering and forgetting. We all reconstruct the past to make it more acceptable and more interesting, depending on the context of the telling, our present needs and moods, and the responses of our hearers.

Reminiscence Is Used as an Escape from the Present

Some believe that people should not be encouraged to use reminiscence as a refuge from present reality. Whatever a person's reality may be, it is essential to try to understand what purpose or purposes reminiscence is serving and to respect the individual and to appreciate each person's needs, feelings, and time preoccupations. Some people with a history of mental illness involving the distortion of reality may require specific reality testing therapy. Increasingly in dementia care, confidence is growing about encouraging caregivers to share the reality and time scale of the person with moderate or severe dementia and to validate the feelings associated with whatever time period is significant to them. Further information about using this approach with people with dementia and the role of validation and reality orientation is given in Part III.

Reminiscence Activities and Multisensory Triggers Seem Patronizing and Demeaning

There can be no place in reminiscence work for condescension, for encouraging people to engage in trivializing or childish behavior, for treating frail adults as children, or for using triggers in ways that belittle or infantalize people. To recall childhood or to reenact aspects of it is not the same as being childish; it is the way triggers are used, not the triggers themselves that may be demeaning. Ethical practice applies to all aspects of reminiscence. It requires genuine respect for people, consultation, and informed choice about participation, programming, and tangible products or outcomes that may be linked with it.

Reminiscence Encourages Emotional Involvement and Loss of Objectivity

Reminiscence raises extremely important questions about the nature of professionalism and professional caring relationships. No longer are professionals required to be remote, cold, detached, aloof, and untouched by the predicament and pain of those they seek to help. There are risks to providing person-centered care unless safeguards of training, support, supervision, and staff care are provided. Staff will only be able to deliver high-quality care if they feel themselves to be cared for and appreciated. Primarily senior managers and employers must carry this responsibility, but it is reasonable to anticipate that their efforts will favorably affect the quality of care that staff provide and the reputation of the organization.

Planned Reminiscence Work Is Unnecessary

Some people believe that spontaneous reminiscence is sufficient. Spontaneous, unplanned reminiscence conversation will undoubtedly occur and give pleasure to those who participate (Bornat, Chamberlayne, Chant, & Pavey, 1998). People who are isolated, egocentric, depressed, or withdrawn may need help to begin and encouragement to sustain social interaction. Considerable additional advantages can accrue from carefully planned and sensitively implemented systematic reminiscence, life review, and life story work for participants of varied ages and backgrounds.

Reminiscence, Whether Formal or Informal, Is Too Time Consuming

Some contend that busy staff are already fully occupied in meeting the physical care requirements of people and that these needs must be the first priority, especially in long-term facilities; time spent listening is an expensive luxury. This objection challenges the philosophy and values of human service organizations. Good physical care, although essential, is not sufficient to meet people's needs. Fortunately, there is increasing recognition of the need for commitment to holistic care to which reminiscence work and related activities can contribute.

Focusing on the Past Results in Bad Practice in the Present

This is the belief that concentration on the past and attributing present behavior to lifetime factors can mean that staff fail to recognize care needs in the present. Explanations of present behavior that staff find challenging may be erroneously attributed to negative past experience rather than recognized as a legitimate appropriate response to unacceptable present circumstances and unmet needs. This may be particularly relevant to people with unrecognized physical problems, inadequate pain control, dementia, depression, or sensory impairments.

Reminiscence May Encroach on the Work of Others

Some staff members worry that existing divisions of labor will be upset and that reminiscence work will overlap or intrude on specialist staff who are employed to undertake counseling, diversional, and recreational activities. Each facility needs to develop its own staffing policies about the allocation of staff roles and responsibilities. Minimally, all staff members need to understand the central importance of reminiscence and have permission to respond attentively when reminiscence spontaneously occurs in their presence.

Confidentiality Is Compromised by Engagement in Reminiscence

Some believe that reminiscence feeds gossip. Clear confidentiality policies need to be set in relation to both spontaneous and planned reminiscence work with individuals, couples, and groups. This issue is closely linked to the need for clarity about the purpose and program of any reminiscence work as well as the particular context in which it is being undertaken. Confidentiality must form part of the agreement or contract developed with participants and is discussed in more detail in Part II.

CONCLUSION

Sharing reminiscences, especially in a group, leads us to identify with other people's life experience. We see in parts of their stories aspects of our own adventures and struggles reflected in the mirror of experience. When we listen to the stories of other people, we are encouraged to consider, reconsider, and reconstruct our own life story or life stories. Each of us, in effect, leads many lives and tells many stories. Just as the French impressionist painter Monet painted many versions of the same scene, as we tell our stories, we recount subtly differing versions. Monet painted multiple canvasses of the west door of Rouen cathedral and another set of pictures of London in the fog. He painted his Rouen series by setting up a number of easels in a house opposite the cathedral. Each day he moved from canvas to canvas, painting as he observed the great west door at different times of day, in changing light, in altered weather conditions, and during his own varied moods and different circumstances. These paintings provide an analogy (but, as with all analogies, not a direct equivalent) for reminiscence and the reconstruction of personal memories. As the circumstances and the audience change, our needs alter and our emotions vary, so the exploration of our memories produces subtly different versions of the same story, with the newer version replacing the previous one and, in turn, becoming the basis of future revisions.

In reminiscence work, we try to take people beyond mere recollection. We try to enable them to recapture the intensity of pleasure, to feel afresh and experience again the reconstructed, partially transformed recollection. This enabling requires empathic listening and sensitive prompting by stimulating different senses. Memories of a day at the seaside, for example, will be enhanced by actual, recorded, or imagined hearing, seeing, or feeling: the roar of the waves, the cry of gulls, the sound of fairground music, water lapping on a shingle beach, the feel of sand between the toes or the fingers, the texture of shells, the smell of seaweed, the feel of handling a bucket and spade, and the taste of ice cream. All of these sensations are possible in reminiscence work, and some or all will add immeasurably to the richness of the recall and the varied gains that it brings.

This chapter has reviewed several formulations of the reasons for undertaking reminiscence work and the different functions it serves, and it has paid particular attention to Webster's empirically based RFS. The chapter has also explored the widespread desire to achieve a sense of coherence in later life (interpreted as viewing the world as comprehensible, manageable, and meaningful) and how people with depression may be assisted by integrative and instrumental reminiscence and life review. Similarities and differences between oral history and reminiscence work were summarized, and common objections to reminiscence work were addressed. Chapters 4 and 5 show how to implement different kinds of reminiscence work to achieve these various functions; before that, however, the contribution that reminiscence work can make toward developing the knowledge, values, and skills of staff is considered.

Chapter 3

Staff Development Through Reminiscence

In all health and human service professions, the competence and commitment of staff largely determine the quality and effectiveness of the services provided. Their salaries, training, and continuing education constitute the majority of recurring expenditures faced by service providers. It is crucial that staff training and development actually influence attitudes and develop knowledge and skills in ways that affect the quality of the services provided. Although the principles and philosophy of adult education (Cross, 1991) have become imbedded in the basic professional training of most helping professions, these principles are too frequently ignored in the development of less well-qualified staff who provide most direct care.

Direct care providers undertake the greatest amount of face-to-face care in hospitals, residential facilities, adult day centers, and home care services, yet they often have had only rudimentary preparation. This group of staff has the greatest potential for immediately influencing the well-being or ill-being of those in their care and is likely to benefit most from engaging in reminiscence work. They are also likely to be most missed by care recipients if low job satisfaction and low wages result in constant staff turnover (Beck, 1999).

Managers and senior clinical staff who provide leadership and supervision must be responsible for creating opportunities for direct care staff to extend their horizons, deepen their relationships, reconsider their attitudes, and extend their knowledge and skills within a climate that encourages inquiry, constructive criticism, personal growth, and professional

Photograph courtesy of Encore Theatre, Eugene, Oregon.

development. Good intentions and a desire to serve others, although essential characteristics, are no longer sufficient qualifications for working in a caring context. All professionals striving to respond to the health and social needs of people of all ages are increasingly required to demonstrate competence and to use treatments and interventions that have been carefully researched and recognized as effective. Caring establishments are required by law to meet rigorous standards and to respect the rights of the people they serve.

This chapter explores issues concerned with developing staff competence and the relevance of research to reminiscence work and related interventions. The chapter concentrates on staff involvement in reminiscence work. Reminiscence as a tool for promoting staff development has received relatively little attention, yet its potential for changing staff attitudes and influencing staff behavior by enjoyable, nonthreatening means is considerable (Gibson, 1998b). The developmental gains for staff arising from their involvement in reminiscence-related activities could be one of the greatest benefits from reminiscence work (Bornat, Chamberlayne, Chant, & Pavey, 1998).

If successful, reminiscence should result in observable changes in staff attitudes and behavior that affect the quality of the care provided. The staff members involved develop greater personal confidence and increased job satisfaction. Competence and satisfaction are intertwined, and both should positively affect the quality of service. Staff development involves acquiring, integrating, and using knowledge, values, and skills in ways that improve the quality of services and the quality of relationships with service users and their principal relatives. It also means that the staff members experience increased competency, improved morale, and greater commitment. Related issues concerning the importance of research and the development of international guidelines to underpin good reminiscence practice are also explored in this chapter.

ASPECTS OF STAFF DEVELOPMENT

This section explores nine aspects of staff development deriving from direct participation in planned reminiscence work either with individuals, families, or small groups. These aspects are most relevant to health and social care organizations, although most can also be translated across to other practice contexts. Some of the categories overlap, and several gains are likely to be achieved simultaneously from the same reminiscence practice experience.

Changing Staff Attitudes, Values, and Behavior

Attitudes and personal and professional values influence behavior. How we behave toward others arises from how we feel toward them, how we value or respect them, and what we believe about them either as individual people or as members of a group or category. Care staff often have negative views and prejudices toward older people and people with disabilities (and sometimes toward younger people, migrants, and members of minority ethnic groups). These people are often labeled or categorized with general titles such as juvenile delinquents, prisoners or ex-offenders, alcoholics, sex abusers, or drug addicts. Stigmatizing attitudes result in negative behavior and reduce the amount of effort staff members are prepared to make with and on behalf of those in their care. If staff members perceive someone as old, useless, boring, demoralized, unable, unwilling to learn new things, or lacking anything interesting to say, then they are unlikely to make very effective efforts to engage with this person. They will be inclined to limit the time spent in his or her company and will concentrate primarily on attending to routine physical care tasks. If through reminiscence work staff members catch a glimpse of the person as he or she used to be, their attitudes—hence, their behavior—can change dramatically (Clarke, Hanson, & Ross, 2003; Goldwasser & Auerbach, 1996).

Engagement in reminiscence provides a sense of continuity across time because people become known as individuals rather than anonymous members of a stigmatized group. As older people talk about their lives, the conviction grows that they are not part of the group viewed by society as the elderly. Despite all external appearances, the individual person stands out as essentially being the same as in past times. Staff members who are quick to judge people too frequently limit opportunities for people to join reminiscence groups because of strongly held negative preconceptions about how they will respond if invited. Staff who believe "she seldom joins anything" or "he will never come because he is always preoccupied complaining about his illness" need to be challenged to reconsider their preconceptions. These premature or mistaken opinions usually dramatically change when confronted with the enthusiasm that people labeled as uncooperative often develop for reminiscence activities once given the opportunity to participate.

Mills (1998), who undertook extensive life story work with individuals with severe dementia who attended a day hospital, found that she became more aware of their special characteristics as her informants' cognitive impairments increased. She realized that in bequeathing their stories to her she became their beneficiary. As a consequence her respect, understanding, and acceptance of each person grew. She unashamedly loved these people; they became her friends, and she grieved greatly when they were lost to her, either because of the ravages of their advancing dementia or through death.

Encouraging caregivers to write and reflect on their own life story has been used as a means of positively influencing the attitudes of mental health aides, nurses, and social workers (Burnside, 1984, 1990; Ross, 1990). Burnside (1990) wrote persuasively that reminiscence was the single most effective way to reduce ageism in nursing students. Petrukowicz and Johnson (1991) found that adding positive biographical details about patients to their charts countered the stereotypical attitudes of staff and resulted in more personalized staff–resident interactions. Other identified gains have included increased staff identification with older people—seeing the person as being "just like me," acquiring new learning ("he brought history alive"); and developing affection ("I couldn't help loving him"). Dobrof highlighted dramatic changes in staff behavior:

> And then the Butler article came out and was read and talked about and our world changed . . . In a profound sense, Butler's writings liberated both the old and the nurses, doctors, and social workers; the old were free to remember, to regret, to look reflectively at the past and try to understand it. And we were free to listen and to treat rememberers and remembrances with the respect they deserved, instead of trivializing them by diversion to a bingo game. (1984, p. xiii)

Individualizing People Through Knowledge of Their Lives

It is easy to say that everyone is unique; it is much harder to treat everyone as unique, especially if a number of people share common characteristics such as advanced age, ill health, low mood, minority status, or communal living arrangements. Personhood is easily eroded in the face of physical frailty or mental disability. If respect and dignity are to be preserved in advancing years, then it is essential that caregivers continue to relate to people as individuals and not in terms of any general group characteristics that may be unconsciously assigned. Examining the ways in which we address people is a good way of checking our ability to relate to each person as an individual. High-quality care is synonymous with respecting individuality. Encouraging care staff to review their own lives can bring a heightened sense of their own uniqueness and, by implication, the uniqueness of the people whose lives they share in the course of their daily work. In a simple consciousness-raising training exercise, for example, staff could be asked to name or list three to five characteristics that make them different from other people. This provides rich material for discussion about sameness, difference, and our need to be seen as unique individuals yet members of a group.

Involvement in reminiscence work highlights the personhood or humanity of each participant, and this, in turn, evokes a human response from the worker or caregiver, as Forster (1998) and Gibson (1998b) both found. Forster, an oral historian employed in a large rehabilitation center, compiled life histories that she summarized on storyboards and placed beside the person's bed. These boards provided a personal record showing continuity across time; they were a celebration of the life lived and were a means of informing nursing staff about the individuals:

> There is no doubt that when you get to know someone a bit better, your attitude changes. The resident is no longer just a resident. She has had an interesting life that you have just discovered where you can now treat her and think of her as a friend. I feel closer to the residents now. Instead of knowing them only in their later years, I feel as if I have also known them as young people. (1998, p. 61)

Through engaging in life history work, staff members glimpse the older person as he or she used to be. With new eyes, they see the long, intricate, often heroic journeys traveled by each individual. This new view radically shifts perceptions and changes relationships. Through this fresh understanding, care can be transformed. If staff members become intrigued by these intensely unique histories, then not only do their conversations become more meaningful but also their sympathy and empathy for the person—regardless of current frailty, mood, and behavior—is greatly enlarged. Molly Coulter, a residential facility manager, discovered this while participating in a reminiscence group:

> My whole relationship with Mr. Brown is transformed . . . I had always found him very difficult. I never understood why he hated being here. Now I understand. Suddenly we have something in common, something to talk about and share an interest in.

Enhancing Caring, Coping, and Interpersonal Skills

Doing specific, detailed life history work with people, including people with dementia who exhibit behavior that challenges care staff and disrupts life for others in care contexts, can contribute to staff development. It helps staff to learn that each person has distinct needs (Puentes, 2000). It can increase confidence and bring great personal pleasure and increased job satisfaction because staff members learn to be less frightened, less defensive, and less overwhelmed.

Involvement in reminiscence work improves communication and enhances relationships as staff members realize that effective care needs to be based on respect for each person's values and history. Knowledge of the past gained through reminiscence and careful listening is particularly indispensable in dementia care, where it can help caregivers decode puzzling speech and bizarre behavior. Killick sought to understand people with dementia by means of attentive listening. He described how he decodes their conversation, and then returns their words to them as poetry:

> It seems to me that the language used by people with dementia is a metaphorical one—where what they say often does not make sense in the usual literal way but has a poetic or symbolic meaning. People express themselves in language nearer to poetry than they used before. One lady, for example, talked about her experience as a monkey-puzzle, and another expressed a yearning for freedom as riding on a swing. (1994, p. 16)

Assessment Care Planning and Managed Care Skills

Assessment is the gate through which most people enter care. It is also the ongoing process by which their continuing needs are subjected to regular review and service responses are refined and adjusted. It is very important that all staff in significant contact with an individual, as well as the person and his or her family representative, have opportunities to contribute to assessments and reviews. Assessment is frequently a very formal process, which can be experienced as intimidating and unhelpful. Frequently, service users or care recipients feel they have not had an adequate opportunity to participate and to be heard. The direct care staff who know the person best often are not included in case conferences. Bender, Baukham, and Norris (1999) recognized the valuable contribution group reminiscence could make to the assessment process for people thought to have dementia. In a psychiatric hospital setting, Bender et al. used a structured reminiscence group co-led by a nurse and occupational therapist, instead of the conventional individual testing done by a clinical psychologist for making initial assessments. They suggested that a reminiscence-orientated group is less intimidating than an individual interview, its informality and focus on reminiscence topics encourage easy conversation and provide rich opportunities for staff observation.

Gearing and Coleman (1996) developed a biographical approach to individual assessment of frail older people who were facing the possibility of admission to residential care. They created a semistructured biographical assessment format that could be completed in one or two interviews, each lasting approximately half an hour. The interviews were undertaken by professional social workers within the context of a sympathetic and informal relationship. This was not a research instrument but a person-centered tool used for reaching a mutual assessment. The biographical focus enabled the workers to make more appropriate, comprehensive assessments and to agree on the content of care plans. Staff undertaking these assessments developed the capacity to locate present frailties within a life course framework, to appreciate individuality, to respect personal preferences, and to suggest agreed rather than imposed care plans. Through such life history methods, staff enhanced and extended their conventional assessment skills and had the added satisfaction of knowing that the people being assessed were more confident about the process and more content with its outcomes.

Owning Emotions and Using Personal Strengths on the Job

Reminiscence gives staff the freedom to be themselves, to express their own emotions, to demonstrate their humanity, and to be appreciated. In reminiscence work, staff are permitted to have feelings, to express feelings, and, in a reflective and disciplined way, to develop an awareness of past influences in their own and other people's lives.

Bornat recognized the potential of reminiscence in staff development when she reflected on the response to the original three recall tape/slide audio-visual trigger packages that fueled the growth of reminiscence-related activities in the United Kingdom (*Help the Aged*, 1981):

We began to hear accounts of how, by taking part in reminiscence sessions, staff became aware of their own particular competencies and strengths. Care staff in residential settings were then, as now, typically poorly paid, low in the hierarchy of responsibility, and undertrained. Yet evidence from the field suggested that reminiscence work was bringing out hidden strengths and enthusiasms. Some people emerged as natural group facilitators, whereas others became keen collectors of objects . . . It is the potential for the recognition and development of staff's skills and involvement that I see as possibly the most significant contribution of reminiscence work, certainly as significant as its potential for the quality of life of older people themselves. (1998, p. 46)

Staff members bring many strengths and skills to their work. Engagement in reminiscence work enables them to utilize many natural and acquired abilities. Reminiscence groups, which are usually warm, sociable, and happy occasions, provide nonthreatening contexts within which staff can showcase their organizational, display, photographic, recording, archiving, information technology, writing, music, dance, dramatic, and graphic skills. Involvement in reminiscence is important because it assists staff to discover practical, artistic, creative, and emotional resources within themselves and to develop the courage and confidence to express these in the workplace for the benefit of others. Enhanced motivation and increased job satisfaction have been linked to involvement in reminiscence work, which can become stepping stones to further training, advancement, or promotion.

Acquiring Historical and Cultural Knowledge

Staff report that gaining historical knowledge and the skills to elicit and organize historical material is the most common outcome for themselves from reminiscence (Levine, 1996). This knowledge is usually highly valued because of its infectious authenticity. Hearing an eyewitness say, "I was there when . . ." carries interest and conviction that far surpasses written or published accounts. If staff members prize the richness of verbal culture above more conventional ways of learning about the past, then these direct accounts will open up new worlds. For some people, the oral account will encourage them to explore related historical documentary sources. The transmission of cultural knowledge and experience is invaluable for individuals, families, and society. This exposure to firsthand witnesses frequently proves to be a particular fascination in intergenerational and ethnic minority projects (Basting, 2001; Perlstein, 1995).

De Souza (1995, 2003), for example, initiated an elementary school project in Brazil that provided a rich source of cultural and historical information for everyone involved. She introduced older people into elementary schools in various neighborhoods in Brasília. The teachers said that the presence of the older people in the classroom was very beneficial. The project brought new meaning to their work, broke established routines, stimulated the development of new relationships between different age groups, and changed the attitudes of the children toward old age and older people. In turn, the older people themselves reported improvement in self-assessed health status. Many other examples of intergenerational work could be cited from around the world.

Challenging the Status Quo

Reminiscence can often be unsettling and subversive because it challenges conventional relationships among staff of residential facilities and residents, especially older people or those with disabilities (Dunn, Haight, & Hendrix, 2002). It upsets the usual institutional power balance between caregivers and those receiving care. It challenges staff to revise and reorder their priorities and to think about how residents perceive them. People and listening to people may become more important than maintaining present practices and prevailing regimes where the first priority is usually the provision of physical care. Reminiscence can democratize institutions. When residents find their voice, however, and grow more confident in expressing their opinions, staff may not necessarily view this positively. What may well be empowering for residents and service users may be perceived as disempowering for staff. If this happens, then opportunities for genuine change will be lost, although some staff may develop insight into power relationships and how they contribute to creating, sustaining, and perpetuating inequalities within hierarchical institutional structures.

Learning to Collaborate with
Professionals, Volunteers, and Family Members

Learning to work cooperatively across professional and disciplinary boundaries is crucial for delivering high-quality care. Too often, staff members find it hard to work cooperatively with members of other professions. Interprofessional respect and collaboration is usually hard won. Sharing reminiscence work across professional boundaries has proved to be an effective way of lowering defenses, sharing expertise, and broadening knowledge and skills. Volunteers often identify different but similar problems of competition and insecurity in their relationships with paid staff, and the potential for strain and lack of trust between professionals and family caregivers is also well recognized. Such problems need not be insurmountable, but relationships based on respect grow best from shared endeavors. Mutual involvement in reminiscence work, in which all contribute and all feel valued can break down many real and imagined barriers.

Tutoring, Supervising, Consulting, and Mentoring

Various approaches are used to develop staff members' confidence and competence in reminiscence work. *Tutoring* tends to emphasize teaching or instruction. *Supervising,* the most commonly used of these terms, suggests oversight, instruction, and encouragement of self-reflection. *Consulting* indicates sharing superior knowledge on a take it or leave it basis. *Mentoring* stresses example setting, informal discussion, and advice giving. Too frequently, the approach and style adopted by those responsible for delivering staff development reflects their own experience of training and development. Instead of a careful appraisal of the needs of staff members and what is likely to be most effective within the particular context in which people are working. Careful planning must underpin all reminiscence training and development efforts.

INTRODUCING STAFF TO REMINISCENCE TRAINING

An organizational framework is required if the potential of reminiscence work in promoting staff development is to be realized. Reminiscence needs to fit within an explicit overall staff training and development policy that is implemented by means of strategic plans and operational actions. The gains identified in the previous section will not happen automatically when staff members become involved in reminiscence work. Several conditions are necessary for high-quality reminiscence practice to flourish and staff to benefit from being involved in it. They will need assistance to develop the skills required to undertake such work and ongoing support to integrate the learning arising from it. Senior staff must endorse reminiscence work as a legitimate part of the worker's job, for without this formal explicit backing, reminiscence work is unlikely to flourish.

When intending to introduce a reminiscence program into an adult day center or residential facility, the initial step is to provide basic information about the value of reminiscence, including planned and spontaneous reminiscence, to all staff throughout the facility: managerial, administrative, care, domestic, and maintenance. Every staff member needs to be alerted to the importance of responding sympathetically to spontaneous reminiscence. Consciousness-raising exercises usually succeed when they are multifaceted and lighthearted. There are many ways to raise awareness about the importance of valuing personal memories. Competitions and prizes heighten interest. Some could span several weeks. Possibilities include the following:

- Small exhibitions in public areas of artifacts or especially interesting or ambiguous memorabilia that provoke discussion
- Photographic guessing competitions during which staff and service users exhibit personal photographs of themselves as children, adolescents, and young adults
- Historical quizzes
- Enlarged photographs of the neighborhood in days gone by or the facility in earlier years
- Newspaper accounts and photographs of local and national events for the approximate period of 1930–1980
- Simple explanatory brochures or flyers

There needs to be a continuum of training that draws on a range of expertise and creative learning opportunities suited to adults, some of whom may have limited formal education and little confidence in their ability to learn. Introductory short courses are run by various specialist agencies (see Resources) and may be available on an extramural or in-house basis. If an agency intends to undertake its own training, then the material contained in Chapters 1 and 2 of this book, supplemented by experiential reminiscing exercises that involve participants in actual memory work, could provide a basis for two induction sessions, each lasting approximately 2 hours. Chapters 4 and 5 could provide a basis for two further training sessions concerned with beginning to undertake reminiscence practice. Individuals who do not enjoy reminiscing are unlikely to become skilled reminiscence practitioners, so it is important to provide reminiscing experience as a part of the training for people to experience the process first hand.

The awareness-raising exercises should be quickly followed by the identification and selection of staff members who will undertake an initial induction to reminiscence work. Some staff from this group will progress to become involved in actual reminiscence work. Because reminiscence requires competencies that are best learned by doing and then reflecting critically on this practical experience, the actual practice needs to be accompanied by some form of supervision or consultation to encourage critical self-reflection. The content of basic induction training should cover the following:

- What is reminiscence?

- Why do it?

- What outcomes might be expected from the process, for whom, and in what circumstances?

This material is best presented informally, with ample opportunities for participants to reminisce themselves and to discuss and analyze the process so they can identify what reminiscence means to them. The induction training needs to be reinforced by simple handouts. It is important to demystify the process while simultaneously lending a vision about its possibilities and honestly responding to any anxieties about its potential complexities.

Involvement in actual reminiscence practice (preferably with a small group) will build confidence. No trainee should be a passive observer in a group, and no new worker should be left to begin reminiscence group work alone, if at all possible. Instead, an inexperienced worker should share an active role as a co-facilitator who carries defined responsibilities for some aspects of a session with either an individual or a small group. It is assumed that planned group work will be co-led and that each session will be preplanned and debriefed. In addition, supervision is ideally available so that a novice worker can examine his or her own involvement and reactions in more detail and be helped to link the reminiscence practice with wider job responsibilities.

It is desirable to follow this initial period of practice relatively quickly, within 2–3 months, with a further practice opportunity that provides increased leadership responsibilities. Whenever possible, this practice should again be accompanied by ongoing supervision, which does not necessarily have to be on a one-to-one basis or provided by a line manager. Some staff will require further advanced tutoring or training to enable them to develop special knowledge and skills relevant to specific working contexts and particular client groups. As they grow in skill and confidence, they are likely to want to develop other related aspects of reminiscence work concerned with presentations and displays and various artistic, expressive, and performance skills related to the creation of tangible outcomes arising from reminiscence activities. The Reminiscence Trainer's Pack (Gibson, 2000a) contains tutoring materials relevant to working with individuals and small groups; members of ethnic minorities; and people with lifelong learning difficulties, dementia, various sensory and speech disabilities, and depression. The pack also contains various experiential exercises, teaching notes, transparencies, and student's notes that can be photocopied.

If participants in a training course gain an explicit understanding of what reminiscence or life story work they will be expected to undertake within a defined time period, then better outcomes from the training are likely to be achieved. Modest, realistic, specific goals should be encouraged. These action contracts or learning pledges are best written down and should contain a small number of precise objectives and identified action intentions or targets. Completion of a standard learning contract form can help cement good intentions. Some tutors like to reinforce initial training by telephoning the participants after some weeks to check on progress and provide advice, information, and encouragement. This approach is particularly effective if initial training is then followed by a period of application before a subsequent recall day takes place. The purpose of the recall day is to review practice experience, share learning, and work on areas of concern identified by the participants. A recall day needs to be built around presentations made by each participant of the work done or planned but not yet done in the intervening period. Participants need to be encouraged to reflect critically and report on the following:

- What was attempted, with whom, and how it went
- What was achieved

- What obstacles or difficulties were encountered
- What other colleagues thought
- What might be done differently next time

Such presentations provide invaluable material for discussion and are an excellent device for reinforcing positive learning.

TYPES OF SUPERVISION AND SUPPORT

Throughout this book, the importance of training and supporting reminiscence workers both initially and continuously has been stressed as a means of ensuring competent practitioners who will deliver high standards of work. Different types of supportive supervision are possible. Figure 3.1 summarizes various approaches to providing staff supervision and support, development, management oversight, and worker accountability. The approaches identified are tutoring; individual supervision; consultation; group supervision led by a supervisor; and supervision undertaken either in a peer group, a pair or a work team, and mentoring. Figure 3.1 identifies where responsibility for various identified functions, tasks, or responsibilities is vested. It refers in particular to supervision of the part of a salaried staff member's workload that is concerned with developing and sustaining reminiscence practice, although any supervision will inevitably have implications for other aspects of the workload. It refers to formal arrangements while recognizing that a great deal of learning and support also occurs informally and spontaneously within all work groups. Related issues concerned with recruiting, preparing, and supporting volunteers and family members involved in reminiscence work, particularly in relation to dementia care, are discussed in Chapters 9 and 10. All of these approaches or types of supervision and support have been used to increase knowledge, refine skills, reinforce learning, and improve competence. Each profession will have its own conventions and expectations about job-related learning. These can be used to develop an approach that is compatible with the working context, cultural and educational backgrounds, and identified developmental needs of the staff concerned (Kadushin & Harkness, 2002).

REMINISCENCE WORKER	TUTORING	INDIVIDUAL SUPERVISION	CONSULTATION	GROUP SUPERVISION	PEER GROUP SUPERVISION	TANDEM OR DYAD SUPERVISION	TEAM SUPERVISION	MENTORING
WORKER STAGE OF DEVELOPMENT	Inexperienced, new to subject, likely to be anxious	May be either new or experienced in terms of overall job	Experienced worker with considerable autonomy	Usually matched for competence, experience, and qualifications	Experienced workers, willing and able to contribute, shared areas of competence	Equally matched with considerable sympathy for each other's style of work and respect for each other's competence	Varied membership in terms of experience, training, interests, and competence	Usually inexperienced or new to type of work but not necessarily so, especially if other support or expertise is unavailable
TO WHOM ACCOUNTABLE FOR REMINISCENCE PRACTICE	To supervisor	To supervisor	Not provided by consultant	To supervisor	Not vested in group	Not to peer partner but to designated line manager	Team leader or line manager	Team leader or line manager
LINKAGE TO AGENCY	Through supervisor or line manager	Through supervisor or line manager	Not provided by consultant	Through supervisor	Through line manager	Mutual	Team leader	Team leader or supervisor
EVALUATION	By tutor	By supervisor	Not provided by consultant	By supervisor with each individual worker	Mutual	Mutual	Mutual	Mentor, supervisor, and possibly team leader
DEVELOPMENT	Emphasis on teaching either formally or informally	Discussion	Emphasis on teaching	Emphasis on teaching through group discussion	No formal teaching, development achieved through discussion	Peer group and dyad partner	Mutual and team leader	Team leader or other line manager
INITIATIVE IN CONVENING SUPERVISION MEETING AND SETTING AGENDA	Either supervisor or worker	Either supervisor or worker	Worker	Supervisor	Agreed agenda by common consent	Agreed	Team leader or shared by members	Worker

PERSONS INVOLVED	May be supervisor, team leader, external tutor, or knowledgeable and experienced staff member	Supervisor	Consultant	Designated supervisor	Agreed chair or rotating leader	Workers of equal status and experience, indentified roles may be rotated	Team leader and members	Usually one to one, older person gives benefit of experience, popular with women
NUMBER OF PERSONS INVOLVED	Any agreed number	One to one	One to one but other workers may sit in	Group of workers	Six–ten	Two	Six–ten	Usually one but could be a small project team
POWER AND AUTHORITY	Favors tutor	Favors supervisor	Shared between consultant as 'expert' and worker as implementers of decisions	Supervisor	All members seen as equal	Equalized	Favors team leader but equalized between team members	Supervisor or line manager, not mentor who carries moral authority only and commonly volunteers expertise
MANAGEMENT OF REMINISCENCE WORKERS	Either supervisor, worker, or line manager	Supervisor or line manager	Not provided by consultant	Shared	Line manager	Line manager	Line manager	Worker and team leader or worker and line manager
RESPONSIBILITY FOR IMPLEMENTING DECISIONS	Worker	Worker	Worker who is free to accept or reject advice	Agreed within group	Agreed within group	Agreed between partners	Agreed within group	Worker

Figure 3.1. Supervision and support of staff undertaking reminiscence work.

Many members of staff who provide direct care in health and social facilities have had no formal professional training and will benefit immeasurably from being introduced to reminiscence work through appropriate induction training and ongoing supervision of direct reminiscence practice. It is now widely accepted that improved standards of care practice are best achieved by combining learning arising from direct practice experience, training, and supervision (Bender, 1994; Nomura, 1997). Whatever approach is used for ensuring accountability and professional development, it must be based on respect for individual learners and appreciation of each person's own life story. It should value each staff member's own life experience and prior learning. It should demonstrate a belief in each person's ability to learn and to grow, and it should provide tangible evidence of the organization's commitment to assisting all staff to achieve best practice standards. The particular approach to supervision used will depend on the traditions, philosophy, and resources of the agency and the identified needs and resources of its staff.

Mentoring

Mentoring has become very popular, particularly in community service agencies. Mentoring is a formal arrangement, although most often the mentor is serving as an unpaid volunteer. The mentor is an experienced person who undertakes to provide one-to-one support, information, and encouragement over a period of time to another person who is usually, although not always, a younger person. Mentors may be senior agency staff members or retired professionals now working as volunteers, who wish to use their expertise acquired during years of paid employment to assist their community. Mentoring is a way of assisting someone to set and achieve goals, develop skills, and manage his or her own learning and development. A mentor works to develop trust, explores goals, provides information, makes introductions, and motivates and actively encourages self-evaluation of performance and achievements.

Personal Reflection on Reminiscence
Practice and Using Critical Incident Records

Tutoring, consulting, supervising, and mentoring only work satisfactorily when reminiscence workers assume major responsibility for their own learning and development. A characteristic of effective adult learning is that the learner develops the confidence to become self-critical. Other people can play a role in this process, but they can only encourage, support, and assist. If supervision is to influence practice, then it needs to be systematic, regular, and ongoing rather than casual, sporadic, or used only as a crisis response. Workers—either singly or along with co-workers, team colleagues, consultants, supervisors, or mentors—usually find that it is helpful to reflect on practice overall and then on each separate reminiscence session.

Making a record is a key technique for promoting self-critical appraisal. It is strongly recommended that workers keep some records for the purpose of improving their interpersonal skills (Berman-Rossi, 1994). Making audio or video recordings of a session may be intrusive or inhibiting and will certainly be extremely time consuming to replay, view, and analyze. It is nevertheless increasingly common to use such comprehensive recordings for data collection and analysis in research designed to illuminate the processes and effectiveness of reminiscence and for the training of reminiscence workers. Reminiscence practitioners will find that briefer written records of critical incidents are practical helpful learning tools.

A short, focused critical incident record is useful for analyzing and evaluating those parts of sessions that the worker considers have been either very successful or problematic. All of the following need to be written down: details on what immediately preceded the critical incident chosen for recording; who said what to whom; the accompanying emotions (especially the worker's feelings at the time), either expressed or withheld; and the consequential actions by participants and workers. Such a record makes it possible to examine what worked or did not work, to recognize both good and poor practice, and to formulate alternative ideas and explanations. This reflective analytical process also helps the worker to identify and rehearse what might possibly have been a more effective response. Such brief but focused records provide invaluable material for discussion in supervision sessions whether these take place with a supervisor, consultant, mentor, or colleague. The following questions may assist the process of writing such a record, guiding its critical analysis and encouraging second-guessing:

- Where did the incident take place?
- How long did it last?

- What else was happening, if anything, at the same time?

- What immediately preceded the selected incident?

- What was the content of the interaction and who was involved?

- What was the person(s) feeling at the time and afterward?

- What were you feeling at the time and afterward?

- What do you think was being communicated and by whom?

- What did you do that assisted or hindered the incident?

- What else or who else contributed to the success or failure of the incident?

- What happened afterward?

- What would you do the same or differently again?

Other kinds of records and their purposes are discussed in Chapter 4, and various examples of types of record forms are contained in the appendices.

NEED FOR MORE RESEARCH

There are differing views about what are acceptable and relevant means for researching the nature and functions of memory, reminiscence, and recall. A considerable gulf exists between quantitative scientists researching memory unrelated to personal meanings, such as in randomized word cuing and laboratory-based experiments, and those interested in studying how autobiographical memory actually operates in day-to-day life. Increasingly, reminiscence practitioners are turning to the writings of narrative and autobiographical memory theorists to underpin their applied memory work as well as drawing from oral history, literature, and the creative arts.

The evidence-based movement in medicine exerts inexorable pressure toward restricting the range of acceptable research methodologies. At the same time, increasing numbers of researchers of psychosocial interventions appear to be turning to qualitative methodologies, especially single case studies. These are used to demonstrate the specific impact of a particular technique or approach and are considered by many practitioners to be a more appropriate, feasible, and preferred methodology (Fischer, 1994;

Kropf & Tandy, 1998; Sokolovsky, 1996; Woods, 2002). The tensions concerning methodology are most evident in health-related professions in which reminiscence, if represented as a therapy, is required to measure up to the rigorous demands of randomized control trials of efficacy (Cook, 1998; Spector et al., 2000).

Some reminiscence researchers and practitioners vigorously argue that quantitative approaches are too crude and inappropriate to capture the fine gradations of behavioral change and subjective experience of people with complex conditions such as dementia or depression. These researchers believe that single case studies based on the analysis of extensive video recordings and other ethnomethodological approaches are more likely to capture the fine-grained characteristics of people and the changing nature of their disabilities and life circumstances.

Research concerning aspects of reminiscence and life review practice as a psychosocial intervention continues apace, but many aspects await investigation. In order to establish whether reminiscence works, studies need to focus more on specific groups or clearly defined diagnostic categories than has been so in the past. The term *works* is taken to mean something that improves the health, well-being, or life satisfaction of individuals and groups, or improves care practice and care staff competence and morale, which in turn affects the well-being of individuals in defined, positive ways. It is accepted that both the objectives of any research and the means by which it is carried out, in whatever context, will be subject to the rigorous application of accepted ethical principles; this includes research with people not normally regarded as competent to give informed consent (Post, 1995).

Webster (2002) identified a number of limitations of past reminiscence research: the absence of differentiation between reminiscence and other related terms; methodological shortcomings, including poor experimental designs; sampling limitations; and a lack of appropriate, standardized, reliable, and valid psychometric instruments. In the past, too many studies used undifferentiated, or mixed populations whose characteristics were described in very broad, general terms or not at all and whose results were unpersuasive. Successive critical reviews of the research literature have exposed these shortcomings (Haight, 1991; Haight & Hendrix, 1995; Hendrix & Haight, 2002; Merriam, 1980; Molinari & Reichlin, 1985; Spector, Orrell, Davies, & Woods, 2000; Thornton & Brotchie, 1987).

Increasingly, studies are using experimental designs—including carefully specified controls, variables, and interventions with data compared at pretest and posttest points in time together with longer time intervals between—to demonstrate the persistence of effects. Continued caution will be necessary before generalized conclusions about effectiveness are widely substantiated. This is not easy to achieve as types of intervention multiply, functions served remain diffuse and ill defined, and an ever-widening range of research populations are studied.

As the reviews already listed suggested, however, steady progress continues to be made. Increasingly sophisticated and more rigorous approaches to research methodology are developing in parallel with interest in researching populations other than people who are English speaking, Caucasian, and older (Webster, 2002). Reminiscence research as well as practice is being constructively influenced by multinational, multidisciplinary, and multiprofessional collaboration. Ethnic differences in terms of reminiscence functions, program content, and outcomes are beginning to attract research attention (Atkinson, Kim, Ruelas, & Lin, 1999), as are a widening variety of research methods, practice contexts, and client groups. There is also a growing interest in defining where and how reminiscence work fits with artistic creativity, oral history, autobiographical memory, and narrative studies and with the exploration of spirituality, meaning making, life satisfaction, and quality of life.

It is not easy to undertake quantitative research in reminiscence with people who have dementia because of the idiosyncratic course of different types of dementia and the considerable variability in symptoms, behavior, and rate of decline. Nor is it easy with such a vulnerable population to gain access to sufficient numbers of people to enable intervention and control groups to be established and maintained over a sufficient period of time and thereby obtain adequate baseline and retest measures. There are also serious ethical concerns about withholding interventions or treatments for the purpose of achieving control groups, although people waiting for service provision are increasingly used as controls.

Research concerned with response to activities, including reminiscence undertaken with people with dementia, shows that most types of psychosocial interventions achieve positive results in cognitive, social, and psychological effects, with reminiscence showing the greatest effects (Brooker & Duce, 2000; Droes, 1997). This finding once again raises the specter of a scattergun approach to research—namely, that it does not matter much what you do by way of intervention as long as you do something. The study of specific interventions for specific types and degrees of impairment associated with dementia is likely to yield more valid and reliable results, and a more focused approach would also permit replication of studies that now only rarely happens.

There is a growing determination worldwide to try to understand the experience of people with dementia, to appreciate the view from the inside (Hirsch & Mouratoglou, 1999). Strenuous efforts are being made to listen to and comprehend the voice of people with dementia speaking about what it is like to have dementia and what kinds of assistance are acceptable and helpful in what circumstances (Davis, 1993; DeBaggio, 2002; Friel McGowen, 1993; Henderson & Andrews, 1998). This is a huge challenge that demands a considerable repertoire of clinical, research, and creative communication skills (Allan, 2002; Killick & Allan, 2001).

Regardless of whether people have dementia, much reminiscence work utilizes various artistic activities by means of which people portray, interpret, and communicate their life stories. Therefore varied research approaches will be required to illuminate the ways in which individuals use and benefit from these creative approaches. No one research approach is likely to be comprehensively adequate or universally applicable in the study of reminiscence and related work being undertaken for multiple purposes with diverse people in widely different practice contexts. If reminiscence work comprises both art and science, then it can reasonably be suggested that both rigor and creativity must find a place in any associated research.

Defining Good Practice

Even when rigorous research indicates what is required to achieve effective practice, there is unfortunately no guarantee that such findings will be widely disseminated and implemented. Many factors besides ignorance conspire to restrict the application of research findings to reminiscence practice. The contribution of training and supervision has already been explored, but there is also a pressing need to identify minimum standards as a guide to good practice. Because reminiscence work is such a loosely defined set of ideas and embraces such a disparate range of activities undertaken by people with such varied professional and personal backgrounds in many diverse contexts, this is no simple task. If some national and international standards of agreed ethical practice principles are to emerge, then organizations such as the International Institute of Reminiscence and Life Review and the European Reminiscence Network, together with other national umbrella groups, need to work together to begin to articulate them. Agreed standards would give some protection to vulnerable people who participate in reminiscence work to ensure that they are treated with respect and are empowered, not disempowered, by becoming involved in reminiscence activities. A statement of principles would assist resource holders, researchers, practitioners, and participants to set realistic, attainable goals and indicate the parameters within which accountability, monitoring, research, and evaluation might reasonably occur. It is beyond the scope of this discussion to do other than identify the need and suggest some of the core areas that could be addressed. These include considerations of selection, risk assessment, accessibility, equality of opportunity, consent, contracting, confidentiality, clarity about objectives and methods, partnership, and the competence and accountability of workers.

Guidelines could also refer to desirable expectations concerning training, preparation, and supervision of reminiscence practitioners and the responsibility of employers concerning these matters. Workers and volunteers need to be aware of their own limitations and personal needs, which include awareness of their own attitudes to memory work and meaning making and the significance of reminiscence and recall in their personal and family lives. They need to be open to discussion, self-scrutiny, and responsible criticism from others. They must be both reflective and reflexive so that they come to understand how involvement in reminiscence, recall, and life review affects themselves as well as others.

Workers and volunteers must be willing to respect and accept a participant's version of memory and to be sensitive to differences in culture, ethnicity, and age. They need increasingly to develop understanding about the impact of broader historical, cultural, and political events related to the times and places through which people of different ages involved in memory work have lived. If any material resulting from reminiscence is to be made public, then the agreement of the people concerned must be secured, preferably in writing. Confidentiality must be negotiated according to the people and circumstances involved and the context in which the reminiscence work is taking place. Guarantees of absolute or blanket confidentiality are rarely possible or desirable and contractual and legal liability considerations must be respected. If referral to another agency is required, especially for clinical reasons, then workers should inform themselves beforehand of the services available, proceeding only with the agreement of the people concerned and in ways that are acceptable to them. It is recognized that this is only a brief examination of complex issues that may have far-reaching resource, ethical, and professional implications.

CONCLUSION

If the potential of reminiscence as a tool for influencing the development of staff's knowledge, skills, attitudes, and values is to be realized, then staff development needs to become an explicit mainstream objective, rather than an incidental by-product, of reminiscence work. If we are to understand the value it could have for staff, then, as in most aspects of reminiscence, we need to be more precise about terminology, more explicit in our methodology, and more rigorously critical in our evaluation of outcomes. By learning about and participating in reminiscence practice, staff can begin to free themselves from constraining preconceptions, negative attitudes, limiting stereotypes, and rigid interpretations of behavior. Through involvement in reminiscence work, staff can become more open to a fresh vision of people as unique individuals and to a more generous assessment of their capabilities. Reminiscence work changes the nature of the caring task because it changes the quality of relationships. If only some of the gains identified in this chapter could be realized, then the quality of care experienced by people of all ages and the job satisfaction of staff who work with them would be immensely improved because of mutual involvement in reminiscence work.

PART II

REMINISCENCE PRACTICE

P art I has provided the background for this second applied section that seeks to provide a guide to good basic reminiscence practice. In Chapter 4, planning and preparation are considered, whereas Chapter 5 describes various different ways of undertaking reminiscence work with individuals, couples, or small groups depending on the objectives sought and the people and places in which the work is undertaken. Chapter 6 explores how to translate individual or group reminiscences into tangible products and Chapter 7 considers how reminiscence, closely allied to oral history, is being used to promote and encourage the social inclusion of marginalized groups in society. Reminiscence workers are often apprehensive because they lack detailed historical knowledge of the times, events, and experiences that will be discussed by people reminiscing. To assist them, Appendix E contains an abbreviated 20th-century chronological chart listing major events that either occurred in or centrally involved the United States; it also identifies presidential terms of office. If used in conjunction with the quick age reference grid in Appendix F, then it will be easy to establish approximately how old people were when certain public events occurred and to relate these to the personal memories being recounted.

These chapters are geared toward a beginning reminiscence worker—perhaps an experienced health or social care worker, community worker, teacher, librarian, or artist who may already know much about the general health, social, educational, and recreational needs of people of various ages and who is experienced in working with people in small groups.

For the experienced reminiscence group leader, these chapters will deepen and extend your knowledge by challenging you to think in novel ways about aspects of your established practice. If knowledge and skill remain static, they quickly grow stale and deteriorate. Knowledge about reminiscence and life review will grow and develop by reflecting on each reminiscence encounter, hearing of other workers' experiences and from exposure to research findings.

Chapter 4

Planning and Preparation for Reminiscence Work

This chapter gives general guidance about deciding whether to reminisce with individuals, couples, or small groups; the need for contracting with participants; and how to use multisensory triggers to encourage reminiscence. A commitment to ethical principles of good practice should underpin all reminiscence work. These guiding ethical principles are concerned with respect for and sensitivity to individual's holistic needs and specific circumstances. This means appreciating each person as a unique individual with emotional, spiritual, physical, intellectual, and social needs, especially the need to be able to communicate satisfactorily and to have opportunities to form satisfying relationships. This implies that although each person is a unique individual, we are all social beings who have expectations of other people and obligations toward them.

The conceptual framework used here provides structure for reminiscence work with individuals, couples, or groups. The terms *reminiscence worker, leader, enabler,* and *facilitator* are used interchangeably. Likewise, *participant* and *group member* are synonymous. So too are the terms *phase* and *stage,* which apply to an entire piece of reminiscence work, sometimes called a *project,* as well as to each separate interview or session within it. Awareness of the overall stage and the stage within each single session helps alert the worker to the kinds of roles, responsibilities, and tasks re-

Photograph courtesy of Teaching Old Dogs New Tricks, Coleraine,
Northern Ireland.

quired at that time and to the associated range of emotions that leaders and
participants are likely to be experiencing.

The approach adopted here is humanistic and person centered. It
draws from many sources and influences, including literature on counseling (Rogers, 1969; Sherman 1981, 1991a) and the reciprocal, mediating
approach to group work. Although this model of group work emphasizes
process, it can also include negotiated, agreed-on, task-oriented work
(Berman-Rossi, 1994; Schwartz, 1971; Shulman, 1999). The life skills
helping approach of Jones (1993), cognitive counseling, autobiographical
approaches (Kenyon, De Vries, & Clark, 2001), and clinical psychosocial
therapeutic literature (Stock & Whitaker, 2000) are also relevant. There
are many parallels between the approaches proposed here and those of
many therapists who work through graphic arts, music, mime, and dance
and emphasize creativity, imagination, nonverbal communication, expressiveness, and performance (Clair, 1996).

THE FOUR PHASES OR STAGES
IN THE REMINISCENCE PROCESS

Regardless of how many individual sessions or group meetings are held, four stages apply: the preliminary or planning stage, the beginning stage, the middle stage, and the ending stage. All planned work with individuals, couples, and groups move through these four stages (Shulman, 1999). It is not possible to be prescriptive about how long each phase lasts, but in loose terms, the beginning and ending phases will likely cover two or three sessions each in a total of approximately ten to twelve sessions. Time during the preliminary phase will vary greatly, although it is indisputable that the eventual success of planned work largely depends on the care taken during the preliminary or planning phase. The middle or work phase needs to be as long as is required to achieve the desired objectives, including the completion of any intended tangible products.

This division into stages or phases is not used with opportunistic, spontaneous, unplanned reminiscence conversations. The worker, however, still needs to be alert to how these conversations are brought to an end and to the feelings that may be aroused. The discussion that follows refers primarily to time-limited, planned reminiscence group work, although it is also relevant to planned work with either individuals or couples. The preliminary phase is covered in this chapter and the other three phases are discussed in the following chapter.

THE PRELIMINARY PHASE: SETTING THE STAGE

A newcomer to reminiscence work will experience both positive and negative emotions when facing the prospect of this experience. It is important for a newcomer to acknowledge to him- or herself how he or she is feeling and to be clear about why he or she is embarking on this adventure. A number of decisions need to be made at the outset before detailed planning and preparation can begin.

Deciding to Use Reminiscence
with Individuals, Couples, or Groups

Deciding to work with an individual, a couple, or a small group is absolutely basic. In reaching this decision, it will be helpful to have some preliminary information about potential participants, the characteristics of the place or context in which the reminiscing will take place, and the reasons why it is to be undertaken. Meeting potential participants and determining their initial views is also very helpful. It is important to know about the opportunities and constraints imposed by the context and to begin to formulate ideas about the functions or outcomes desired from the reminiscence work.

The first consideration in deciding whether to work with an individual, couple, or small group must be the person or persons concerned but equally important are the purpose, functions, and objectives. The personal or professional background, preferences, and experience of staff also influence this decision, as do many practicalities concerned with resources and accommodation, such as staff availability, participants' availability, time, program possibilities, and whether any tangible products or outcomes are intended. It is therefore neither possible nor desirable to lay down hard-and-fast rules but, rather to identify the areas in which early decisions are required while keeping in mind how important it is to listen to the views of the people you wish to involve in reminiscence and related activities:

> All too often, elderly people do not have a voice. Decisions are made on their behalf. It may be said that they are unable to participate or that they won't want to. It is clear to me that they do want to and are willing to try all sorts of new things. (Davies, cited in Sim, 1997, p. 4)

It is not always easy to decide whether individual work, couple work, or group work is likely to be more effective. Figure 4.1 summarizes indicators concerning the relative suitability of each. The context in which the work is to be undertaken and workers' preferences often determine this decision, but the choices of the people likely to be involved should be preeminent. Individual work can become a bridge into group work for people who initially may lack sufficient social confidence to join a group. Likewise, a couple may in time benefit from the wider social opportunities available in a group. Also within group work, it is often desirable to include opportunities to work with an individual, a couple, or a subgroup as well as with the whole group. So in many ways, the distinction between individual work and group work can be artificial.

Inexperienced staff members initially seem to prefer to undertake individual work, perhaps thinking it is easier and will leave them less ex-

Reminiscence with individuals	Reminiscence with couples	Reminiscence with groups
Provides an opportunity for a person to experience undivided personal attention without competition or distraction	Provides an opportunity to sustain and strengthen a mutually supportive, well-established relationship	Provides an opportunity for experiencing a warm, accepting, mutually supportive group
Eases communication difficulties for people with speech, sensory, or cognitive disabilities	Increases conversation, interaction, and appreciation between partners	Eases apprehension about the perceived intimacy and intensity of a one-to-one relationship
People who are socially isolated, introverted, profoundly depressed, habitually tearful, obsessional, markedly agitated, or so aggressive as to threaten others are unsuited to group work but may respond to a one-to-one relationship	Decreases a sense of isolation and reduces emotional burden of both partners when one develops dementia or other disabilities by reliving and integrating past shared positive experiences	Group membership appeals to social extroverts and enjoy the company of others
People who have experienced difficulty in coping with a problematic past and who have restricted opportunities for learning new coping skills in the face of present challenges will probably not benefit from reminiscence, but may be helped by cognitive approaches.	Parent–child or grandparent–grandchild reminiscence provides opportunity to bequeath the family history to the next generation.	People who desire to preserve and transmit personal memories as a contribution to the public record and the creation of collective memory

Figure 4.1. Indicators for reminiscence with individuals, couples, and groups.

posed, less likely to lose control. On the contrary, sharing joint leadership of a small group with a supportive co-leader is likely to build confidence faster than working alone. Collaborative co-working provides opportunities for alternating roles and responsibilities, thus enabling a wider range of skills to be developed. It can also provide a positive experience of knowing that you have contributed to multiple, varied gains for a number of people arising from their participation in a small group. Some staff members have deeply ingrained preferences for individual work or group work and may feel very reluctant, even fearful, of venturing into other ways of working. Perhaps they should be encouraged to try a new method. The primary reason for choosing to work with an individual or a group should depend more on the needs and wishes of the participant and less on the needs and preferences of the worker.

People's living arrangements and personal characteristics also influence this choice. Sometimes particular living arrangements and practical difficulties of transport and geography will prevent group participation; for example, people with specific sensory impairments or disabilities may find group work too difficult. This is not always such an obvious or inevitable decision as the circumstances might suggest, but if the obstacles to including an individual in a group are so great as to limit the possibility of the person's successful participation, then it is better to proceed with individual work. It is preferable to have positive rather than negative reasons for making this choice. A person may be too depressed or lack sufficient energy to engage with more than one other person. Hearing or speech impairments or other singular characteristics of race, age, ethnicity, class, social, or educational background may make successful group participation doubtful. It is usually not desirable for only one person with a particular characteristic to be in a group—for example, one man or woman or one member of a minority ethnic group. Being the only representative can lead to feelings of being burdened with responsibility, frustration, low levels of inter-personal participation, isolation, and the increased risk of being scapegoated by other members.

No one should be urged to participate in a group if the worker, having considered risks and personal preferences, is not reasonably confident that the experience will prove to be positive, enjoyable, and constructive. So at this crucial point of decision making, the worker needs to consider all available background information and make a preliminary assessment. The worker may also need to take into account the views of family members and colleagues before reaching a decision. It is worth remembering that even though a person may live in a group care situation, such as a nursing facility or retirement community, it should not be assumed that group work is preferable. Although the advantages of group work are considerable, an individual may welcome the all too rare opportunity to receive undivided personal attention. This is also true for children and young people who inevitably spend much of their time as members of groups—at school, home, camp, clubs, or residential care groups. An individual child may blossom if given the opportunity for intensive personal attention when compiling a life storybook or doing a similar individual project.

Working with pairs or dyads provides an intermediate position between working with either an individual or a group. This most often involves another family member, usually a spouse or adult child. Sometimes it may involve a grandchild or other younger relative, close friend, or paid home caregiver. Dyad work can also include separate sessions for parallel life reviews and for shared or tandem reminiscence. Guided autobiographical and creative writing groups combine opportunities for each individual to work alone and also in a group (Birren & Cochran, 2001). Chapters 9 and 10 describe other variations that involve spouses, friends, and other family caregivers of people with dementia reminiscing both at home and in groups. Yet another variation is often used in oral history work in which the material gathered in a series of interviews with individual informants is used to compile a coherent composite account. Sometimes differences in the accounts given by individuals are noted and contributions individually identified; at other times, contributions are treated anonymously within composite accounts. In this approach, an individual process is used to achieve a common outcome although the contributors may never meet each other or talk together.

CO-WORKING AND MULTIPLE LEADERSHIP

Shared leadership of groups is highly desirable, but because of resource implications, it may not always be possible. Successful co-leadership and multiple or team leadership require time and effort to achieve. Both co-working and multiple leadership demand mutual respect and require careful preparation, capacity for self-criticism, and willingness to give and receive honest, constructive comment. Competitiveness between leaders or lack of agreement about objectives and ways of working will undermine any group whose members quickly discern tension between leaders. Roles and responsibilities should be explicitly assigned both generally overall and within each session. Rotation of roles is strongly recommended to provide opportunities for personal skill development but also to extend the experience for group members. Such an approach models mutual respect and cooperation; it can form a valuable part of the learning that takes place within a group. It is highly desirable that all leaders attend all sessions so they are aware of developments and are an integral part of the group. Serial leadership, in which leaders take turns being present, is not recommended. Time is required outside group meetings for preparation, debriefing, and supervision, different types of which have already been discussed in the previous chapter.

Generally, tasks can be divided between housekeeping matters and facilitating the process of discussion, but this division of labor risks oversimplification. Clear responsibility for the opening and closing of each session should be allocated beforehand. Responsibility for facilitating the discussion and for obtaining and introducing triggers into the discussion, if these are to be used, needs to be agreed on. If some work within a group is to be done in pairs or small groups, then this is usually planned beforehand, and team members may be allocated special responsibility for particular individuals with whom they work more intensively at certain times. Supporting any members with sensory impairments will be important, as is attending to any member who becomes distressed. Not everything can be planned in detail, especially regarding the group process, the ebb and flow of conversation, and the expression of emotions. There will be dynamic, spontaneous, unexpected happenings because all groups develop a life of their own. This is part of the challenge as well as part of the satisfaction of successful group work. Co-leaders will quickly learn how best to support each other. Each will bring different strengths to the group. Each will be tuned to read and respond to the group process in different ways, and through cooperative, sensitive, responsive working together, successful outcomes can be achieved.

If people with sensory or cognitive impairments are included in a group, then the demands on a single leader are likely to be onerous, and co-leadership or multiple leadership is strongly recommended. Multiprofessional leadership enhances reminiscence groups because each leader brings particular expertise and life experience. Groups led jointly by a staff member and a volunteer provide a useful mix of outsider and insider perspectives. The involvement of a volunteer can encourage a day center or residential facility to meet its obligations in terms of a regular commitment of a staff member's time and ensure that the group meets according to plan.

In a residential facility, an outside visitor who provides an important link with the local community and its resources is a considerable asset.

Volunteers bring a fresh perspective and can be a tangible reminder that other people, those from the outside world, have not forgotten the establishment and its residents and staff.

> I just love the day our reminiscence group meets and Mrs. Yates comes in. She is different and she helps us think about other things. I have nothing against the staff here, but we all get set in our ways and it's good to talk to people from outside. (Barbara Irwin, residential facility resident)

Multiple leadership is even more complex than co-leadership. It requires considerable time, effort, and sensitivity to ensure that all helpers, including volunteers, feel equally valued. "We only made the tea—we had much more we could have offered," said a disgruntled volunteer. Her experience of being involved with professional staff who failed to appreciate and to use her abilities was personally disappointing and a wasted opportunity for the group. Volunteers need to feel valued, so particular care about preparation and allocation of roles and responsibilities must be exercised if professionals and volunteers are to work together without friction (Bell & Troxel, 1997, 2001). Chapters 9 and 10 further discuss working with volunteers.

THE PLACE WHERE REMINISCENCE IS UNDERTAKEN

Individual work may be undertaken with agreement in a person's home or in any other acceptable and accessible venue that affords adequate privacy, quiet, and comfort. These criteria apply equally to the choice of location for group meetings. The kind of organization or agency sponsoring or promoting the reminiscence work and its particular ethos and values greatly influence both its purposes and processes. The place or context in which the work takes place also exercises a subtle influence. Group reminiscence in a nursing facility, for example, is likely to be very different from group reminiscence in a local community museum, neighborhood center, library, or youth club. This comes about not only because the people and the objectives may be different but also because the place is different. This may seem rather obvious, but it is worth reflecting on the likely advantages and disadvantages associated with different physical locations and the possible gains from forging new partnerships instead of perpetuating long-established boundaries between organizations.

A regional museum and a neighborhood women's health center both recognized their mutual desire to engage in outreach work. Both organizations needed to involve new users. The museum wished to extend its educational services to groups other than children. The health center was keen to address the health needs of older women. An education officer from the museum collaborated as co-leader with a health promotion officer from the center to recruit a group of older women that met in the center for six weekly reminiscence sessions. The topics were agreed by group members and followed a thematic life span perspective that addressed childhood, school, looking good and going out, war years, courtship and marriage, and raising a family. Discussion of health issues, remedies, and treatments naturally permeated most sessions, and many comparisons emerged between remedies, past and present, and home and professional treatments. The *Memory Lane Group*, a title suggested by the members themselves who did not like the word *reminiscence,* compiled a book of memories incorporating their personal and collective stories. Few group members had ever visited the museum, although all had lived their entire lives within a few blocks. The museum co-worker invited the group to hold its last session in the museum and arranged for the costume curator to display some of its vast fashion collection. The women greatly enjoyed admiring, handling, and modeling some of the garments. As changing fashion had been a recurring topic in many of the meetings, this visit provided a natural culmination of their time together; it gave immense pleasure and made a community resource accessible that was previously outside the experience of the women. Either of the two sponsoring partners could have run a reminiscence group on its own. By recognizing their separate but mutual needs and by pooling physical resources and expertise, both organizations achieved their desired outcomes in ways that were immeasurably richer and more rewarding for all concerned (Ferguson, 2000).

Reminiscence groups meet in immensely varied locations. Each location needs to be physically accessible and emotionally acceptable to potential participants. Apprehension about the location or the ethos of the meeting place should not be added to the usual anxieties associated with embarking on a new experience. Reminiscence may be only one part of a comprehensive activities program, such as in a day center, or it may be the sole purpose for coming together, as in a free-standing reminiscence project. Whatever the status of the group and the auspices under which it is meeting, the ambience and arrangement of furniture can either facilitate or obstruct discussion. Seating needs to be flexible rather than fixed so that chairs can be easily arranged in whatever size circle or semicircle is required at different times during a session to encourage informal discussion. An acceptable alternative is to seat participants around a table or a number of small tables if artifacts are to be displayed or if writing, painting, and similar activities are to form part of the program. Leaders should always be distributed throughout the group.

Serving refreshments is highly recommended. The arrangements need to be thoughtfully planned and the timing carefully considered. Some residential care facilities, retirement communities, and day centers for older people are establishing reminiscence rooms with décor, furniture, and fittings matching the 1930s, 1940s, or 1950s to create an atmosphere that readily encourages both spontaneous and planned reminiscence and recall. These dedicated spaces are conducive to recall, but they are by no means essential. Reminiscence gardens planted with older varieties of fragrant plants, trees, and shrubs are also increasing in popularity (Hoover, 1995; Pollock, 2001). If such gardens allow space for newcomers to bring and plant cuttings or favorite plants from their own gardens, then this could add familiar touches and increase pleasure. These places can be a considerable resource if laid out with safe wandering paths and with attractive places for sitting, relaxing, socializing, and for actual gardening, retiring to the tool shed to inspect old-fashioned tools, or just puttering about. They are congenial spaces that encourage recall and conversation as well as provide sensory stimulation, socialization, and opportunities for physical exercise and interesting activities.

THE IMPORTANCE OF CONTRACTING

The concept of contracting or reaching an agreement is central to all democratic group work and person-centered individual work. It demands that the worker is open, honest, genuine, and explicit about what he or she and the person or persons involved might agree to do together. Although the term may sound legalistic, the process does not need to be particularly formal. It does not have to culminate in a simple written statement, although this may be desirable in some circumstances and for some people, particularly those with short-term memory, speech, or hearing problems. A contract is a positive working tool that benefits both leaders and participants. It means that at the time of contacting potential participants and issuing invitations or of meeting participants for the first time at a session, the worker has to be reasonably clear about what is being proposed.

The leader needs to be able to explain in straightforward terms the objectives of the proposed work, what means will be used to achieve them, and the time commitment envisaged. This information is crucial, as it becomes the basis on which people decide whether to find out more. An initial exchange of ideas is usually described as a *preliminary contract,* which is further clarified, refined, and agreed in the beginning phase of work. A contract can be modified or renegotiated at any time, but it provides a secure framework within which the work can proceed. Before each session, time should be spent contracting, in which the program for the session is laid out and agreement to proceed is sought. If a one-time session is envisaged or the membership of a group is open, meaning that it changes from meeting to meeting, then the process of contracting will be much attenuated. In an open group, the worker should still explain without using jargon what is intended and reach for feedback from those present to make sure that they understand and accept what is being proposed.

To plan effectively, leaders need to have considered the following questions, even if some of the answers at this early planning stage can be only tentative or suggestive:

- What are the desired objectives, outcomes, or functions?
- What will the group be called?
- Is the group to have open or closed membership?

- Will there be a single leader or co-leaders, and how will they be selected?

- Will additional helpers or volunteers be involved, and how will they be recruited?

- How big should the group be?

- Who decides who should be invited?

- Who will do the inviting and how?

- Will the group be time limited or open ended?

- Where will it meet?

- What program of work is envisaged?

- How many sessions will be held?

- How frequently will the group meet?

- How long will each session be?

- Will potential members be interviewed before the first session?

- How will members get to meetings, and what will the transport arrangements be?

- What resources—including finance for possible materials, refreshments, triggers, and equipment—will be needed to reach the desired objectives?

- How will the various resources be provided, and who will be responsible for procuring them?

- What ground rules do the leaders and the sponsoring agencies believe are desirable?

OPEN AND CLOSED GROUPS

In some care contexts—for example, hospital wards or short-stay respite care and assessment units—it will only be possible to run groups with an open membership because of the ever-changing population using the service. In a group with open membership, members join and leave at any time. Those just beginning reminiscence are likely to be experiencing feelings of anxiety and insecurity, whereas established members will be confident and keen to progress with the program. This imbalance usually means that groups with open membership seldom develop the same degree of trust, intimacy, and personal disclosure as groups with closed membership. In an open group, each session may be a new beginning for some members and an ending for others. Nevertheless, the group, assisted by its skilled facilitators, will develop ways of constructively handling repeated changes in membership.

Introducing newcomers into a reminiscence group in neighborhood clubs, day centers, residential communities, or nursing facilities, however, may assist them to settle in and begin to develop new friendships. If an established group is committed to its agreed program of work and confident about its progress, then it will be relatively easy to assimilate a newcomer from time to time.

In an open group, topics will need to have wide popular appeal and address universal themes, preferably within the life experience of all the participants. The emphasis should be on enjoyment, social stimulation, and pleasure derived from having one's life experience validated and celebrated. A single well-run open session can still achieve considerable benefits for people who may be feeling lonely, isolated, anxious, or uncertain about their present circumstances.

Closed membership means that everyone joins at the beginning stage, and all members are expected to remain for the agreed duration of the life of the group. In the early sessions, some members may drop out and others join but generally throughout its life, the membership remains constant. If any members leave for whatever reason, then it is customary not to replace them. Because of familiarity and continuity, a closed group can be expected to develop trust and intimacy between members. Groups of people who are older, have disabilities, or are frail are always liable to lose members through ill health, hospitalization, or death. Such events need to be openly acknowledged in group meetings, but it is also desirable to begin with a sufficiently large number of members so that the viability of the group will not be threatened if some members are lost.

GROUP SIZE

Eight to twelve members is a good size for groups undertaking general reminiscence work. Very experienced co-leaders may be able to cope with larger groups. There will be many times when considerably smaller groups are more appropriate, especially if members have sensory or cognitive impairments. It is important not to have too many people with special needs in a mixed group because it becomes difficult to respond to everyone.

GROUP TIMING

Meeting once per week for 2 hours per session allows time for gathering together, reminiscing, having refreshments, and dispersing. However, the people involved, the available resources, and the desired objectives will determine how many sessions are held. Time-limited rather than open-ended groups are easier to run and more likely to be effective. A total of 10–12 weekly sessions gives a group time to form, cohere, undertake constructive work, and disperse with confidence. It should be noted that people with specific needs, such as dementia or learning disabilities, will benefit from more frequent but shorter sessions whereas particular types of programs will require more and possibly longer sessions.

GROUP MEMBERS

In forming groups, try to identify naturally existing groupings or commonalities among people. People may, for example, have grown up in the same neighborhood, attended the same school, emigrated from the same country, followed a particular interest or hobby, worked in the same industry, or now occupy rooms on the same corridor of a residential facility. They may be people who are facing the same uncertainties in life, coping with illness or bereavement; they may be newcomers to a facility or recent arrivals in a neighborhood. Some groups are formed through a public invitation or through professional referrals, which can identify people who may benefit but who are unlikely to take the initiative, unless encouraged to do so. In whatever way people hear about the possibility of undertaking reminiscence work, it is important that they freely consent to participate.

It is best for the group leaders to issue the invitations as this enables them to make preliminary contact with each potential participant, but sometimes it is better to get a familiar trusted staff member to do the inviting. There is no single best way of handling invitations. Often, a notice on a communal notice board or in a newsletter or flyers inviting people to attend a meeting without commitment works well. Remember, however, that a fair way of forming a group is necessary if too many people initially respond, which often means planning for subsequent reminiscence opportunities.

If possible, meet prospective members individually before the first group meeting. This provides the opportunity to explain about the proposed group, gather brief background biographical information, and tentatively explore ideas about the work of the group and the themes or topics that it might discuss. If using a summary life history form such as the one included in Appendix A, remember that some people are suspicious of filling out forms and may be deterred from joining if they feel threatened by what they perceive as unwarranted intrusion into their private affairs. Never make completing this form a condition of membership. In some contexts (e.g., a person attending a day center or living in a residential facility), some background information will already be available. This is, however, often surprisingly meager and is no substitute for meeting the person. It may also be possible to gather information from family or friends or from health and welfare professionals, if appropriate and acceptable.

DEVELOPING A REMINISCENCE PROGRAM

The term *program* is used in two ways. It refers to everything that is planned to take place in a group throughout its life as well as to the activities and experiences planned for each separate session. In an open group, the program will need to be planned with little or no prior consultation, as the participants will change from meeting to meeting. In a group with closed membership, there will be considerable consultation, and after the first session members will be involved in making plans for subsequent sessions. The interaction between people is called the *group process*. This term, however, oversimplifies the complex interweaving of talk among participants and cooperative work to produce tangible products or outcomes linked to the reminiscence process (see also Chapters 6 and 8).

When we recall a memory, it becomes much easier to recall it or a closely related memory again. So in constructing a program, if a theme or topic has already proved fruitful in eliciting recollections, then it is wise to build on this foundation in future sessions. It is also usually more productive to use various topics related to a general theme rather than to address an entirely separate topic in each session. Common themes or topics are usually selected. Some popular themes include 1) a chronological life course order from birth through old age, with sessions devoted to childhood, adolescence, young adult life, mid-life, and later life or 2) aspects of a particular period—for example, childhood and growing up, with sessions devoted to school life, family life, games, toys and recreation, hobbies and special interests, friends and relations, holidays and trips, adolescence, and growing up.

Some groups may have a major interest in the history of a particular town or local neighborhood. Others may have all worked in the same trade or occupation, followed a particular sport or recreation, or belonged to a particular club. Another group may decide on themes such as "The most beautiful thing I ever saw," "Places I have lived," "The most memorable holiday I ever had," "Birthdays," "Unforgettable characters," or "Pets." Whatever the content, programs should provide opportunities for all the group members, regardless of personal differences in age, race, ethnicity, sexual orientation, cultural background, and religious belief to feel respected, validated, and appreciated as unique individuals.

Research shows that women generally are more interested in recalling memories related to people and relationships, whereas men commonly recall more work-related memories. Adult memories tend to be more chronologically structured than children's memories. Children are inclined to recall more vivid, disparate, unconnected memories than adults do, and their sense of chronological time will be less well structured and far less important. Late childhood, adolescence, and young adult life appear to be the richest periods for recall and provide a good starting place for groups unsure of a theme.

There are innumerable ways to explore themes or topics. Such versatility and flexibility make reminiscence work immensely attractive and readily accessible. What is important, however, is that both the purpose and the program through which it is achieved are negotiated and agreed on with the participants. When planning the content of the program, it is necessary to take into account the stage of the group's development and the nature of the participants' relationship. Topics or themes chosen for new groups should not demand too early or too great personal disclosure. At first, members will be testing whether they feel they can trust the leaders and members. It takes time to develop trust and confidence, for relationships to evolve, and for groups to cohere. Once the group has reached the middle or work phase, warmth, shared pleasure, and growing confidence energize members for accomplishing agreed on tasks. At this stage, people who have access to treasured memorabilia are usually pleased to bring items to a group meeting and to share very personal intimate recollections.

CONFIDENTIALITY

It is highly desirable that the pleasure, enthusiasm, satisfaction, and achievements of group members are widely communicated. Reminiscence is contagious. It is usually designed to promote conversation, among other objectives, and this will probably be impossible to contain within the confines of a session. Yet some safeguards will be necessary. It is advisable for leaders, co-leaders, and other helpers to have an early discussion concerning the nature and extent of confidentiality. They will then be able to raise this issue early in the life of the group, desirably in the first session, so that an agreed-on view becomes accepted as an integral part of the contract. The arrangements are likely to differ from group to group or from person to person. The contract needs to include decisions about any records that are kept and also what participants may or may not discuss with other people outside of sessions. Too strict an approach to confidentiality can defeat the purpose of reminiscence, whereas too free an approach may breach the privacy of individuals.

In general terms, it can be agreed that people and their contributions are treated with consideration and that no one should be demeaned or belittled. Beyond this general understanding, it can be suggested that from time to time if a group member discloses a very intimate or distressing recollection, then the facilitator will address its confidentiality before the end of the session. The facilitator should engage in precise contracting around this specific episode by acknowledging the personal nature of this memory and suggesting that participants keep this recollection confidential within the group.

Confidentiality is extremely important and must be treated seriously and frankly, but it is not an inalienable right. Health and social care facilities as well as other types of community agencies will already have relevant written policies that staff and volunteers should be required to read, understand, and apply appropriately to their reminiscence work (Wooly, 2002).

Record Keeping to Assist Accountability

There are two types of records: 1) those kept to further the agreed purposes of the work and that meet the administrative and accountability requirements of the sponsoring agency and 2) those kept to assist with the worker's knowledge and skill development and ideally form the basis of supervision discussions. (See Chapter 3 for discussion about this second type of critical incident record that is intended to assist the worker's development.) Even if not obliged to keep either accountability or developmental records, it is still highly desirable to do so to assist the worker's own careful reflection, analysis, and evaluation of work undertaken. The appendixes contain examples of four forms:

- Appendix A: Background Personal History Form

- Appendix B: Sessional Group Attendance Form

- Appendix C: Group Activity Form for Use with People with Dementia

- Appendix D: Permission to Use Material Obtained During Reminiscence

If possible, plan to complete relevant accountability forms jointly with other leaders and helpers immediately following the end of each session. The group forms can be easily adapted for use with individuals or couples. All records should meet agency requirements in terms of confidentiality and security. Good practice principles concerning record keeping include the following:

- Clarity about the reasons why records are to be made

- Openness with participants about what records are being kept, their purpose, and who has access to them

- Agreement before each session about who is to be responsible for formal record keeping and, if possible, rotation of the responsibility among leaders

- Distinguishing between process and outcome records, where possible

When a reminiscence project has been completed, agree about secure storage or disposal of the records.

RESPONDING TO SAD MEMORIES

The expression of strong emotions, particularly sad emotions, is an inevitable dimension of reminiscence and life review, and workers need a plan for responding to sad memories. Everyone's life consists of happy and sad experiences, of achievements, failures, gains, and losses; life breaks everyone, but some are strong at the broken places (Mills & Coleman, 2002; Sandford, 1990). Loss of many kinds is an inevitable part of life and few, if any, reach mid life, let alone old age, without experiencing loss and grief. For to live is to suffer the ordinary sorrows of life that are never felt as only ordinary by the person affected. Inexperienced reminiscence workers are inevitably fearful about arousing pain or doing harm. (For learning to cope with the worker's own and other people's emotions when called on to respond with empathy during the reminiscence process, see Chapter 5.) Tears and anger are not to be feared or viewed as necessarily harmful or as an excuse for an anxious worker to retreat into avoidance by providing superficial distraction. Rather, emotion indicates that a person is engaged in exploring deeply personal issues in the presence of others. Christina Rossetti believed it was "Better by far you should forget and smile. . . . Than that you should remember and be sad" (cited in Sisson, 1984, p. 35). This is not, however, the experience of everyone; many people still prefer to remember rather than forget, even if the remembering means paying the price of being sad. Just as reminiscence may trigger the recall of sad memories, so too memories can become a resource to assist people in coping with their distress by reminding them of good times and how they have managed to cope in the past when overwhelmed by sadness.

Part of planning and preparation work needs to include consideration of arrangements for supporting any person who becomes seriously disturbed as a consequence of reminiscence work and who may need to be referred for counseling or psychotherapy. This is rarely necessary, but good practice requires that an appropriate referral source is available should it be required. Chapter 3 discussed supervision and support for workers and their need to have opportunities to reflect on how engagement in reminiscence and life review affects themselves. No effective reminiscence worker will be untouched by the stories heard, but the developmental challenge for each worker is to learn to extend the ability to listen and to remain open to hearing the story without fear, judgment, or retreat into his or her own preoccupations.

MULTISENSORY TRIGGERS

Reminiscence work uses many different kinds of triggers or memory joggers (sometimes called props)—that is, something that stimulates a memory and encourages its emergence as conscious recall. Using triggers is much less common in reminiscence work with an explicit oral history orientation that relies on semistructured verbal questions as the starting point for gathering information. Proust (1981), the French novelist-biographer, wrote at considerable length about the vividness of memories sparked spontaneously by some chance or coincidental experience that brought vivid images of long-buried memories to consciousness. He described the whiff of a long forgotten smell, the taste of a cake, stumbling on a stone, or the unexpected sight of an old glove (De Botton, 1997). Triggers can be invaluable, especially in the beginning phase of a session, because they assist individuals to overcome initial anxiety and start to engage in exploring and sharing their own life experience. As the work develops, triggers usually become less necessary.

An initial word of caution about using triggers: Many reminiscence workers, especially inexperienced ones, become enthralled by their quest for triggers. The search for triggers and the triggers themselves are interesting, exciting, and rewarding. Unless used in a disciplined way, triggers can become a distraction or hindrance rather than tools to facilitate shared conversation. In reminiscence work, artifacts are valued but secondary. The primary purpose is to stimulate the recall of personal memories so that these memories may be processed, integrated, and shared. In reminiscence work, triggers are essentially means to an end.

Triggers should stimulate all of the senses but should be used sparingly; otherwise, people feel bombarded, overloaded with insufficient time to recall and process the memories aroused. Inexperienced workers are prone to use too many triggers, especially if they have gone to considerable trouble to assemble a collection. Triggers can and should include everyday objects and events, equipment, tools, and machinery; daily domestic routines; the immediate surroundings; newspapers; magazines; music; radio programs; changing seasons with their different colors, trees, and plants; the scene outside the window; children going to school; people out shopping; the weather; and passing traffic. Family photographs and personal memorabilia such as jewelry, clothing, hats, shoes, scarves, and handbags are effective triggers.

When considering the place of triggers in reminiscence with either individuals or groups, begin with the people, not the triggers. Discover what interests them and what concerns them. Only when the worker has done this can he or she hope to locate relevant triggers and use them effectively. Because people have personal preferences and one of their senses may be either more or less dominant or possibly impaired, particularly vision or hearing, it is important to use every possible sensory pathway to stimulate recall of long-term implicit and explicit memories. If various triggers are available, then they need to be used economically and sequentially. If presented simultaneously or in too quick succession, then people are liable to feel overwhelmed. Visual images shown alone and then with accompanying speech or music followed by opportunities for handling and passing around related artifacts can be extremely effective. Many people find that taste and smell are also useful in stimulating memory. People need time to observe, listen, consider, savor, touch, taste, or smell because the sensory stimulation as well as the memories being evoked arouse many emotions. It takes a while to respond to two separate but linked time phases, the immediate present and the recalled past, so the worker should not be in a hurry; he or she needs to slow the pace and take time.

Although visual triggers are the most readily available, auditory triggers, especially music, are probably the most effective. The more closely triggers relate to the backgrounds, interests, and experience of the people concerned, the more evocative they are likely to be. Considerable care is necessary when using film, video, and recorded sound. If the technical nature of the presentation is allowed to dictate the structure and pacing of the session, then opportunities for conversation about memories aroused by the visual and auditory stimuli will be jeopardized. If verbalizing the recall has to be postponed until the end of the film, then the memory may be lost in the meantime. The session risks becoming just another film show, television program, or recorded music session, passively enjoyed but not actively promoting reminiscence. All triggers are aids used to stimulate recall and to encourage personal reflection and communication between people about the memories aroused and other matters of personal significance.

Personal possessions and cherished objects brought by members can provide effective triggers. Sensitivity is required if some people no longer have access to personal possessions, although such an exercise does not have to exclude them. An invitation to describe a particular object that is seen in the mind's eye is usually sufficient for most people to be able to describe it in fine detail. Other people's triggers can stimulate memories of similar objects, but sensitivity to gender issues and interests is important so no one feels excluded. An example of how other people's triggers can stimulate memories in an entire group follows.

A woman who brought her sewing box to a women's group was displaying her entire adult life. The box contained her cherished silver thimble, scissors inherited from her mother, buttons, buckles, tape measure, spools of thread, bits of tape, ribbon, elastic, and a suspender end. Every woman in the group immediately identified with the contents. Animated conversation was unstoppable as they enthusiastically exchanged stories about family life and parents, especially mothers, and how as children they had been taught to sew.

Visual Triggers

Photographs are personal, documentary, or artistic. The most evocative photographic triggers combine the personal and documentary. Those featuring people and action (not just buildings, empty streets, or landscapes) are more effective. Newspapers, magazines, books, advertising posters, invitation cards, theatre and concert tickets and programs, church magazines, alumni publications, postcards, comic books, photographic slides, cinema, video, and many types of memorabilia and ephemera are relatively easy to locate. Local newspaper offices; public libraries; community museums; archives from schools, colleges, institutions, churches, synagogues, mosques, clubs, industries, and businesses; family albums and scrapbooks; and professional photographs and photographic collections are all poten-

tial sources. Many commercially published packages are suitable for reminiscence purposes. Photocopying, scanning, color printing, and enlarging
are simple to do and costs are relatively modest. Laminating helps preserve
visual materials and assists their safe storage. Local history librarians and
museum staff can advise on these matters and may be willing to offer this
kind of assistance as partners in reminiscence projects.

Auditory Triggers

Memory for sounds can be extremely vivid and instantaneously evoked. As
already suggested, music is particularly evocative, provided that it is music
with which the person was once familiar and still appreciates; here age, cultural, ethnic, and individual preferences are particularly relevant. It is important to gather information about the type of musical preferences that
people have developed throughout their lives because preferences built on
familiarity and use that have become well integrated into long-term memory may alter over time. Clair identified how musical tastes can change:

> Some people may have liked rock and roll music in their young adult
> years. Although they still listen to it in later life, they may have also
> expanded their musical tastes to include various types of jazz, some
> classical music, and rhythm and blues. (1996, p. 10)

Having such background information reduces the need for trial and
error and informs and accelerates the stimulation of memories associated
with music. Because of most people's acute sensitivity to music and the
wide variations in people's tastes, having to endure music that is not integrated into a person's life preferences can be experienced as intrusive, perhaps offensive, even physically painful. If forced to listen, irritation, agitation, or disengagement can result.

Auditory and visual memories are often closely intertwined. By triggering one, both are readily evoked. Other types of auditory triggers can
also be effective. It is easy, for example, to read aloud poems, rhymes, sacred texts, extracts from stories or speeches, and items from newspapers or
magazines. People can be reminded of famous speeches such as President
Abraham Lincoln's Gettysburg address or the inaugural speeches of President Franklin D. Roosevelt ("The only thing we have to fear is fear itself";

March 4, 1933) or President John F. Kennedy ("Ask not what your country can do for you"; January 20, 1961). Martin Luther King's "I have a dream" speech delivered at a civil rights demonstration in Washington, D.C. (August 28, 1963) is another well-remembered speech. Many different kinds of quotations can be used to introduce sessions. People might be asked what they were doing at the time particular events took place, what they remember of their own and other people's reactions, or how, on reflection, they now believe these events and speeches influenced their personal lives and public affairs.

Much repetition in childhood of poems, rhymes, songs, hymns, sacred texts, prayers, and pledges means this material is so imbedded in long-term semantic and episodic memory that it can be recalled either wholly or in part, despite some deterioration, well into advanced old age. This kind of recall can also be pleasurably shared with much younger people. Quizzes and guessing games based on musical memories, proverbs, wise sayings, and poetry are usually very popular with people of all ages. Content can be cumulatively recovered when a number of people working together contribute snippets or fragments; the rhythms and physical actions often associated with rote learning and singing and stored as procedural memories are similarly recalled. Use the sounds and the memories aroused to stimulate further personal memories and encourage people to share their remembered experiences with each other.

Recorded sounds, speech, and music of all types and periods are easy to obtain on cassette tapes, CDs, DVDs, and videotapes. Ensure that the equipment and type of recording used provides high quality sound reproduction and that volume levels are acceptable to listeners, bearing in mind the special needs of people with impaired hearing and the widespread use of hearing aids. Seek advice, if necessary, from a music therapist, an audiology professional, or a sound recording professional about sound equipment and its use.

Using Equipment

Audio recordings and video recordings, if used appropriately, can speed up the process of stimulating the recall of memories (Ives, 1995). Often audio and video recordings may also be made as part of the ongoing process to be used as reminders and triggers in later sessions. Making a permanent record in various formats is often an integral part of the agreed work. A digital or ordinary camera can be immensely valuable. Several principles of good practice that follow concern using equipment and making recordings. Related ethical issues are discussed in Chapter 6 in reference to making tangible products part of reminiscence activities.

- Always seek permission and explain the reason for wishing to use any camera, recording, or filming equipment.

- Develop confidence and competence in using equipment by undertaking instruction and practice before using it in a session.

- Assess how any equipment is likely to affect participants and the reminiscence process.

- Seek advice from knowledgeable people before purchasing equipment.

- Read a simple guide on how to make good quality audio or video recordings and, if necessary, undertake appropriate instruction.

- Clarify ownership rights concerning any records or tangible products, their possible use, and arrangements for the distribution of any financial gains that may accrue from their exploitation.

- Always obtain signed release forms from all relevant people (see Appendix D).

- Use any technology as servant, not master. Be very vigilant about the time it can consume and the distraction it can cause.

Tactile Triggers

Handling objects, with or without visual accessibility, can produce immediate recall. As Mastoris (2003, p. 11), a museum curator, said, "It is in the small things of everyday life that the greatest power to evoke meaningful memories resides." The very act of feeling and examining an object, holding it, and then passing it on to another person links people together, encourages speculation, and stimulates animated conversation about the object, its characteristics, and its uses. Objects invite demonstration; household domestic appliances and working tools evoke associated long-term procedural memories. It is as if the allied actions remain stored in the very bones and muscles of people long after the capacity to name them has become elusive. Many everyday objects demand activity; they encourage shared opinion and stimulate lively conversation. Strange objects with less obvious or ambiguous characteristics provoke vigorous debate and even healthy argument. An entertaining warm-up exercise for a group invites participants to feel and identify objects hidden in a bag or box that is passed around a circle. Turning this into a type of "pass the parcel" guessing game can add to the fun. Guided by touch, each person takes turns in choosing an object, then displaying it to the group and sharing a memory it evokes. Avoid using valuable, fragile antiques that can only be viewed from a distance or handled with anxiety. Although not denying that aesthetic and artistic appreciation enrich experience, reminiscence work seeks to use every day, domestic, or work-related artifacts to stimulate personal recollections.

Touch will be especially important to people with a visual impairment, but not only to them. Seek appropriate triggers and try to include different textures and types of material such as metal, stone, sandpaper, velvet, leather, silk, cotton, nylon, polyester, elastic, lace, linen, plastics, polystyrene, cardboard, and paper. In childhood, touch is used extensively as a means for exploring the world and memories of how things felt can be vividly recalled many years later. If other senses are impaired, then touch can again become significant as a means of knowing the world and reactivating past knowledge. Remember to ask people about the sensory aspects of memories that they recall. They may not think to tell the worker about these important characteristics unless specifically asked, and a rich dimension may be missed as a consequence.

Tastes and Smells

Even if taste and smell deteriorate with advancing age, they can still be very evocative when used alone or combined in sequences with other triggers. Memories associated with particular tastes or smells seem to survive, etched in long-term memory and capable of fine-detailed recall. It is particularly easy and inexpensive to make a smell collection by putting various liquids and powders into small bottles that can then provide sensory and cognitive stimulation. Both similar and contrasting smells of varying strengths can be presented. Identifying and naming the smell and sharing related memories quickly helps a group to develop camaraderie and to enjoy the guessing, speculation, and the conversation that invariably occurs. Once again, background information about the life experience of participants and their preferred sensory pathway will assist in matching smells to individuals, although some smells, particularly those associated with childhood, food, and home remedies for illness have wide, almost universal appeal. Lavender; eau de cologne; perfume; toiletries; eucalyptus oil; menthol; childhood medicines; soap; baby talcum powder; various household cleaning and disinfectant products; herbs; spices; and many flowers, vegetables, trees, and shrubs are widely recognizable by smell. Particular locations, events, or people such as a kitchen, bathroom, farmyard, hospital, school, shop, neighborhood, or occupation, not to mention Mom's home baking, can all be remembered in the imagination as much by their smell as for any other distinguishing characteristics.

Likewise, taste, again subject to degradation in later life, remains a potent memory trigger. Food has great significance in most people's lives, regardless of age. Ordinary family meals, celebrations of anniversaries, birthdays, weddings, bar mitzvahs, high days and holidays (e.g., Thanksgiving, Christmas, the end of Ramadan), and many other cultural celebrations conjure up memories of special food. There will be memories about its preparation, the places and events with which it is associated, and, most of all, the people who shared the occasions when it was eaten. As with music and other sounds, even if actual food is not available as a tangible prompt, people can be encouraged to imagine what it smelled like; recapture how it was prepared, looked, and tasted; and with whom it was eaten. Recipes may be recalled and details of the ingredients and their preparation can be discussed. Engaging in actual food preparation and cooking as part of a reminiscence session is a natural way for launching into reminiscence. Then, eating the prepared food in congenial company enhances and reinforces the memories by providing present pleasures that in turn become associated with earlier reconstructed memories in the future. Very few people are unable to call to mind colorful, detailed emotional recollections involving past sights, sounds, touch, tastes, and smells. They can undertake a reminiscence journey into their past with nothing more than a question or a prompt because memory and imagination are virtually inseparable (Warnock, 1987).

DETERMINING PREFERRED REPRESENTATIONAL SYSTEM

The literature concerned with neurolinguistic programming provides another justification for using multisensory triggers. This approach suggests that everyone has a Preferred Representational System (PRS), a preferred sensory pathway or sensory modality for processing information. A person with a visual PRS will attend to images and facial expressions. A person with an auditory PRS will focus on sounds. A person with a kinesthetic PRS will focus on bodily sensations, tactile experience, and felt emotions. People use the words *see, hear,* and *feel* as indicators of their preferred way for retrieving sensory information (Hossack & Standidge, 1993). It therefore makes sense for reminiscence workers to be sensitive to each person's dominant sensory pathway and to use triggers that mesh with it. If this is done, then it is assumed that each person's recall will be speedier, more intense, more confidently engaged in, and more personally satisfying. The recalled memories can then become a resource that the person can continue to use to enhance well-being and affirm personal identity.

This approach could be particularly fruitful when undertaking reminiscence with an individual who at first may be poorly motivated or lacking in confidence, possibly because of depression. Hossack and Standidge (1993) used this technique with depressed people who were encouraged to create imaginary scrapbooks by recalling earlier positive experiences in chronological sequence and then rehearse their positive memories repeatedly as a way of rebuilding self-esteem and self-confidence that had been eroded by illness, bereavement, or other stressful life events. The experience of Elijah illustrates this approach.

They described Elijah, a retired and self-critical man who had been a seaman and a firefighter and was hospitalized with clinical depression and agoraphobia following a series of traumatic life events. After discharge, a psychologist determined his PRS was largely kinesthetic, meaning that he responded best to emotions and touch. Visual images and sounds were much less important to him. An imaginary scrapbook was created consisting of recalled life events that demonstrated achievements, satisfaction, and appreciation. The first memory entered in the scrapbook was of Elijah winning a school swimming competition. He was encouraged to recall the details of this occasion and to feel the winning medallion in his hand, to hold the weight of the winner's cup, and to again experience, in memory and imagination, the firm congratulatory handshake. He was prompted to feel the flush of pride as he noticed the audience and to hear again the sound of the whole school cheering his efforts. Five positive images of successful life events were entered into the memory scrapbook. These included an image of a particular event when his bravery in the navy was acknowledged, giving friends a gift of his own paintings, decorating his house, and being appreciated by others for a verbal contribution in a retirement group. All of these memories were systematically used together with reducing medication and relaxation to reestablish his confidence and assist his successful recovery.

EXAMPLES OF REMINISCENCE THEMES AND TOPICS

To demonstrate various ways in which a theme can be explored and the types of readily available triggers that can be used to assist recall, the following section outlines in detail three themes: school; work; and dressing up, going out, and having fun. Some tangible representations or products are also suggested. These illustrations are intended to be suggestive, not prescriptive. Workers should feel free to develop their own ideas with flair and creativity and to use their skills to enable themselves and the people with whom they are reminiscing to reconnect with their own unique pasts.

School

The topic of school or education presents many opportunities for drawing on long-term, implicit procedural, and explicit declarative memory. General and specific facts, concepts, actions, and knowledge learned through much repetition, all colored by emotions associated with the circumstances and people involved, will be recalled. Opportunities for triggering cumulative memories abound, and there is much enjoyment and considerable satisfaction when combined group effort recovers a whole poem, quotation, or song. When this happens, little additional effort is needed to encourage people to talk about school-related events and personally significant people (see Figure 4.2).

The richness in reminiscence comes from encouraging people to recall the detail that paints a fuller picture and encourages the recall of further memories. School, as a theme, rarely produces only happy memories, as few of us pass unscathed through this formative period of our lives; ambivalence over some aspects is almost universal. Usually, along with the

First day at school or early memories	The journey to and from school
Learning to read and write	A significant teacher
A favorite/feared teacher	An embarassing/triumphant experience
My best friend	What I kept in my satchel
Telling tales/being punished	What I kept in my locker/under the desk
Playground games	Notes I sent (or received)
Homework experiences	School reports
The principal or college president	Looking after brothers or sisters
Moving to a new school	Gangs and hide outs
My best (or worst) memory	Lessons I liked (or hated)
Lunch times	Newcomers
Missing school	Challenging authority
Sporting achievments	Leaving school and making career decisions
Lost opportunities	Significant turning points
When I realized I was no longer frightened of teachers (or children)	School trips/excursions
Parties and dances	Minding or teaching younger children
Concerts, plays, and performances	Special events or celebrations
Class reunions	Sports, special matches, athletes, and cheerleaders

Figure 4.2. School topics or themes.

recall of academic, sporting, and social achievements; effort rewarded; and accomplishments acknowledged, there will be memories of acute embarrassment, pervasive anxiety, punishment or bullying, and painful failure. These too can be reviewed and people helped to form a fresh, more balanced view. Whatever intellectual or emotional burdens associated with school and educational attainment (or lack of it) people have allowed to persist throughout their adult lives may now be put to rest. School as a theme of reminiscence and life review produces very rich opportunities for developing a more kindly, less censorious perspective about oneself and other people.

School Topics

Many of the separate topics listed could be grouped together as a theme—for example,

- Journeys to and from school
- Teachers and classroom experiences
- Sporting events and attainments
- Friendships and gangs
- School social activities
- Poems, songs, proverbs, or wise sayings remembered from school
- Lessons for life

Chronological periods relating to elementary school, high school, and college could provide an alternative framework for structuring a number of sessions.

Multisensory Triggers

Many relevant visual and auditory triggers can be obtained with only minimum effort. Possibilities include pencils; ink wells and ink pens; fountain pens; biros; chalk; rulers; erasers; crayons; wall charts and maps; exercise books; text books; reading and poetry books; bags or satchels; lunch boxes; school reports; skipping ropes; marbles; whistles; medals; certificates and trophies; photographs of individuals, special occasions, and class groups; concert programs; newspaper cuttings; and sporting memorabilia. Playing a recording of children reciting multiplication tables, singing hymns or songs, or ringing a school bell immediately produce recall.

In addition to lighthearted recall of school memories, some triggers will promote more reflective discussion about negative aspects of school life, even if recounted with humor.

The group could validate achievements, appreciating the pain of failure and the sadness of regret for those people whose achievements were limited or who lacked opportunities to excel, perhaps because of family circumstances, economic constraints, or other reasons.

Tangible Products

There are many ways of presenting tangible outcomes or products of reminiscences related to school. Many products require prior planning and preparation; some are achieved spontaneously. The possibilities, for example, of transforming memories into theatre, either scripted or spontaneous, are endless. A group might decide to become a class of children of a certain age and act scenes from school life (late arrivals, playground events, classroom misbehaviors), with or without costumes and props, to entertain themselves or inform others. Imaginary class photos could be posed or school plays or events reenacted.

If identity preservation and the maintenance of self-esteem and life review are objectives, then participants could prepare "report cards" giving a summary of accomplishments and future prospects. These cards could then be read aloud to the group members, who can provide validation, respect, and understanding. Scrapbooks, yearbooks, photographic exhibitions, and simulated school reunions complete with time-appropriate music, dancing, clothes, and refreshments could be organized. Memoirs, diary extracts (real or fictional), stories, essays, poetry, letters, art, and graphics could be produced in the format of a school publication to be shared with family members and the local community.

Work

Work, like school, is one of the most common human experiences. It involves an immense variety of mental and physical effort undertaken in countless organizations, locations, and circumstances. It provides associations with innumerable people, as very few of us have not worked at some time to earn a living, raise a family, or constructively pass the time. Work and its associations, therefore, provide a potentially limitless reservoir of memories to be retrieved by means of reminiscence.

Almost everyone remembers work as having been a most significant part of adult life, whether it was enjoyable and satisfying or just endured and filled with hardship and disappointment. It will have occupied much time and effort and is also likely to have been a source of friendships and recreation. Work is highly significant in terms of how people define themselves, their successes or failures, and their place in the world. Retirement from paid employment is generally regarded as a major branching point in most people's lives. Any discussion about work (or lack of it) will be accompanied by many varied positive and negative emotions, often strongly felt and vigorously expressed. Discussion is likely to reflect marked differences between men and women and between women who stayed at home after marriage and those who worked outside the home after marriage. There will also be very marked differences in people's recollections about work linked to differences in status, remuneration, and achievements, so lively and energetic discussion should be anticipated.

Work Topics

Although there will be vast differences between the work experiences of unskilled workers, agricultural workers, blue-collar workers, and white-collar workers, general themes concerned with work do exist, and shared experiences can still be identified. These may include feeling the anxieties of job searching and leaving home; establishing oneself in new locations; making new friends; acquiring qualifications; becoming unemployed; and experiencing the satisfactions, achievements, and disappointments related to employment.

Younger reminiscence workers may find it harder to identify with hardships recalled—periods of unemployment, industrial unrest, low wages, poverty, and economic downturns. If these events have been outside the personal experience of the reminiscence workers or their parents, then it is sensible for them to gather some historical background information. They may need to turn to local newspapers or film archives to learn about economic and labor history, general and local labor disputes, and ways that individuals and communities were affected. Some popular topics include the following:

- My first job and how I got it
- My first pay and how I spent it
- Leaving home and finding a place to live
- People I worked with—friends and foes, mates and bosses
- Pay and working conditions—illness and accidents
- Belonging to a trade union—strikes and lockouts

- The Great Depression—being unemployed

- Different types of urban and rural work and work locations—farm, factory, shop, office, hospital, and home

- Wartime work experience

- Being in the military

- Relinquishing paid work to stay home and raise children

- Experiencing retirement

Multisensory Triggers

Because triggers are also likely to be more closely related to specific places, types of work, and chronological periods, it may be more difficult to identify triggers unless people have worked in similar jobs, industries, or locations. In locating suitable triggers, local public libraries, oral and community historians, newspaper archives, local industries, or resourceful individuals may be very helpful. If a facility is serving the retired members of a particular trade union, profession, or industry, then work-related reminiscence and the availability of relevant triggers will be easier. Without them, verbal prompts will need to be carefully prepared to stimulate group participation.

Sometimes when searching for triggers, relevant human resources are also discovered. People employed in relevant industries or businesses may provide "human" triggers. Bell and Troxel (1997, 2001) described a local fire department that began bringing its mascot Dalmatian to visit a retired firefighter in a nursing facility. Novels and autobiographies can provide excellent trigger materials for reading aloud or for extending limited personal experience. McCourt's autobiographies, *Angela's Ashes* (1996) and *'Tis* (1999) are such examples. The first describes McCourt's Irish childhood, adolescence, extreme poverty, and immigration to the United States; the second describes his innumerable unskilled jobs, military service, college education, and eventual 30-year teaching career in New York City high schools.

Tangible Products

Ideas for tangible products, if desired, will grow out of group discussion. Photographic exhibitions, memoirs, stories, plays, poems, oral histories, paintings, drawings, visits, and excursions may all be relevant and feasible, depending on local circumstances, interests, and resources. Visits to previous work places may be possible.

Dressing Up, Going Out, and Having Fun

People rarely tire of reminiscing about dressing up and going out. It generally represents the lighter side of life, although no topic can be guaranteed safe or pain free. This theme is very popular, has wide general appeal and considerable potential if one of the objectives of the reminiscence work is to promote staff training and development. The interest and sympathies of young nursing staff can be dramatically extended when they experience the animation and excitement of older people enthusiastically and energetically talking about dressing up, being in love, and having a good time in their youth. Staff members catch a glimpse of what the person used to be like. They can more readily identify with them as they used to be, not as they now are, perhaps frail, timid, dependent, demoralized, depressed, or even difficult. Old men glow with pride and pleasure as they recall past enthusiasms for fast cars, fast motorbikes, and the girlfriends who accompanied them on adventurous outings.

There is a risk of retreating into nostalgia or of seeing the past through rose-colored glasses and the present as all bad, but it does not have to be so. There can be genuine rejoicing over things that once were, even if they are no more. There can be celebration of good times and acceptance that although life has changed, the changes do not cancel out past pleasures. Young staff members become interested, even fascinated, by the emergence of the unique individual with an interesting past, and in this dramatic shift of perspective their sympathies are enlarged and their care transformed.

Dressing Up Topics

There are innumerable related topics, some likely to interest women more than men, but in a mixed group, all interests should be included. There are so many possibilities that the problem will be in making a selection and keeping the ensuing discussion within reasonable bounds. Some possibilities include

- Changing fashions—evolving styles, materials, buttons and trimmings, accessories, designer names, prices, home dressmaking, and shopping trips

- Going places—dance halls and music halls, big bands, movies and film stars, plays and musicals, parties, dances, home entertainment, car outings, picnics, trips, and holidays

- Different ideas of having a good time
- Changes in entertainment over time
- Musical styles
- Romantic outings
- Embarrassing and entertaining moments

Multisensory Triggers

Many triggers are available. Clothes, jewelry, shoes, scarves, hats, and handbags may still be found in grandparents and parents' closets and attics. Photographs of film stars, old films, memorabilia, books, magazines, and musical recordings abound. Local museums and libraries are rich sources of information and artifacts. Mail-order catalogues, fashion magazines, and dressmaking paper patterns could all be useful. A collection of handbags, each containing small objects linked to going out—such as lipstick; powder compact; comb; perfume; fan; train, bus, or theatre tickets, and handkerchiefs—could be used to stimulate conversation. A toilet bag with shaving soap and brush, various sorts of razors, collar studs, and cuff links or a collection of assorted neckties, bow ties, and suspenders also could be used to stimulate conversation with both men and women.

Tangible Products

Presentations, music, mime, and dancing are all appropriate to reenact experiences. Fashion shows always give great pleasure. Compiling a tape or CD-ROM of remembered dance tunes, popular hits, and political songs of the times could provide stimulation for future sessions or for listening to at home. Creating displays of posters and programs with related personal recollections added, making collages or scrapbooks, viewing old films and following up with discussion, putting family collections of memorabilia in order, taking trips and outings to remembered places, or going to contemporary shows or concerts are some of the many possibilities.

INTERGENERATIONAL ACTIVITIES

Reminiscence work with people of different age groups is extremely rewarding but requires meticulous preparation and planning. Careful recruitment, selection, placement, and evaluation are all necessary. Many successful projects linking neighborhood care facilities and local schools have been reported (McGowan, 1994). Schools in close proximity to health and social welfare establishments serving older people have ready-made opportunities for forging friendships and engaging in mutual service. "The day I go to school is my best day of the week," said a day center member who each week visited first-grade children in the local school. She served as a proxy grandmother, an honored visitor, a history informant, a renowned storyteller, and a listening ear for children needing extra reading practice. Obviously, such relationships need careful nurturing; they seldom happen without effort, but their potential for shared benefits across generations is enormous.

In any intergenerational project, clarity about the mission and objectives that meet the aspirations of all involved are essential. The objectives frequently include aspirations to overcome age segregation; foster interaction between participants, and encourage the discussion of values, knowledge, beliefs, and attitudes. Three types of programs can be distinguished:

1. Young people serving older adults

2. Older adults serving young people

3. Young and older people serving the community

Intergenerational friendships take time to develop, so a realistic time frame is important. The appropriate amount of time overall as well as the length of each separate contact or session needs careful planning with consideration for the age, abilities, and health of all participants (American Association of Retired People, 1993; Lutz & Haller, 1996; Perlstein, 1995; Tietze, 1998).

Using older people as direct historical informants who visit schools and share their experience of public and private events with students of all ages has produced many educational and social benefits. Hearing firsthand from eyewitnesses usually fascinates children. Authentic accounts carry an authority and immediacy that make a profound impression in ways very different from and usually more persuasive than information gained from books and the Internet. Children are also interested in comparing then and now accounts of relevant experiences. Many aspects of the curriculum can be explored and enhanced through linking younger and older people together in shared work of mutual importance. Social, civic, intellectual, artistic, and personal objectives are all possible. There are many examples of children energetically working on projects in which they are encouraged to gather data from grandparents or other older informants through personal interrogation and to reflect on the material gathered as well as the processes of discovery in which they have engaged. Provided that such projects are carefully prepared and sensitively managed, both groups benefit from enlarged understanding. They grow in respect and sympathy for each other, whereas previously they may have dismissed, ignored, or even feared members of the other group. Even if grandparents are separated by distance, increasing access to information and communication technology is making it much easier to keep in contact and exchange information. There has never been a better time for developing electronic friends and surmounting limitations imposed by distance or disability. These opportunities should, however, provide additional contact rather than become substitutes for face-to-face meetings.

CONCLUSION

This chapter has considered a four-phase model for reminiscence work and emphasized the significance of the preliminary or planning phase of work and the importance of contracting with participants. The essential tasks to be undertaken in the preliminary or planning stage were identified, including deciding whether to work with individuals, couples, or small groups and the desirability of gathering background information. The valuable contribution of multisensory triggers in reminiscence work and some of their limitations were discussed and many different types of triggers identified. Three popular evocative reminiscence themes of school; work; and dressing up and looking good were developed together with suggestions about related triggers, activities, tangible outcomes, linked intergenerational programs, and possible implications for participants. It is inevitable that sad memories will be recalled from time to time, and the expression of sadness should not be avoided or regarded as harmful, although it is essential that workers develop good empathetic listening skills so that they feel confident in responding supportively. The chapter stressed the need to anticipate and plan for the rare eventuality that a small number of people may require professional clinical support as a consequence of being involved in reminiscence work. Brief guidance about the use of audiovisual equipment was mentioned, and principles of good practice concerned with various types of records were outlined. The beginning, middle, and ending phases of reminiscence work are elaborated in the next chapter.

Chapter 5

Engaging in Reminiscence Work

This chapter outlines the general knowledge, skills, and understanding required by reminiscence workers to develop their reminiscence practice with individuals, couples, or small groups. It emphasizes the importance of working to achieve satisfying, agreed-on outcomes through the processes of remembering, recalling, reviewing, reconstructing, and sharing personal memories. Workers are encouraged to think about how to apply these general principles to their own particular circumstances and the people with whom they wish to reminisce.

Many different factors, especially the needs and characteristics of the participants, determine what is done and how it is done. The approach described here assumes that some regularity of meetings across a reasonable time span is required for a worker's relationship to develop with an individual, couple, or small group. A weekly meeting is assumed, unless other reasons linked to the needs of the people involved or the requirements of the work they are intending to undertake indicate that more frequent and intensive work sessions or a longer time span than 12 weeks is desirable.

The group work literature refers to many different models or approaches, in which aims and objectives, leadership styles, responsibilities and methods of working vary greatly. The reciprocal group work model used here fits well with the philosophy and values that underpin reminiscence work. It sees the reminiscence worker as a facilitator or enabler whose responsibility is to ensure that the mutual needs and interests of the individual, couple, group, and the agency under whose auspices the worker is functioning are satisfactorily fulfilled. Although acting democratically, leaders

Photograph courtesy of Encore Theatre, Eugene, Oregon.

have clear responsibilities. It is their responsibility to bring people together, help them agree what they wish to do, assist them to work constructively together to accomplish an agreed program with satisfaction, and disperse with a sense of achievement. The worker simultaneously has obligations to the individual, couple, and group and to the sponsoring agency.

THE BEGINNING PHASE

With the preliminary planning phase completed and organizational arrangements in place, it is important to attend to how the workers and others are feeling as they get ready for the first meeting or session. Participants are likely to initially see the leader as an authority figure, which means the worker will need to work hard at establishing a more mutual, equal relationship from the outset (Dunn, Haight, & Hendrix, 2002). The leader of a reminiscence group is an enabler, not a historical authority, so behaving as a teacher is inappropriate.

Participants and leaders alike begin new encounters with some apprehension or tentativeness, wondering whether it is sensible to expose themselves to this experience. A mixture of hope and anxiety, most likely arising from previous experience of joining groups or being in new situations, will influence everyone's attitudes to this latest experience. It is essential that the workers appreciate their own feelings of excitement, probably tinged with apprehension. Even if the preparation and planning has been meticulously undertaken, the first meeting is always approached with a mixture of expectation and uneasiness. If not, the worker is probably bored or uncommitted to the enterprise. Workers need to tune in to their own feelings as part of their preparation and to be fully available to participants as they arrive (Shulman, 1999).

The First Meeting

First impressions are paramount. Meeting potential members beforehand will make the first meeting much easier. This first meeting should not be wholly devoted to contracting and planning. There needs to be an opportunity for engaging in simple enjoyable reminiscence.

People should be greeted personally. Everyone needs to feel warmly welcomed. Refreshments served at the beginning can help to break the ice and assist people to relax and informally meet each other. A number of tasks need to be accomplished in the first meeting. These include making introductions, making a clear statement about the purpose of the group, and explaining why the workers and the host agency are involved. Collecting feedback is essential to make sure that there is reasonable understanding and agreement among the leaders and members and to allow any divergent views or misunderstandings to be explored or any perceived obstacles to working together to be identified. Conversation among members should be encouraged. All members need to begin to feel that the group belongs to them and that it promises to be an enjoyable experience.

Some new groups begin by having everyone introduce him- or herself. This works well enough for the socially confident but can be quite daunting for shy people. However introductions are managed, make sure that they are handled in an age-appropriate way and are acceptable to all participants. It is usually desirable to use large nametags for the first few meetings. Never do anything that embarrasses anyone or draws attention to possible difficulties of remembering names or other specific information.

A brief statement about the aims and objectives of the proposed reminiscence or life story work needs to be made. Ideas about the possible program as well as expectations about attendance, participation, and mutual responsibilities need to be explored and tentatively agreed on. A link can be made to the earlier interviews with individuals, if these have been undertaken. The possibility of any tangible outcomes should be mentioned, if any are envisaged. It is customary to suggest some simple ground rules concerning respect for divergent viewpoints and giving everyone equal opportunities to participate as well as mentioning confidentiality and record keeping.

After these preliminaries, the leader should introduce reminiscence, perhaps using a small number of relevant triggers. Simple questions such as, "What does this remind you of?" or "What does this take you back to?" are usually sufficient to start people talking.

It is important to read people's emotions, not just their words, and to respond to both. Reach out reassuringly to anyone who looks uneasy, and value everyone's contribution. Some people will dominate the conversation out of natural confidence or maybe as a way of covering up initial insecurity; others may be relieved because this takes the pressure off them to speak. Friends and acquaintances may talk to each other while appearing to ignore other people. More than one conversation will probably go on at the same time, and the facilitator may feel that he or she is losing control. It is tempting to abdicate responsibility if this happens and to let the group become a free-for-all. This seeming chaos is typical of the beginning phase in the life of a group. It usually does not take long for the leaders to relax, and when they do, so too does the group. As a group settles down and confidence and trust develop, problems of domination tend to disappear. Likewise, silent members usually grow more confident, more willing to speak.

Just as the beginning of the first session is important, so too is the end of this session. Watch the time, and stick to the agreed arrangements. Do not let the group overrun the planned time, as this is likely to cause inconvenience. Before the first session ends, there needs to be a brief summing up of the ground covered. Arrangements for the next meeting should be outlined, with ample opportunities provided for participants to give feedback and to check out their understanding of what is being proposed. Workers, in their initial anxiety to succeed, may attempt too much in a first session. Purposefulness needs to be matched with relaxed pleasure for members, leaders, and volunteers. All participants need to leave the first session feeling that they have had a good time together and would like to return, and that each person has a valued contribution to make toward what it is agreed that they intend to do together.

THE MIDDLE PHASE OF WORK

It usually takes two or three sessions for a group to feel at ease, committed to an agreed-on program of work, and energetically engaged in pursuing it. Some of the various matters raised initially will need to be discussed again and clarified at subsequent meetings. Then, groups can move into the middle phase—the work phase. Now, initial tentativeness is set aside; trust, respect, and courtesy emerge as people willingly undertake agreed work and accomplish allotted tasks. They begin to learn to listen to each others' stories, to appreciate the complexity of people's lives, and to find their own voice. Feinberg gave an example from a reminiscence group formed for isolated recent Jewish–Russian immigrants.

> Group cohesiveness evolved quickly during the second meeting as members began to disclose emotional material. The images of deprivation, oppression, and suffering presented at this stage seemed to have a contagious effect on the group as a whole. The impact was to draw group members together and to begin to identify as a group. Each group member felt the urge to tell his or her story of personal tragedy. By the third meeting, all members demonstrated a willingness to speak and to listen to each other. (1996, p. 49)

At the start of each meeting, sessional contracting about how the time together is to be spent needs to be undertaken. People are only likely to invest time in concerns that are important to them, give them pleasure, and promise satisfaction in moving toward achieving personally significant goals. Sometimes communication may be indirect, even symbolic. This may cover up ambivalence or resistance and needs to be recognized as such and converted into energy for the work at hand. At the beginning of each session, it is the leader's responsibility to welcome people on arrival, check out concerns, briefly link back to the previous session, anticipate the intended program, and start the discussion. By means of an agreed-on division of responsibilities, leaders provide the framework, give encouragement, make suggestions, pose possible alternatives, mediate disagreements, strive for consensus, procure resources, and move the whole process forward.

As trust grows, reminiscences are likely to become more complex. Early simple, safe stories of happy times or good old days usually give way to more reflective, complex accounts. Earlier stories may be repeated with subtle changes and more elaborate details. There will be stories of achievements that will need to be acknowledged or even celebrated. There will also be accounts of opportunities lost, mistakes made, or regrets of roads not taken. In the middle phase, it becomes very important for the worker to be aware of and to cope effectively with the simultaneous legitimate demands and needs of both the group as a whole and each individual member while remaining aware of the interaction between the two. Although it is important to be sensitive to an individual's concerns, no individual should monopolize attention to the detriment of other people, and the worker's attention must focus on helping the individual and the group to find ways of working constructively together.

If a member expresses strong emotions, then other members may initially want to protect themselves by appearing to be uninterested or unwilling to engage in discussion of what is being said. The worker must do everything possible to link the individual who is expressing these emotions with the rest of the group by encouraging the members to identify from their own experience times when similar events or related emotions occurred in their own lives. Sometimes this is called *making a feeling link* between members or establishing common ground, and it is also an important skill in working with couples. Moments of strong emotion are not in themselves a diversion or a hindrance to achieving the agreed objectives. They are part of the work and only become an obstacle if ignored by leaders or members who fail to acknowledge their expression and respond to their implications.

Leaders may need to encourage people to elaborate their stories, to move from generalities, to fill in more specific details, and to speak about what really matters to them. The discussion will constantly move from the general to the specific and from the specific to the general. Specific memories provide opportunities to link with the experiences of other people and behind a general statement lies the possibility of a specific story someone would like to tell if encouraged to do so. Discussion in groups at any stage is seldom neat and orderly. At times it will appear irrelevant, fragmented, or out of sequence. Sometimes members will test the willingness of others to listen by tentatively telling part of a story to which they may return only when the group feels safer. Subtle skill is required to appreciate timing or pacing while also being able to make a demand for work and hold the group to achieving its agreed purposes (Shulman, 1999; Stock-Whitaker, 2000).

The overtalkative group member is probably the most feared. It certainly is desirable that each person feels content with the amount of time and attention given to him or her, is satisfied with his or her own contribution to the group, and believes over time that his or her life experience has been validated. If there is competition for time and attention, then members can be reminded about the original ground rules agreed about each person having a fair share of the time and everyone's contribution being respected. Retiring members can be encouraged to participate by introducing a topic on which the person concerned has particular expertise or by using an "asking around the group" type of exercise in which everyone takes turns (Osborn, 1994). If one member continues to dominate the discussion, then it may help to seat this person next to a leader so it is not as easy to make direct eye contact with the leader. Most groups soon develop sufficient confidence and security to be able to regulate themselves in ways that provide mutual satisfaction for all the members. Only in the most extreme situations and as a last resort is it necessary for a leader to take a member aside to discuss in private his or her style of interaction within the group.

Group Process

As the middle phase of work continues and the program unfolds session by session, it is often the most ordinary and commonplace triggers and the most everyday topics that awaken the richest memories. This may have less to do with the actual significance of the trigger, topic, or theme as with the associations of place, people, and emotions stored in memory. These surface as a consequence of sensory, social, and intellectual stimulation and growing confidence in participating. Once stimulated, it then takes little additional encouragement for people whose memories have been so aroused to talk of related associations, places, and people with energy, enthusiasm, and intense feeling. In a group session, one person may recall a fragment of experience, retrieved from the vast storehouse of memory, that will trigger another person to recall a similar experience. Each person interacting with the other members helps to create a composite story that, although not belonging completely to any one person, is richer as a consequence of being a shared creation. It has come from the memories and imaginations of many people and rightly belongs to them all.

Furthermore, the story's very creation may never have occurred without the separate but related building blocks retrieved from each person's own sedimentary memory and now reconstructed in the presence of others. The new story, whether it is an individual or collective one, then becomes a fresh memory for each person who has heard it; in turn, it too becomes available for future recall and further revision. Additional refinements and other stories will follow because it is the nature of reminiscence and recall to move from one memory to another, to build on the stories already told, and to develop newer versions instead of being limited to the one already told.

Although each group is unique, there are common characteristics that help guide workers in their efforts to achieve the best possible outcomes for everyone involved. Moods and energy levels vary both within sessions and between sessions. There will probably be times when a group appears to stray from its intentions or is less committed. Talk may dry up, and interest may flag. Leaders may feel depressed or discouraged. There may be challenge, resistance, or even overt hostility expressed among members or between members and leaders. If this happens, then it is crucial for the leaders to read accurately and respond appropriately to the mood of the group. They must endeavor to understand what is at stake and be open and honest about confronting, not ignoring, the difficulties, which can have many different causes. At times such as these, supervision or consultation can help workers to understand what is happening and their part in it. The leader needs to assist the group to identify and address, rather than avoid, the issues or obstacles. Members will need assistance to refocus, and if necessary renegotiate, the original agreement to secure a commitment concerning how the remainder of the group's time together should be spent.

Members tend to wait until the middle phase to disclose very painful memories, some that they may possibly never have talked about before. These may be about harm experienced or harm done to others, perhaps in cases where forgiveness, restitution, or reconciliation is no longer possible. There may be expressions of grief, anger, and regret over different types of past experience, including unresolved grief caused by loss of many kinds. People of all ages experience loss, but in late life, loss is cumulative with little time for recovery. Loss of lifetime partners, friends, health and strength, homes, possessions, pets, and many other kinds are commonplace and felt acutely.

The leader should mobilize the group as a resource for its members by enabling powerful emotions to be expressed and encouraging members to hear each others' distressing stories and reach out in comfort and solidarity to one another. It is his or her responsibility to hold the group to listening through difficult and happy narratives, to encourage attentive listening, and to support the group as a whole as well as each member in the group.

Workers need to cope with strong emotions at any time during their reminiscence work. Inexperienced leaders often find it difficult to encourage reminiscence groups to recall painful memories. They need to learn to cope with others' pain as well as with their own and develop the skill and confidence to let people talk about their pain instead of damping it down and hurrying everyone on to safer territory. Very likely, members of the group will be more experienced in coping with loss than the leaders. They are resources to each other. Reminiscence groups go through frequent shifts in mood. They move from laughter to tears and back again. These mood changes are natural, as memories come wrapped in accompanying emotions. Reminiscence work should be as much concerned with the emotional component as with the actual content of the memory.

Most people are frightened by silence. A skilled worker is able to respect silence and encourages the group to do the same. People need time to get in touch with their feelings, and silences should be respected, particularly when strong emotions have been aroused. Wait out the silence until the person expressing the pain indicates he or she is ready to move on. Assist by acknowledging the feelings that have been expressed by naming them, and encourage the group members to make a link between these feelings and their own emotional reactions to what they have just heard or seen.

Many people who lived through a large part of the 20th century have encountered profoundly traumatic experiences linked to world events such as recurrent wars, famine, revolution, and migration. Many appear to cope well with extreme trauma until late life, when the pain resurfaces or perhaps emerges for the first time (Hunt, Marshall, & Rowlings, 1997). It is important for workers to be able to place personal distress arising from

public events within a larger historic frame and to know something about
the enormity of suffering that so many have endured (Coleman, Hautamaki, & Podolskij, 2002; Feinberg, 1996; Kaminsky, 1988). The timeline
in Appendix E may be of some assistance, although it includes few international points of reference.

THE ENDING PHASE OF WORK

Ending a session requires the worker to undertake the tasks of summarizing; generalizing or finding connections between the stories of different
members; and identifying specific next steps, including making plans for
the next meeting. Workers may also provide encouragement by briefly
outlining the content of future sessions. At times it can be difficult to end
a session, as the approaching end sometimes causes participants to release
a fresh burst of energy. People begin to talk animatedly, sometimes for the
first time. It is helpful if the facilitator anticipates the ending by reminding people that time is almost up and then begins to wind down the session by engaging in the ending tasks of summarizing and forward planning. The leader should bring a session to a formal close even if some
members linger on afterward for informal conversation.

In individual work, the most significant communications are liable
to occur just as the worker gets ready to leave. These are known as *doorknob
communications*. Again, the impending ending seems to release an urgency
to communicate, an opportunity that is easily overlooked if the worker is
rushed and fails to perceive the significance and respond appropriately.

Overall, the ending phase can be exceedingly problematic if not managed with considerable skill. Groups should not be allowed to drift on,
fade away, or slowly disintegrate because of a worker's inability to handle
endings. Often as the end approaches, leaders are pressured to agree on an
extension of time. There needs to be a very positive reason for extending a
group beyond its originally agreed life span. Because of their own ambivalence about endings, workers may allow themselves to be persuaded
to extend a group for no other reason than that they lack the confidence to
undertake skilled endings work. The leader should, however, anticipate
the ending by reminding the group of the number of sessions remaining
and the work still to be completed.

As the end approaches, some absences may occur. Other members may begin to show anger, disappointment, or resentment. Some participants may feel relief that the group is over. All of these emotions need to be overtly addressed. Mixed emotions may be credited to other lost relationships or earlier experiences of endings, and the varied feelings associated with endings need to be openly acknowledged. Shulman (1999) suggested that groups that have courageously addressed negative feelings as well as positive ones throughout their time together terminate with far less anxiety. Their members have gained strength and developed confidence through their group experience so that they feel ready to move on to whatever the future holds for them.

Many groups like to celebrate their time together with a farewell party of some kind. Too often this denies an opportunity to consider the negative feelings associated with endings, which form a legitimate part of the life and work of any successful group. Sometimes it is better to hold a celebration before the actual last meeting. The final meeting can then be used for a constructive evaluation of the group and its work and for reaching a balanced, agreed understanding about what has been accomplished and what is to be written up and reported to others about the overall experience.

Workers also need to openly acknowledge the various emotions they experience during the ending phase. They may, for example, feel relief that a demanding, if enjoyable experience, is ending; they may feel guilty that more was not accomplished; they may be apprehensive about leaving vulnerable people to manage without the kind of support provided through a reminiscence group. Their task is to encourage the group honestly to review and evaluate its work, celebrate its achievements, and express confidence in moving on. If people are going to undertake further reminiscence work, then some endings may be more accurately described as transitions, and preparation can ensure a smooth transition.

REMINISCENCE WORK WITH INDIVIDUALS

There are many reasons why reminiscing with an individual or a couple may be preferable. *Life history* and *life story work* are the terms more commonly used when referring to *reminiscence* with individuals, but the three terms are often used interchangeably. Life story work suggests a more dynamic composition than life history, which conveys a fixed or static account, more often compiled by someone else, instead of being created by the individual. All the approaches overlap, so a strict classification is impossible. The interests, skills, professional backgrounds, and employment contexts of workers influence the type of work undertaken, the extent and depth to which personal issues and emotional conflicts are explored, and the type of outcomes sought and achieved.

Particular living contexts, specific types of disability, or multiple disabilities may mean that group work is not feasible for some people. In these circumstances, life story work will provide opportunities for concentrated personal attention. More attention to the evaluative and counseling elements of reminiscence and life review usually occurs during the course of individual work because of the greater emotional closeness and affection associated with one-to-one relationships. The worker needs to ensure that the interests of the person and the agreed purposes of any planned work, including a tangible outcome, are adequately explored and mutually agreed. Just as in group work, the how, when, where, and why of the suggested life story work need to be agreed on, and work needs to be facilitated throughout the four phases already described.

Life story work uses the interplay between memory and imagination to construct a story that assists the person to locate him- or herself within his or her own family's history and often within the broader framework of public history. It provides a sense of continuity, stretching back into the past and forward into the future. This is not always, however, experienced as helpful. It may exaggerate the sense of immediate isolation experienced by people—for example, those who are depressed, have dementia, or have lost touch with their families because of circumstances or their own or other people's behavior. The ethical worker must carefully assess the risk of possibly doing harm or of leaving a person worse off rather than better off as a consequence of engaging the individual in life story work. People should be given a genuine choice, reach their own decisions about participation, and be permitted to freely withdraw at any time.

Before examining planned life story work, the importance of seizing opportunities for unplanned, spontaneous reminiscing needs to be stressed. These openings occur naturally, without planned prompting. Everyday occurrences, such as putting a small child to bed or reading stories, may bring to mind memories of other times and places. With nursing facility residents, daily living routines can stimulate conversation. Assisting with intimate physical care such as bathing, dressing, wound care, or bedtime preparations frequently prompts spontaneous conversation about significant memories. Staff members need to realize the importance of these openings and to respond with respect, interest, and appreciation of what is being tentatively related. If staff members are only concerned with accomplishing the physical task at hand as quickly as possible, then wonderfully rich opportunities for significant conversation about the past and the present will be lost, possibly never to occur again. Staff members who are good communicators are able to exploit opportunities as they arise as well as to create special occasions to mine the riches of personal memory.

Spontaneous occasions are precious, but too many busy caregivers are satisfied only with such opportunistic reminiscence. They too easily dismiss the additional benefits of planned or prompted work. Clearly some circumstances are more likely to lead to reminiscence than others. Alumni weekends, camp reunions, anniversaries, family parties, weddings, or funerals naturally create expectations or provide surroundings that prompt reminiscence. Both spontaneous and planned approaches are valuable. One approach does not have to compete with the other; each brings its own rewards (Garland & Garland, 2001).

Using Triggers with Individuals

If people are living in their own homes, then triggers abound. Photographs, ornaments, pictures, furniture, and possessions provide a focus for reminiscence. Simple open-ended questions easily lead to conversation about the circumstances in which memorabilia was acquired, who is in a photograph, or the significance of a particular object. If actual objects are not available, then people may nevertheless respond if asked which objects from the past they most cherish and why (Sherman, 1991b). Is there, for example, one object or phrase that best represents a person's life? If this is too difficult a question, then inquire about the names of a small number of possessions most valued in terms of personal significance. These possessions may be drawn from different periods in the person's life. This can lead on to an age-stage discussion. A conversation thus begun can move backward and forward in time and branch out into questions about the objects' appearance, associations, manner of acquisition, and reasons for being treasured.

Another easy way to start a reminiscence conversation is to ask a person to imagine the house where he or she lived in as a child. Invite the person to walk you through the house, beginning at the front porch or the front door, moving down the hall, exploring other rooms as you go. Talk about décor, use, and contents of significant rooms. Inquire who else lived in the house, what they did, which games and toys were shared with other members of the family, and who came to visit. Encourage conversation about favorite and least-favorite rooms; memorable events; and family, friends, and neighbors. Perhaps draw a simple plan. Let the storyteller linger; imagine the smells; describe the furniture, fittings, and fabrics; relive events; and expand on the story. Memories are likely to crowd in thick and fast once this process is begun. Particular rooms or parts of rooms can be recalled in considerable detail. A woman could, for example, be asked to imagine a shelf or cupboard in her kitchen and talk about its contents. A man could be asked to describe what he kept in his garage or his toolbox. A keen gardener could walk you around the backyard in imagination and tell you what was grown at various times of the year. There are endless possibilities once we see and help others to see the importance of ordinary things and how the seemingly mundane gives meaning to our lives.

Engaging Individuals

All of a worker's engagement skills are needed to overcome natural self-effacement and lack of confidence. Many people initially declare they have done nothing sufficiently interesting to talk about. Usually once this lack of confidence is gently challenged and exploration begins, enthusiasm is released and energy mobilized. Provided that the hearer values the life story as it unfolds, self-esteem grows and pride emerges. This lack of confidence seems to be less of a problem for men, although this observation risks making a gross generalization because there are many exceptions. They more readily associate personal significance with their paid occupation and only later begin to speak about the importance of relationships and family life. So a more fruitful starting place for a conversation with a man is likely to be his occupation, profession, or place of work. Cars once owned, especially the first one, may come next and only then do recollections of wife and children and memories about other significant personal relationships emerge.

Sometimes reminiscence is easier and more natural if undertaken along with some mutually enjoyable practical activity such as cooking, washing, cleaning, polishing, sewing, knitting, needlework, or tapestry. Walking, gardening, carpentry, car washing and polishing, painting, or sanding provide similar opportunities for productive, companionable conversation about times past. These encounters may be experienced as less threatening, more relaxed, and more conducive to the easy recall of memories. The order of exploration is not important, provided that the reminiscer derives pleasure and satisfaction from the reminiscing experience. Having considered simple reminiscence with individuals, it is now time to consider a number of more structured or systematic approaches to memory work with individuals.

Life Story Work with Individuals

Life storybook techniques, or life story work, first appeared in the child care professional literature in the 1960s and 1970s and have since been adapted for other age groups (Ryan & Walker, 1997). Life story work can be undertaken with people of all ages in many different practice contexts. Although it is sometimes appropriate at the point of crisis, especially with children and others who may be unable to verbalize their feelings, it has many applications in times of chronic difficulty, major life transitions, bereavement, and life-threatening or anxiety-provoking circumstances. This approach attempts to discover, discuss, restore, and document information about family origins and childhood experience for children (and others) who have been denied the opportunity to acquire this knowledge, which is normally gained by growing up in or with access to their birth families.

Life Story Work with Adults Facing Transitions

Life story work has been undertaken with adults who have developmental disabilities and need assistance in relocating to small community homes (Atkinson, 1994; Hussain & Raczka, 1997; Porter, 1998). For older adults likely to be faced with moving into protected living situations either because of deteriorating health or other vulnerabilities, life story work can provide a valuable focus for effective communication. It can assist the person, his or her close family members, and involved professionals in making and implementing momentous, life-changing decisions. It can help prepare for the move and assist significant people in the new location in getting to know and beginning to form a relationship with the newcomer (Forster, 1998).

Chapter 6 lists ideas about the many different formats used to record life stories and reminiscences. It is reasonable to ask why life story work with people of all ages is not undertaken more frequently if its advantages are so obvious. When is it used? Why is this used more often with children than with adults? Basically the answer is that younger age groups are widely believed to be more likely to benefit from psychotherapy, counseling, and other psychosocial interventions than are adults, especially older adults. Even with troubled children, family members and professionals often resist when asked to assist in life story work. They may resent the demands on their time; they may feel insufficiently informed and ill equipped; they may believe that it will be difficult, if not impossible, to locate relevant information; they may fear losing family photographs and other memorabilia (although copying is simple and inexpensive); and they may be reluctant to have information about the family become more widely available.

Part of the work lies in dealing with such resistance, in patiently explaining its importance and likely benefits, and in genuinely respecting differing viewpoints. Some wish to protect children from their unhappy pasts, a course of action that is unlikely to be successful if access to life history information is denied, or fear stirring up memories of their own unsatisfactory childhood. Many professionals simply do not see the point or genuinely believe that the perceived obstacles are greater than the anticipated benefits.

Life story work is most often done on a one-to-one basis, although there are examples of the same skills and techniques being used in small groups, particularly with troubled adolescents. Participants' dawning realization that they are not the only ones to have endured unpredictable, threatening changes and the discovery of common ground assists the individuals to reach more balanced evaluations of their own problems.

Life story work is the preferred term because it does not limit the type of documentation to book format. Some agencies have begun to use digital formats, including video and CD-ROMs, as alternatives to books. The people involved should agree on the format, bearing in mind interests, skills, and available resources. The process of engagement as much as the form of the record is always important.

Life Story Work with Children and Young Adults

Life story work is employed as a way of assisting children or young people who are preoccupied with or confused about their past, unhappy in the present, and uncertain about their future. It is used to provide a personal story and to promote resilience, which Grotberg defined as "a universal capacity, which allows an individual person, a group, or community to prevent, minimize, or overcome the damaging effects of adversity" (1995, p. 7).

The children and young people who undertake life story work are likely to have experienced repeated changes in care arrangements and living locations. In addition, they often experience deep insecurity due to absence of or removal from their birth parents because of family breakdown, neglect, abuse, institutionalization, death, adoption, foster care, or other disruptive events.

Life story work has also been used effectively with children and adolescents who are confronted with life-threatening illnesses, terminal care, or chronic disabilities and has sometimes been used with their siblings, whose feelings of fear, sadness, loneliness, guilt, jealousy, and anger need to be recognized and processed. Common approaches include video diaries; life storybooks; writing imaginative symbolic stories, often illustrated with the child's own drawings and paintings; and acting out feelings through puppets, clay modeling, storytelling, and games. All are helpful ways for children to communicate about the past, present, and possible future, and these methods often pave the way for related conversation about personal and family predicaments and their associated emotions. Such approaches may also directly assist the child and his or her siblings to understand the nature of an illness or disability and its related procedures and treatment. These approaches may also help to explain the role of the numerous people involved in providing care and treatment. If more than one child within a family is working on a life storybook, then it is usually more beneficial if each child is able to have a different worker so that individual needs and wishes can receive concentrated attention without arousing competitiveness or envy.

The children and young people are assisted to review their past and present circumstances and to plan for the future by making a written and pictorial record of their life story, mostly in their own words. Visiting and photographing former places where the child lived and attended school, unearthing records, locating old photographs and memorabilia, and writing descriptions may all be part of this work. It can also involve interviews with relevant informants who know about aspects of the child's past. This way of working is not suited to all children, nor should it be used as a cheap, quick substitute when longer-term therapy is required. Careful listening to children and respect for their views are central to life story work. Social workers, foster parents, adoptive parents, or birth parents may assist in the process of creating the life record, which becomes a continuing chronicle of the child's journey toward adulthood. The objectives of life story work include

- Helping to examine and develop a positive self-image and enhance self-esteem

- Helping to develop a strong sense of personal identity

- Promoting relationship building between the child and key worker

- Assisting birth parents to contribute to their child's well-being

- Helping substitute parents to acknowledge the child's past, understand the child better, and contribute to the child's ongoing development

Life story work can only be successful if the child fully engages in the process. It is essential for the child or young person to feel in charge of compiling the record. The child must determine the interpretative slant, speed of compilation, and people who will have access to the record. The actual process of talking about a problematic past, however, is usually considered more important than any actual record that may be created as an outcome. Once again, the worker can only be an enabler, not a director or owner. Such work can make heavy demands. The worker requires considerable skill to support the child throughout what will inevitably involve considerable pain before acceptance of the past, integration of memories, and emotional growth toward maturity is established. A trusting relationship, time, and commitment are all essential. Adults fear the pain involved for the child in uncovering the story's details. Yet many speak of how resilient the children are and how generous and accepting they can be of parental shortcomings once the facts are known and honestly explained. The record becomes a tangible challenge to the child's idealized fantasies, tendencies toward self-deception, and fears of the unknown. It provides a structured way for children and young people to talk about themselves and to confront their past, present, and anticipated future concerns.

In doing such work with children, memories of a worker's own difficult childhood inevitably arise. When workers share their painful memories in a disciplined way, children may come to appreciate that other people too experience pain, that the fault or cause does not lie in the child, and that there is no need to feel guilty or responsible for parental behavior. There are many issues, both ethical and technical, concerning life story work with children that require more exploration than is possible here. Any adult intending to undertake such work needs advice, supportive supervision, and commitment to see the process through to a mutually agreed, satisfactory end (Ryan & Walker, 1997). There can never be any finality to the story, as it will always be open to further revision, expansion, and development. This is a process that cannot be rushed, and although at times it may be extremely demanding, even painful, it can bring relief and hope to troubled children and to those who live or work with them.

Similar techniques have been used with young adults. Some may have been abused as children or may now be experiencing many vicissitudes, perhaps doubting their capacity to parent or behave responsibly toward their own children who may be in trouble or may have been removed from parental care. Some of these young adults have only hazy recollections of their own childhood and can be assisted by retracing their own developmental and family history. They can be helped by reflecting on tangible evidence of places lived, home and school life, parenting and substitute parenting experiences, and formative life events. Again, a counseling-type of trusting relationship is important, but talk alone may be insufficient compared with active engagement in the process of producing a tangible record of real or simulated documentation. Assistance in drawing family trees (a task now greatly simplified by readily available computer software), help in gaining access to official records, companionship on visits, photography, and research can all assist, together with crucial ongoing discussion, as the information is uncovered. This demanding, skilled work requires management support and appropriate resources if it is to help arrest the spiral of transgenerational parenting failure and the costly cycle of repetitive abuse.

Children whose parents are in the process of separating or divorcing or are already divorced may benefit from life story work. Here issues of conflicting loyalties, self-blame, feelings of burden or assumption of responsibility for the marital breakdown, concern for the well-being of younger siblings, and anxieties about the future can be addressed. Inevitably in times of family breakdown, children want to rehearse the past in seeking to understand and accept what is happening to them in the present, so skill in doing memory work is very relevant to many aspects of contemporary child care practice.

Jackie, age 8, moved to a children's home after three foster placements had broken down, mainly because of her aggressive, uncooperative behavior and the poor health of some of the foster parents. Her social worker of 3 years hoped that Jackie might eventually be adopted, as she had never known her birth mother and no other relatives appeared to exist. During the course of Jackie's relationship with this social worker, she gradually showed increasing interest about her origins. One day she began questioning the social worker more directly about her earlier life and seemed especially curious about her mother. The social worker asked Jackie if she would like her to find all of the information she could and Jackie agreed. She also responded enthusiastically to the suggestion that they work together on a life storybook so that whatever information was discovered could be written down to help her remember in the future. The agency file contained very little information about Jackie's childhood and the social worker only knew the most recent foster parents, so the search for the absent life history details began. For the next year and a half, the two had regular sessions consisting of making visits, taking photographs, having conversations, and writing and drawing sessions. Jackie liked to do most of the writing herself. She put things in her own words; drew pictures, simple maps, and diagrams; and arranged photographs of herself and other significant places and people as the information was uncovered. Throughout this time, Jackie talked about what she was learning, taking time to absorb the details that were slowly unearthed. The process of coming to terms with the numerous changes and losses in her life so far and the gaps in information that still existed was turbulent and painful. Two of the three previous foster parents were located, and the first foster couple invited Jackie and her social worker to visit. These foster parents were able to tell Jackie what she was like as a baby, when she began to walk and talk, and how they had celebrated Christmas together. Photographs were loaned and copied. Jackie was able to visit the maternity hospital where she was born and the street where her mother had lived and to photograph the three foster homes and the present children's home. As the storybook took shape, she began to suggest that she would like a new family and a successful search for adoptive parents took place. When Jackie, now nearly 10, moved to her adoptive home, the book went with her as a cherished possession, and her new parents undertook helping her to keep her story up to date.

Children of parents with HIV/AIDS may be involved in providing care for an ill parent over an extended period of years. They may also have to care for and support younger siblings while facing the possible death of the parent, their own grief, and probable stigma and isolation. Life story work with these children and sometimes with the parents as well, provided that it is flexible and adaptable, can bring pleasure and satisfaction. It can provide a focus for addressing the past, the painful present, and the inescapable anxieties and grief to come for both the adults and their overburdened children. Weishaar (1999) reported that using visual format life review with adults who have HIV/AIDS is helpful, although Vaughn and Kinnier (1996) found some problems when attempting life review with this group. Chapter 6 discusses the use of memory boxes with African families affected by HIV/AIDS.

Another contemporary example of different but related work refers to young offenders who have been arraigned on homicide charges and are awaiting trial in Reno, Nevada. Often these young men are poorly educated and unable to verbalize their frustrations or to present themselves persuasively in court. An imaginative project encourages them to take responsibility for writing the lyrics of a three-verse song that they then sing in court to a tune that they all seem to know, the childhood song *Twinkle, Twinkle Little Star*. This brief presentation sung to the judge encapsulates their past experience, their present situation, and their future fears and hopes. Sands (2002) reported that this songwriting and singing enables these young offenders to take public responsibility for themselves, their behavior, and their own lives in ways they have previously avoided.

LIFE REVIEW

In the 1930s, two Viennese psychiatrists made the earliest systematic reference to life review in clinical literature when they identified a tendency for all older people to be concerned with a balance sheet of life (Sherman, 1981). Frenkel-Brunswick (1963) and Buhler (1968) believed this process involved consideration of retrospective experiences in anticipation of death. Butler (1963) described life review as the return to consciousness of past experiences and unresolved conflicts, which can be revisited by means of reminiscence and reintegrated into the personality. He argued that this process could have both positive and negative consequences, leading either to greater candor, serenity, and wisdom or panic, guilt, and depression. Reminiscence with a life review emphasis is now commonplace, as evidenced by diary writing during adolescence and older people writing their memoirs and autobiographies.

The term *life review* is frequently used in a generalized way but also refers to a carefully structured approach to evaluative reminiscence undertaken with older individuals (Haight & Burnside, 1993). In this second precise sense, *life review* refers to a process that is guided by another person. It aims to assist an older person systematically to review the past, face old conflicts, develop new perspectives, and reach an acceptable formulation of life as a preparation for facing death with minimum fear or anxiety. Assisted by an empathic listener who is equipped with counseling skills, the person is systematically encouraged to review his or her life chronologically from childhood to the present, reflect on it, resolve issues, reorganize, and reintegrate whatever aspects of the past may be troubling or preoccupying him or her. The process can be thought of as putting one's house in order by walking through it again and seeing it in a new light. Although the urge to do this appears to be most intense in late life, it can occur at any age. It seems to be precipitated in younger or middle-age people by life crises of various kinds that stimulate reflection on the meaning of life generally and, more especially, the meaning of one's own particular life (Butler, 1996). Such a review involves much more than addressing the final stage of life and the developmental challenge posed by Erikson, Erikson, and Kivnick (1986) of integrity versus despair, accepting life as it has turned out for good or ill. Life review concerns making sense of the whole of life, not just the last stage, by developing a story the teller can live with and is prepared to share with others.

Burnside (1996) and Haight and Burnside (1993) surveyed various definitions and identified distinctions between life review and reminiscence, with particular reference to nursing literature and nursing practice. Life review is usually undertaken with individuals, although there may be some exceptions when families or spouses are involved. It is much more structured and systematically directed than simple reminiscence work, in which there is a more free-flowing exploration of themes, topics, and events, not necessarily pursued in chronological order. Life review seldom uses multisensory triggers to stimulate recall but relies on semistructured verbal questioning to achieve therapeutic, evaluative, and integrative goals. Reminiscence aspires to achieve various social, cultural, artistic, and personal objectives, aspects of which may well turn out to be therapeutic, evaluative, and integrative for some people some of the time. In reminiscence, the worker is primarily an enabler, not a counselor, although empathetic listening and attending skills, among others, are required. Reminiscence is commonly undertaken in small groups and is often accompanied by artistic and creative activities.

Structured Life Review

Haight, Coleman, and Lord (1995) defined *life review* as a short-term structured reminiscing intervention conducted on a one-to-one basis with an older person. The person who conducts the process acts as a therapeutic listener who guides the older individual through his or her memories and helps the individual to reframe troubling events and to move on in thinking about and understanding the memories recalled. Structured life review is undertaken with individuals, not with groups. It is a planned, purposeful intervention to which the participant freely consents and actively engages. It can be undertaken selectively with some people who have cognitive difficulties, provided that they are able to consent or assent (meaning they do not actively object to being involved) and are able to talk about their life and form some evaluation of it as a whole. The meanings or constructions that the person gives to the memories recounted are explored with the therapeutic intention of helping the person to come to terms with the life lived. As a short-term, time-limited intervention, the number of sessions is fixed from the outset, usually involving eight weekly interviews carried out in private.

Conducting Life Review Sessions

Life review sessions cover the whole of the life span from birth to the present, following both a chronological and thematic order. During a structured life review, questions are asked about the person's attitudes to death, grief, fear, religion, school, hardships, sex, work, and relationships. Troubling events are identified and analyzed using reflective counseling skills so that these problematic memories become integrated into the person's life story. The interviewer makes some tangible record, usually a book illustrated with photographs. In exceptional cases, it may be an audio- or videotape. The book that remains the property of the life reviewer is usually not compiled until the review interviews have been completed; then, it will be checked and any requested changes made. The entire review process may be guided and directed by using Haight's semistructured Life Review and Experiencing Form (LREF; see Appendix G). Both this instrument and the process have proved to be widely acceptable to older people and have established validity and reliability (Haight, Michael, & Hendrix, 2000).

Together, the process and the tangible record enhance a sense of selfhood for the individual. The process provides a positive, if brief, relationship and constructing the personal history record, often called a *life book* and sometimes a *life storybook,* is also regarded as a pleasant, predominantly enjoyable activity. The record can become a tool for future communication and reminiscence and is regarded as a useful tool for health care professionals when formulating nursing and care plans. Sometimes a separate parallel life review is undertaken with spouses who act as caregivers. This approach keeps the caregivers constructively occupied and prevents them taking over and telling the life story of the person receiving care. At the same time, it values and validates the caregiver's own life experience. Some modifications to expectations, outcomes, and structure are likely to occur when doing a structured life review with a person who has dementia and may find it difficult to stay within the chronological life stage being explored in any particular session. People with dementia are likely to benefit from more frequent and possibly shorter sessions, and their life book needs to contain briefer captions for the photographs written in their own direct speech. They are likely to switch from stage to stage within a single session, thus making a comprehensive systematic review of the entire life span extremely hard to achieve. In addition, there will probably be a lot of repetition of stories, often in a fragmented or symbolic way, and reaching judgments or evaluations of life overall (as distinct from small parts of it or particular events) may not always be possible.

People with dementia, however, undoubtedly express considerable pleasure and enjoyment within single sessions and enjoy the process. Some people with early or moderate dementia have proved surprisingly able to make coherent, summarizing evaluations of what the whole review process has meant to them. Their ability to do so varies enormously and will depend on a number of factors, such as the extent and nature of each person's intellectual impairment and the amount of time needed to establish a trusting relationship. Haight (1998) suggested that some people with dementia can differentiate between the past and the present and should be encouraged to undertake a life review. It can assist in taking stock of life to date, reinforce a sense of achievement, affirm personal identity, and assist in formulating plans for coping with what lies ahead. It can also help professional caregivers to establish a trusting relationship and to gather invaluable comprehensive information, convey empathic interest and concern, and offer information and reassurance in the face of inevitable anxiety experienced by people diagnosed as having dementia.

Structured Guided Autobiographical Writing

Structured guided autobiographical writing—regarded as a particular type of structured individual life review allied with supportive group interaction—has been widely used and carefully researched (Birren & Birren, 1996). This approach combines individual and group activities. It is a composite method that is customarily initiated and led by a psychologist. It involves each individual person's writing independently and in private on identified themes, then joining with others in a series of regular weekly sessions to read and discuss the individual accounts. It thus combines private and public reflection, individual effort, and group support (Birren & Cochran, 2001; Birren & Deutchman, 1991). Guided autobiographical writing is not intended to be a formal therapy or a prescription for identified diseases. Nevertheless, the process is therapeutic. Memories stimulated by writing are recalled and reflected on in private, but reading accounts aloud in a supportive group promotes further insight, self-acceptance, growth, and development.

Ten weekly meetings with approximately ten older participants are held. In between sessions, each person independently completes a short story of two pages concerned with the following nine aspects of life:

1. History of the major branching points in life or the time and nature of significant decisions

2. Family history

3. Career or major life work

4. The role of money in life

5. Health and body image

6. Loves and hates

7. Sexual identity, sexual roles, and experience

8. Experience of and ideas about death, dying, and other losses

9. Influences, beliefs, and values that provide meaning in life

When the stories are read and discussed in the group, each member receives positive feedback, support, and validation that his or her life has been worthwhile. Self-esteem is enhanced, and opportunities for socializing at a stage in life when other significant relationships may be lost form an important element. Participants gain fresh energy and courage to face the future by realizing, some for the first time, all they have accomplished in the past. Birren and Birren suggested, "The coming alive of old memories and emotions, and the revitalization of power and meaning in life, can be extremely satisfying for all participants in the guided autobiography group process" (1996, p. 289). Other positive outcomes reported include a sense of increased personal power, mastery, or significance. These outcomes are brought about by recognition of successful past problem-solving strategies that can be used to resolve problems and meet present needs. A fresh evaluation of the past leads to resolution of old resentments and negative feelings. A resurgence of interest in past hobbies and activities, together with the development of new friendships and relationships with other group members, brings a greater sense of meaning to life and ability to face impending death with a conviction that one has made a contribution to the world.

Such a method requires skilled leadership; substantial social confidence; verbal and writing skills; and willingness to expose one's experience, values, and personal reflections to other people's critical scrutiny while being willing to engage actively with others in considering their experiences. The process allows inconsistent or persistent negative generalizations to be gently questioned or reevaluated. For articulate, well-educated people, it is an attractive, effective approach that is well-suited to older adults who may be living in their own homes, retirement communities, or nursing facilities. The same ideas have been adapted by using various nonverbal expressive ways of exploring similar life course themes. Drawing, painting, drama, dance, and music all provide absorbing opportunities for people to work, alone or with others, to *re-member, re-work, re-present, re-integrate,* and *re-construct* their life experience.

Spiritual Autobiography and Life Review

There is a growing interest in issues concerned with spirituality and a search for a sense of continuity and meaning in later life. Moberg (2001) believed that this search is an innate part of human existence. It seems as if Butler's (1963, 1996) theme of universal life review has been renamed and represented as spiritual life review. The trigger components for undertaking a spiritual life review are identified as changes in time and space associated with retirement from full-time work, the opportunity for reminiscence and reflection, the changing understanding of what is considered valuable, changing relationships, increasing dependency, and the nearness of death. Awareness of a spiritual dimension to life implies that people seek to be in harmony with the universe and to look for answers about transcendence and the infinite. Some people seek meaning through religion; others seek it in art, music, relationships, nature, and other experiences that produce a sense of awe and wonder. Whether such a sense of awe is innate and universal and whether it exists in childhood but is submerged in adulthood, only to re-emerge in later life, remain unresolved questions. We can be certain, however, that each person who embarks on a search for spirituality travels a singular road and probably arrives at a unique understanding.

When undertaking a spiritual autobiography, much introspection, evaluative reminiscence, and recall are involved. Whether this occurs entirely in private or is shared with others in discussion, writing, or other nonverbal forms depends on personal preferences and available opportunities. Other people can only assist if they are aware of their own search for spirituality and disciplined in not projecting their own needs onto others (Moody, 1995). Diverse approaches provide signposts on the journey, and no one approach should ever be regarded as universally helpful. This applies equally to reminiscence work and to the many different ways in which it is undertaken. Various divinity schools, churches, synagogues, and religious and service foundations offer training in spiritual life review and opportunities to participate in individual and group spiritual life review programs. Clergy, divinity and pastoral care students, and rabbis lead many of these programs, but some are offered within a secular ethos as well as in therapeutic health care contexts such as in hospices or other terminal care programs.

Terminal care presents many challenges for staff and those for whom they care. If the person needing care is to accept it with grace and be able to grieve effectively for their losses, then caregivers must understand the person and demonstrate respect for that person's life story. In late life and especially in terminal care, the challenge is to consent to present necessity and to be able to mourn for what is past and what is now being lost (Viney, Benjamin, & Preston, 1995). Cooley suggested,

> Reminiscence is critical to one's capacity to embrace the diminished life state as good. As the older person reaches the twilight of the life cycle it becomes more important that she be able to bless her single, unique life story. Memory shapes identity. If the older person in a nursing facility is seen only as a patient and an old one at that, it becomes an assault on her personal dignity and sense of personal integrity. If on the other hand that older person is encouraged to remember to tell her story, her sense of personal integrity is validated. (1999, p. 41)

In terminal care, many people will not have the energy to pursue extensive writing, so audio recordings of a series of short interviews or conversations are more customary. Preparation of an illustrated or annotated life storybook or photographic collection may also be possible. A trained volunteer or family member may assist, and work can be sensitively adapted to meet the needs of children who are terminally ill. Many activity programs in hospice day care centers use reminiscence with both individuals and very small groups and frequently combine shared conversation with painting, music, or other nonverbal means of communication.

Creative and Autobiographical Writing Groups

Writers' groups have become immensely popular, although they are not really new (Chandler & Ray, 2002; Ray, 1999). The inspirational work of the poet Koch (1977) provided an excellent model. He established poetry-writing groups for physically frail older nursing facility residents, ages 70–90. The groups met for 16 1-hour weekly sessions and provided proof of hitherto unexpected and underutilized talent for writing. Most group members had little formal education and had worked in low-paying jobs. All were incapacitated, most used wheelchairs, some were blind, others had hearing or speech difficulties, and some had memory problems. Almost no one was able to write because of blindness or muscular weakness and needed assistance with this aspect. Koch used flowers, music, and brief poetry readings to stimulate his frail students. In the spring, he would bring in daisies, violets, chrysanthemums, and hyacinths. People were encouraged to say what the flowers looked like, what they reminded them of, how they smelled, and what they felt like. In some sessions, he suggested writing while listening to music and would begin by reading short extracts to show how poets had talked about music and other subjects. At the end of each session, the poems would be read aloud and commented on. Koch stressed poetry as art and found that through the new experience of poetry writing, participants became eager to talk about what they thought or felt and to express their views with conviction as they emerged from their customary reticence.

Many writing groups have either an explicit or implicit autobiographical orientation. There is little doubt that some people join writers' groups because they lack someone willing to listen to their recollections. They have a story to tell but have no audience. Joining a creative writing or life story class brings a certain discipline to writing and usually also provides a group of listeners, as reading to other members is commonplace.

Some people believe they think best when they write and most find that hearing other people's writing stimulates ideas and encourages confidence.

Beginning writing is the hardest part for many people. Frequent advice is to start with an easily remembered, accessible, and concrete incident and the story can then flow backward and forward as memories emerge. Perlman offered sound advice about using personal memories as a foundation for creative writing. For her, getting started was the important thing. She recommended beginning with "memories that are accessible to you as you rummage about, or those that are called up, somehow, by some present stimulus. Give them breathing space, invite them in, entertain them" (1989, p. 188). She suggested that participants think about it and speculate why this particular memory was recalled, wonder about what it meant at the time and what it means now. Does it have the same meaning or in what ways is it now different? The crucial thing is to overcome the beginning resistance that is usually associated with anxiety. Undoubtedly starting with what comes and letting the rest follow is the easiest way to overcome this initial difficulty and is likely to be far more productive than writing to an imposed chronological prescription or filling in the blank spaces of an already printed memory book. Such approaches seem to stifle rather than stimulate creativity, but they may at least get some people started.

Kent (1999) provided a loose structure to assist people to overcome their fears about sharing life stories, recover from previous negative writing experiences, express individual creativity, and find meaning in memories. She suggested a framework called the *wisdom tree* in which the rings of the trunk suggest the core stories that represent the essence of a person's life. The roots are stories about ancestors, the branches represent people and places of importance, and the leaves are miscellaneous aspects. She used memory-jogging techniques, relaxation, music, and guided imagery to encourage the members of her writing group to generate numerous memories, one of which is initially shared with another person. People then write for 15 minutes and read their stories, poems, letters, or whatever they have written to each other. The timed writing process is repeated for each part of the tree so life stories steadily accumulate. Although it may be easier to start with the core memories, first constructing the trunk, this is not essential as the flexibility of the approach allows for considerable freedom yet provides a secure organizing structure.

The process of writing is like working a patchwork quilt or making a mosaic or a collage. The overall framework may be given, but what is represented within the frame is built up piece by piece. People are advised to include the funny and the ridiculous along with more serious recollections. Usually the more specific the story becomes, the more it connects or resonates with other people's experience. This kind of autobiographical creative writing takes time. It becomes easier once the writing progresses and confidence begins to grow, and most people who attempt it find the outcomes justify the early struggles. The achievement of a written product reinforces the gains in self-confidence and self-esteem that slowly develop. "That is what we are doing. We are paying attention to our lives. To what we have done and been and lived through," wrote Porter (1998).

The Share Your Life Story Group in Galveston, Texas, is one of thousands of writing groups meeting in retirement communities, nursing facilities, college campuses, churches, senior centers and synagogues where older people meet to look back over their lives and write their stories. Examination and excavation of past lives, warts and all, is extraordinarily popular as a way of valuing the years that are gone and making the most of the years that are left. Moody (1995) suggested that through this process, people are searching for meaning, finding a voice, leaving a record, and democratizing autobiography. De Medeiros (2000, p. A14) described this form of unstructured life review work and commented, "people write about relationships and the very small gestures that have made them human." A member wrote: "We are claiming our lives . . . Your life is a bunch of stories, and then you put it down, and it has form. You think, 'This is my life', and its O.K." With the Galveston group the emphasis is on freedom of choice about style and content with the writers being prompted by questions such as "What do you need to work on?", "What is it you want to reclaim, to narrate, to get clearer on?" Reading to the group is as important as writing. Putting it down and then reading it aloud to others is a very powerful tool. Another member, Joy Weiss, married for 55 years and now age 80 wrote a letter to her deceased husband: "You would be proud to know I have become a little more independent, realizing I am on my own and must assume certain duties. You should see me replacing batteries where needed and resetting the clocks and answer machine."

Assisted Biography

Assisted biography provides a bridge between autobiography and biography and is akin to other approaches (e.g., audio or videotaped interviews) or, in this respect, to producing a life book linked to structured life review, in which the burden of production is shared with another person. Such work demands great sensitivity and personal discipline on the part of the amanuensis (the helper who records the account), because to have one's story told by another person or to be presented with an autobiography one has not written or an account that one does not really own can be deeply disturbing. This issue is particularly relevant to life story work undertaken with people who have learning disabilities or other cognitive or physical impairments that require another person to play a major role (Walmsley, 1995).

Mary, age 91, had lived in a nursing home for 5 years. The sudden death of her husband some 40 years ago meant that she was widowed after a long and happy marriage. Because she suffered from severe chronic obstructive pulmonary disease and mild memory loss, she had relinquished living independently. Although settling well in the nursing home and being described as a pleasant woman who made few demands on the staff, she seemed sad and at times withdrawn. She seldom mixed with other residents but remained aloof in her bedroom; however, she always warmly welcomed her two sons and grandchildren, who visited regularly. She proudly displayed their photographs and frequently pointed them out to staff members. She had one other photograph of herself as a young woman with a small child on her knee, and if ever asked about this picture would brusquely change the conversation.

Because of her recurring sadness and underlying depression, Mary was invited to work with a member of the care staff to undertake a structured life review, using Haight's LREF over 8 weeks, and to prepare a life book. From the first interview, Mary seized the opportunity to systematically recall her life from childhood through adult life and old age. In each session, she talked animatedly and energetically, recalling in considerable detail the varied events of her long life. Except for some minor repetition, her memory loss was not evident, and even her chronic chest condition did not impede her eagerness to talk.

When speaking of her married life in the fourth session, she referred to the boy on her knee in the photograph as "him," and except for saying he was born with disabilities, she would say no more. In the next session, when asked to evaluate or comment on her life overall, she said that although she had never had much money, she had never lacked, her marriage had been happy, and her boys had done well.

Then, suddenly, as if for the first time, she found the courage to speak in great detail of the boy in the photograph. This time she named him as Donald, told how he had been born with a severe disability, and was never able to sit up unaided or to eat solid food. She spoke of his death when he was 8 years old as a "happy release," and although she and her husband had loved him very much, they were glad to be relieved of his constant care. During this session, she asked for her handbag, from which she retrieved two very battered small photographs of Donald. The life review process and the memories it triggered provided an opportunity to speak of the unspeakable, to share openly a part of her life from some 65 years before, and to have her love and concern for this child validated.

Mary and her family were delighted with the life book prepared by the member of care staff with the assistance of her sons. It contained both old and recent photographs and copies of other documents with short descriptions and explanations written in her own words. The book became a treasured record of a long life courageously lived, and in the process of its creation, Mary found new freedom and new contentment. When asked how he thought his mother had responded to the life review process, one son said: "She loved it. Her eyes are dancing in her head when she talks about what she has done and looks at her book."

CONCLUSION

This chapter has explored processes in reminiscence work undertaken in small groups and with couples and individuals. It examined the second, third, and fourth phases or work related to beginnings, middles, and endings and the associated roles and responsibilities of reminiscence workers. Behavior linked to phases of work and how to use the group process to support individual members' expressions of sadness and loss during meetings were explored. Various approaches to systematic reminiscence with individuals were also described. These included life story work with children, adolescents, and young adults; structured life review; and different approaches to narrative work including guided autobiographical writing, spiritual autobiography and life review, creative writing linked to autobiography, and assisted or mediated autobiography. These methods are applicable across the life span with people of many different ages, educational attainments, life circumstances, and present problems in living. The next chapter examines how to translate reminiscence and life review work into forms of tangible representation and seeks to raise awareness of some of the associated advantages and pitfalls that might be anticipated.

Chapter 6

Tangible
Representations
of Reminiscence

Most reminiscence products or tangible representations have an extraordinary capacity to evoke memories in other people who see, hear, or handle them. In this way, further reminiscence is stimulated and increasing numbers of people benefit from becoming involved in the process. Tangible records of reminiscence can greatly enhance the experience and benefits of reminiscing, although one must be careful to avoid diverting enthusiasm from the process to the product. In a true sense, the product of all reminiscence and life review is the story (Webster & Haight, 2002), and tangible records are merely ways of capturing the story. It is important to remember that the story can only be known if the memories are translated or transformed into something external. Products can be viewed as a vehicle in which the story resides, a means by which it becomes available to others.

In many reminiscence groups, a product may be central to the whole project, as in a reminiscence theatre group or in an oral history project. In agreeing to participate, people are also agreeing to work on a product and the introductory invitation should refer to this aspect. Much reminiscence work, especially in health and welfare settings, is initially conceived as process oriented, if not frankly therapeutic. The added value of incorporating a tangible outcome only emerges as the work progresses. Such a re-orientation requires honest, open, realistic renegotiation, including consideration of timing, resources, roles, and division of responsibilities, so

Photograph courtesy of Parkmount Day Center, Belfast, Northern Ireland.

that everyone concerned is committed to the changes required to complete the work successfully and to everyone's satisfaction.

This chapter describes possible products as well as guiding principles of producing tangible representations. The ethical implications of creating tangible representations are also discussed.

MOTIVATION, CAPACITY, AND OPPORTUNITY TO CREATE REMINISCENCE PRODUCTS

It is easier to decide to undertake a reminiscence product project with an individual than it is with a group. However, in considering the desirability and feasibility of making a product, either as an integral part of a reminiscence program or as a culmination of it with any individual, couple, or group, three interrelated aspects that apply to both participants and workers must be explored: motivation, capacity, and opportunity.

Motivation

Motivation is the reason for doing or wanting to do something. Motivations vary widely and are very personal and may be of primary or secondary importance. If a tangible product project is to succeed, then there must be consensus or general willingness to proceed, even if it is accepted that some individuals may contribute less than others. Such an explicit agreement is crucial; otherwise, reluctant members will sabotage the work by subtle or not so subtle resistance. Just as time is needed to agree on the themes and content of planned reminiscence work, time should also be devoted to agreeing about the nature and extent of involvement in working on any particular representation. In any group, time must be spent exploring people's motivation to create tangible products.

New leaders—often those who are less skilled or experienced in group work and especially gifted artistically with a keen desire to create—try to persuade an individual, couple, or group to agree on a certain course of action. Sometimes leaders lack the confidence to obtain feedback, perhaps fearing that their idea will be rejected. Some workers have been employed with the expectation that a specific representation will be produced.

Motivation, at least initially, is liable to be influenced by past experience. Adults who had discouraging experiences as children, for example, in painting, singing, acting, or other activities, may need considerable encouragement to overcome fear of failure if similar activities are now suggested. If they enjoyed performing in the past, then they are likely to feel positively about being involved in a new opportunity to use old talents.

Capacity

When considering making a product, it is important to consider the capacity or ability of the participants and workers involved. The experience of producing a product must be positive and enjoyable; failure should be avoided at all costs. This requires careful assessment of present skills and learning potential as well as the demands of the desired tasks. Although high motivation can overcome many limitations and adventurousness is to be encouraged, it is still vital not to overreach the physical, intellectual, or emotional capacity of the participants. It is also important not to underestimate people's potential. It is well recognized that some health care professionals limit opportunities because of their negative views of people who are frail, have disabilities, or face disadvantages. It is vital to identify and build on existing strengths and to be imaginative and visionary but practical in supporting people and in developing ways of compensating for any limitations.

In a group project, each member is likely to bring different knowledge and skills so that by working cooperatively together, the task can be accomplished. By working cooperatively, the agreed product can be immensely more ambitious than is usually possible when each individual works independently to produce a personal product. In the end, despite times of irritation and frustration, a group achievement will bring immense satisfaction and growth in self-esteem for all who shared a vision of what was possible and worked together to achieve it.

Opportunity

The third factor determining successful outcomes is opportunity—or a set of circumstances that makes it possible to do whatever is intended. Clearly, context, resources, and circumstances influence what end product may be achieved. Resources need to be accurately assessed, acquired, and responsibly husbanded. Preparation of a realistic budget at the outset will save considerable anxiety and avoid possible problems. Opportunity also applies to identifying suitable, accessible accommodations if these are required for an intended performance, display, or exhibition. Additional assistance—personal, professional, or technical—may also be necessary from local agencies such as community arts organizations, museums, libraries, schools, and colleges. Many of these organizations are pleased to work in partnership with health and social welfare agencies, contributing their own specialized skills, equipment, and expertise. Forming partnerships at the outset is highly desirable rather than seeking last-minute involvement.

TYPES OF REMINISCENCE PRODUCTS

It is impossible to give an exhaustive list of reminiscence products because of the immense creativity that workers and participants exercise when their enthusiasm for reminiscence work involves them in converting the memories recalled into creative, tangible forms. Nor is it easy to classify these products. Here they are loosely grouped as performance, visual, oral, or written products. These categories are not mutually exclusive because most of the products are multidimensional and many are increasingly multimedia.

Some products are quite simple and easily achieved; others are complex, requiring considerable time and effort to execute. Some are short-lived and ephemeral, and others are relatively permanent. Products also vary in portability and accessibility. Some are created for private or personal consumption, and others are created to attract public attention and appreciation. Figure 6.1 lists some reminiscence products (a few of which are described more fully later in this chapter).

GAINS FROM PRODUCING A TANGIBLE PRODUCT

Both the experience of working on a product and the product itself need to bring pleasure, pride, and satisfaction to participants and leaders. For the people reminiscing, engagement in the task of making a product often aids and accelerates the actual recall of memories; it may also stimulate further spontaneous or sequential recall, reflection, and life review. New skills are usually acquired, confidence grows, and self-esteem is enhanced in the face of proof of a job successfully completed. Many people find that the act of doing or making is less abstract and more satisfying than just talking. For them, the tangible product provides evidence that the experience of delving into memories—perhaps some very painful or problematic, perhaps some emerging for the first time—has occurred without disastrous results. They have faced their past and survived.

The opportunity to bequeath a legacy or testimony in tangible form to their own family or to future generations helps keep faith among reminiscence participants. The urge to preserve and transmit memories as a way of teaching and informing others is considerable. Creating a tangible product can convey a sense of completion, closure, or fulfillment. It is an opportunity to make a statement and may assist people without children or grandchildren to experience a sense of continuity and aid their search for meaning making in life. Neighborhoods and community institutions such as schools, churches, synagogues, trades unions, and clubs are usually pleased to have a record of their history and the people involved in it.

Even ephemeral products such as a temporary exhibition, installation, performance, or celebratory event will remind people of their heritage and strengthen bonds between people. Ellis Island Museum of Immigration, for example, eloquently testifies to the hardships endured by so

Performance	Visual	Written
Audio recording	CD-ROM	Archive
Cooking	Collage	Assisted autobiography
Dance	Display	Autobiography
Drama	Drawing, diagram, or chart	Biography
Gardening	Exhibition	Book
Mime	Family tree or time line	Diary
Movement	Genogram	Letter
Musical composition	Installation	Life story book
Musical show	Jigsaw	Magazine or newspaper
Reading aloud	Map	Memoir
Recitiation	Memory box	Play
Singing	Model	Poetry
Song writing	Mosaic	Postcard
Story telling	Mural	School report
Theatre	Multi-media presentaion	Scrapbook
Trip, visit, or pilgrimage	Needlework and tapestry	Spiritual autobiography
Walking or heritage trail	Painting	Story
	Photograph album or display	
	Pottery	
	Quilt	
	Sampler	
	Sculpture	
	Story board or book	
	Video diary or portrait	
	Wall hanging	

Figure 6.1. Tangible representations of reminiscence.

many in search of a fresh beginning in the New World. It assists each generation that enters vicariously into the migrant experience to appreciate the foundations on which their own lives have been built. For more recent immigrants, the museum resonates with their personal experience. In a similar way but on a smaller, local scale, wonder, appreciation, and respect can be created when the tangible products of reminiscence work are made accessible and shared with others.

Staff members also gain from working on tangible reminiscence products. Products provide proof of work accomplished, skills developed, and effort sustained. Some writers have also suggested that one reason for making a product is to impress funding providers in order to secure money and other resources so that additional reminiscence work can continue in the future (Sim, 1997). A tangible outcome may also contribute to the assessment of practice competence and the evaluation of project success. Displays, performances, productions, and publications are also immensely effective ways for spreading information about reminiscence work; influencing others; and building family, volunteer, and professional interest and support (Golden & Perlstein, 2003).

ETHICAL CONSIDERATIONS

The conditions under which any biographical or reminiscence material and associated products are made publicly available need to be clearly defined, preferably in writing or in some other accessible form appropriate to the capacities of the people involved, taking account of language, educational background, cognitive, and sensory impairments. Both the ends desired and the means for achieving them need to be ethical and agreed on with participants. Although appearing unduly formal, a signed release form is always recommended before any material is publicly displayed or published. The level of release consented to can be varied in terms of time period, usage, and access. A simple general example of a release form that could be readily modified to meet particular circumstances is provided in Appendix D. The complex issues of the nature of informed consent, the assessment of incapacity, and the legality of proxy consent given by responsible relatives or principal caregivers are beyond the scope of this discussion (Kenyon, 1996). When these issues are relevant, workers are advised to seek guidance from senior managers and, if necessary, their organization's legal advisers so that any possibility of future litigation is avoided.

Other issues concerned as much with questions of good practice as with ethics may arise. Artists may, for example, feel that their aesthetic standards are being compromised if a product does not meet their rigorous expectations. They may place undue pressure on participants to relinquish authority for the production or insist that it be altered to conform to the workers' or artists' aspirations. They may also wish to exercise artistic or editorial license in ways that unacceptably alter the representation or accuracy of the original material. Workers and artists may intentionally or unintentionally exploit participants by behaving in ways that effectively de-skill or undermine confidence. If personal confidence and self-esteem are already fragile, then it takes very little pressure from a person perceived to be better informed, authoritative, more gifted, or occupying a professional role to get his or her own way. Challenge may be hard to mount in the face of artistic expertise and professional prestige and power. Funders or sponsors may try to influence various aspects of the work, especially how outcomes are represented. Contributors can also be sidelined or forgotten by workers, managers, and board members who decide to use public displays or events for publicity, fund raising, public relations, political, or other objectives of importance to them and their organization. Although the importance of publicity and fundraising is not denied, ethical policies concerning both need to be adhered to and underpin all aspects of reminiscence work.

A similar problem can arise concerning editing of written text that may not conform to popular opinion or current conventions of spelling or grammar. If corrected, then authenticity may be lost. If uncorrected, then the author risks embarrassment when the shortcomings are publicly displayed through publication or exhibition. Audio and video recordings present related challenges and considerable integrity is demanded in the editing process. Sensitive discussion that respects the needs, rights, and wishes of the people originating the material is essential. It is not possible to give general editorial guidance other than to suggest that each case needs to be carefully considered and that practitioners will find the evaluation guidelines of the Oral History Association helpful (Ritchie, 1995; Yow, 1994).

Reminiscence work inevitably uncovers stories that affect and implicate other people who may be unaware of how they are being represented.

Family members and others may not wish skeletons in the closet to be exposed. Many people who feature in memory work are now dead yet have descendants whose present well-being may be compromised by critical or negative public representations. Meanings may be disputed, and given the social construction of memory, some distortion, inaccuracy, or difference of interpretation is inevitable. Once again, careful discussion with managers and possibly the use of disclaimers is suggested.

Ownership of a product requires careful consideration. It is essential that those who have contributed to producing a tangible record feel identified with it and are enabled to value their part in its creation. They should also be involved in agreeing on issues concerning storage of and access to the materials they have generated. If the reminiscence has been undertaken to assist another party, for example, educational projects with school children, then ownership and ongoing responsibility for the material may be simplified by assigning responsibility to a single organization. Whenever possible, arrangements should be made to involve all the participants in public events linked to any presentation and celebration of productions to which they have contributed. If any monetary benefit is anticipated from a product such as royalties or fees, then these need to be fairly allocated and participants protected from liability for losses. It is strongly recommended that issues such as these be explicitly discussed and agreed on prior to embarking on any production that is likely to generate revenue.

Other ethical issues, including conflicts of interest, are sure to arise from time to time. Each will demand careful thought and open, honest discussion to find agreed solutions. Resolving conflict and overcoming resistance are inevitable parts of using psychosocial interventions; reminiscence work and the preservation and transmission of the memories it generates in tangible formats are no exception. Reminiscence workers should not let these cautions deter them from undertaking reminiscence work involving the making of tangible products. Seek advice, support, and supervision about such issues that are sure to arise sooner or later. Proceed with care, openness, sensitivity, and respect for all involved, remembering that the potential gains for you and many other people are too great to be lightly relinquished because of initial anxiety about possible problems.

EXAMPLES OF TANGIBLE REPRESENTATIONS

Deciding how to develop any product will depend on the people, their motivation and capacity, the opportunities afforded by the context and its available resources, and the agreement reached with all concerned. All of the illustrations that follow can be varied in terms of level of sophistication and the time, resources, and skill required to achieve them. They are only included as illustrations, not prescriptions, and it is worth remembering that simple products can be just as effective as more complex and costly ones in terms of their reminiscence outcomes.

Reminiscence Drama

Avoid thinking that drama, as distinct from a theatre production, is necessarily difficult or requires exceptional skill to achieve. A simple spontaneous reenactment or role play is well within the scope of most reminiscence workers and most members of reminiscence groups (Osborn, 1994). People may scarcely realize that they have been involved in a brief improvised drama when they reenact a memory. Opportunities can arise spontaneously either within groups or with individuals when it is a very natural development to encourage a demonstration or acting out of a shared memory. Acting brings the story to life. If more than one person is involved, then memories can be pooled and the individual stories played out by the group. Imagine, for example, how discussion about school or other childhood memories could develop into a lively performance with different people playing the various parts of children, parents, or teachers. When discussing school days, the leader may begin to act and speak as the teacher or suggest someone else does so and then encourage the group members to act the part of the students. People may swap roles or develop the dialogue through impromptu discussion. Various scenes may develop more or less spontaneously as memories are revived and childhood experiences shared. A larger group can easily subdivide into twos or threes to work up separate scenes taking only some 10 or 15 minutes to prepare before the "play" is ready to be performed.

Alternatively, a group may set out with the intention of producing a "show" based on a script prepared on an agreed theme that represents some fairly common life experiences. There are endless possibilities: Being ill and going to the doctor, getting fired from work and becoming unemployed, leaving home to seek work, going to the movies with a special friend, arriving home later than your curfew, meeting the prospective in-laws for the first time, or joining the army are only a few suggestions.

Reticent people may find it easier to speak and act by using puppets, dolls, or toy animals. Some may find mime easier than speech. Great hilarity usually accompanies efforts to identify and label actions that illustrate occupational activities, housework, games, or family events performed by mime and drawing on implicit procedural memory. It is easy to develop these enactments further by allowing each person in turn to guess the correct interpretation based on a limited number of questions. If people are shy about giving an individual performance, with or without speech, then a group can easily be divided into teams or pairs with people cooperating over their production and performance.

Reminiscence Theatre

There are many different approaches used in reminiscence theatre, an increasingly popular way of representing memories. The range is immense and varies from simple, spontaneous, and improvised to complex, scripted, and rehearsed professional performances. Individuals may perform their own memories. They may contribute to a compilation of group memories as part of a reminiscence-based production written by a professional who continues to assist the originators to perform their own material. Frequently, once the original reminiscence material has been generated and recorded, it may be scripted, produced, and performed by professionals. Some theatre companies consist exclusively of older people who year after year derive great pleasure from working and performing together. Some groups do a single production and then disband.

Our Century and Us by The Good Companions illustrates the process and outcomes of reminiscence theatre. The Good Companions is a reminiscence theatre group of older people, directed by Pam Schweitzer of Age Exchange in London, and all of its performances are based on the members' personal reminiscences. Developed in 1999 in celebration of the Millennium, *Our Century and Us* involved nine women and one man. The idea of a play for the millennium was initiated by the director, then discussed and agreed on by the group, which wrote down ideas that were subsequently developed through discussion and a series of improvised exercises over the course of an intensive week that was led by two experienced visiting directors from a German seniors' theatre company. An example of an early exercise used to stimulate the recall of reminiscences on which to build the performance was to arrange chairs in a chronological line and ask the actors to choose a chair representing a decade that they would be happy to return to, or a time in their lives that they would not wish to relive. Memories of the associated periods were then shared and discussed. The initial week was followed by two to three rehearsals per week for 4 months, culminating in performances at the International Older People's Theatre Festivals in Cologne in 1999 and in London in 2000.

The play was situated within the time period bounded by the actors earliest childhood memories, beginning in the 1920s through adolescence and adulthood, work, courtship, marriage and family life, World War II, and postwar life up to the turn of the century, when all were age 65–85. Throughout the play, life experiences were related to significant national and international events, so personal events were located against the backdrop of wider public events. Mundane but life changing events were also portrayed, and frequently these provided opportunities for humor, dance, and song, which permeated the whole performance. There was a scene, for example, portraying the acquisition of washing machines and what a difference they had made to the women's domestic and working lives.

Many happy and sad memories were recalled, and their inclusion in the play provided the opportunity for further recall, reflection, and revision of points of view. Each woman's wedding day was played with the only man in the cast greatly enjoying his repeated appearances as bridegroom. One woman, Joyce, played the very painful breakup of her marriage when her husband walked out, including the stigma, gossip, and ostracism imposed by her neighbors, reflecting social attitudes of the 1950s; she eventually moved to begin a new life elsewhere.

Although painful for her, whenever Joyce played the episode of her marriage breakup she was always gratified by the number of women who after the show thanked her and talked about how this reflected their own experiences of social ostracism when their marriages had broken up. During the run, Joyce died suddenly on her 80th birthday. In some subsequent performances, her particular scene about the breakup of her marriage was omitted or another more general memory was substituted. In other performances it remained, but another member of the cast introduced the scene by saying, "This is Joyce's story."

Other women in the group recalled their extreme loneliness after their husbands' deaths, for almost all the company were widows, and their experience was portrayed by couples standing back to back and partners walking away from each other while singing a popular period song about lost relationships and distressing loneliness. Retirement was another significant lifetime event recalled and explored. It was dramatized by the image of a clock slowing down, which was followed by accounts of new late life friendships developing and each person's hopes and aspirations for the coming century.

This show proved enormously popular and played approximately 100 times to audiences in day centers and nursing homes, for intergenerational audiences, and at gerontological and oral history conferences. Members of The Good Companions always engage in discussion with the audience after each performance. They experience this process as especially affirming and gratifying. Both they and the audience are stimulated to further reflection and later performances are influenced by subtle revisions and further developments (Bornat, 2001, 2002). This company worked on 10 shows in 11 years. New memories continue to emerge, fresh stories are recounted, and old ones revised to provide the raw material for the next production. It seems that personal memory, reflected on individually and refracted through group performances to responsive audiences, draws on an unlimited reservoir of memories in the making that can be used for personal reappraisal, the building of confidence and self-esteem, the acquisition of new skills, and the entertainment and stimulation of all who participate in creating and attending theatrical performances (Schweitzer, personal communication, 2003).

In the process of creating the play, the older actors undertook a chronological review of their own lives, with personal reflection being stimulated by the use of playback theatre techniques (Boal, 1995). The actors greatly valued the validation achieved through audience appreciation of the public performance of their memories of personal experience. Preparing and playing the show gave them the opportunity to revisit, reflect, and partially revise their life stories and to stimulate audiences to embark on similar journeys of personal exploration.

Usually any planned reminiscence theatre production that is to be played by professional actors begins with tape recording individual or group reminiscence sessions. This initial process may be a novel experience that achieves many of the reminiscence functions already discussed but with the additional explicit understanding that the participants are giving their stories to others who will turn them into a performance. The initial recording may or may not be undertaken by the scriptwriter and actors who will eventually make the show. Schweitzer believed that contact between informants and actors at this early stage "sharpens the actors sense of commitment to the project as well as giving them ideal background for the characters and situations they will play" (2002, p. 7). Verbatim transcripts allow the scriptwriter and actors to draw heavily on the actual idiomatic speech of the informants and to identify with their lived experience. Scriptwriter, director, set and costume designers, musical director, stage manager, actors, publicity, and marketing personnel may then be recruited, sometimes working in ongoing collaboration with the original informants, to bring the production to fruition. Issues around content, emphasis, ownership, and interpretation are best resolved collaboratively, although practice will vary according to the ethos, policy, practice, and resources of the agency mounting the production.

It is common practice to perform reminiscence theatre in venues accessible to people whose life experience may resemble that which is being portrayed. Residential facilities, hospitals, day centers, and clubs as well as public venues all provide opportunities for older people or people with disabilities who do not normally go to live theatre to enjoy the performance. If after the performance the actors engage the audience in informal discussion about the show and the memories portrayed, then people are stimulated to reflect on their own experience and value the personal memories evoked by the performance. Sometimes an accompanying publication containing edited transcripts of the original stories or the script of the performance together with illustrations and photographs is produced as a durable record and celebration to encourage others to undertake similar ventures.

There are several national and many local organizations involved in validating personal memories and communal history through the arts, especially through theatre. (Some relevant addresses are listed in the Resources section.) These groups are predominantly concerned with building memories arising from individual and group reminiscence and general life review into performances. Frequently, performances include singing and instrumental music, dance, mime, and movement. The Senior Theatre League of America's mission is to promote senior theatre, which includes reminiscence theatre, and it brings many older people's theatre companies together for a biannual festival. European and international senior theatre festivals also flourish. Many of the 400 senior theatre groups in the United States use reminiscence-based material, whereas others perform staged readings of published scripts that are not directly informed by personal recollections (McDonough, 1994; Vorenberg, 1999).

Organizations such as the New York based Roots and Branches, Elders Share the Arts (ESTA), and Encore Theatre in Oregon use extensive intergenerational workshops to explore differences, identify common interests and concerns, grow friendships, and assist participants to develop as artists (Basting, 2001). ESTA, a community-based arts organization, serves disadvantaged communities and marginalized groups. It creates performances based on extensive 2- to 3-year commitments to neighborhood groupings, which undertake living history workshops. These are designed for intergenerational storytelling and the creation of community performances that address identified problems and personal development (Elders Share the Arts, 1994; Perlstein, 1995; Perlstein & Bliss, 2003).

When older and younger people work collaboratively both groups come to appreciate the authenticity of each other's life experience. When informants perform their own memories, they are able to exercise relatively more control over the ways in which their memories are represented (Bornat, 2001, 2002). It must be acknowledged, however, that any producer, artistic director, or even reminiscence worker also exercises substantial implicit and explicit influence. Intergenerational theatre productions often have older people play the part of their own parents or grandparents while the younger actors play the older informants as children. This device enables changing times across a considerable time span to be entertainingly portrayed.

Another popular approach is to involve entire classes of school children with older people who serve as informants and raconteurs. Assisted by an actor or drama facilitator playing the role of teacher, the children then work over the course of a day to perform the events and school day experiences recounted by the older informants. A whole show may be based on the memories of a single individual or a composite story may portray several people's experiences. The presence of the older people telling their stories directly to the children brings the past to life, and while the children are having fun as actors, they are learning history. As they replay the stories, the older informants' understanding of their own past also changes. Memories may be reassessed and the whole experience can become the foundation for further contact and new friendships.

Cross-cultural and immigrant experiences make powerful drama. Leaving home, beginning a new life in a new country, and the experience of being an outsider are themes with which many people identify. This latter theme provides particularly rich material for helping second-generation immigrants to appreciate their heritage and the losses and gains that their older relatives have endured.

Memory Boxes

The basic idea that informs the creation of memory boxes or other three-dimensional representations is that we all possess a fundamental core or stable center of our being and that our identity can be represented symbolically in various ways as a sort of life portrait. A memory box consists of a collection of cherished objects; assorted memorabilia; ephemera; documents; brief writings; and photographs assembled, arranged, and displayed within a small box or container. The objects selected will have different levels of personal significance and serve various purposes, such as being reminders of people, places, and events; symbols of personal history and values; proof of continuity; and buttresses of identity. Memory boxes may be created with any number of participants, but the work is labor intensive, especially if run as a group project.

If considering a project such as this, then reminiscence workers should first ask themselves and others working with them what they personally would put into a shoebox or a small container to depict their own life. If a slightly larger box is available, then consider how you would arrange the display and to whom would you be prepared to show it. You may find these questions rather daunting. Imagine the challenge posed for a person who may have lived two, three, or even four times longer than you have. Consider too what sort of support the people in your proposed project may require to complete a memory box.

A memory box project can be richly rewarding if shared with younger people or family members, who may assist with basic preparation, with locating contents, and in reminiscing about the personal significance of the memorabilia selected for display. A willing listener—one who is able to enter into intimate discussion about the actual and symbolic significance attached to the objects selected, rejected, or even unavailable—is essential. The decisions about contents and their arrangement must rest with the owners. A collection of boxes made by individuals working independently or in pairs alongside others similarly engaged can provide an interesting exhibition, and will stimulate further reminiscence by owners and viewers. Once again, the process is as important as the product.

Older people and museums in several European countries and in Taiwan cooperated in making and touring memory boxes between countries in an intergenerational project used to extend understanding across national borders and between older and younger people. The wooden boxes were originally ammunition boxes and were supplied by each country's military so that their conversion into memory boxes also carried great symbolic meaning. The young participants paired with the older informants helped to prepare the boxes by sanding and painting them according to the seniors' instructions. The young people were practical helpers but also listeners, recipients, and beneficiaries of the recollections that inevitably included many memories of the Second World War. This kind of project could easily be adapted and used to promote understanding between majority and minority ethnic communities, between marginalized groups within neighborhoods, or in adult day centers

In South Africa, Uganda, and elsewhere in sub-Saharan Africa, memory boxes are being used as opportunities to remember in order to meet the emotional needs of children affected by the HIV/AIDS pandemic. Many children who are infected at birth do not survive early childhood, but others live only to confront the prolonged illness and death of their parents. A project in the South African province of KwaZulu-Natal is creating memory boxes with affected families as a means of capturing memories and assisting parents to share knowledge about their health status (Denis & Makiwane, 2003). The memory boxes, made with the support and assistance of a memory

worker, contain transcripts and tape recordings of family stories. Small possessions, photographs, memorabilia, or sometimes a piece of cloth belonging to
a dying parent are included. The simple boxes made from any available materials, then are decorated and painted by the children; family members are
encouraged to assist with the objective of promoting resilience in the children by keeping family memories alive and facilitating the bereavement
process (Beverly, 1996; Webb, 1993; Whitfield, 1995; Worden, 1996). This
project emphasizes the importance of keeping a central archival record of
the transcripts in case the boxes are lost. It also stresses the importance
of involving all available family members.

Collages

Personal photographs—or, in their absence, photos from magazines and
newspapers—make excellent pictorial representations or summaries of a
person's life. Collages can also include drawings, paintings, fabrics, or any
other relevant material. Making a collage promotes discussion and helps to
organize what would otherwise be an unstructured, informal life review.
This work is best spread over several dispersed sessions to enable a trusting relationship to develop and to ensure that memories are triggered,
processed, and integrated while their representations are also being accumulated, arranged, and displayed. This approach works well with individuals or couples in long-time relationships who work together to create a
picture of their shared lives (Kurokawa, 1998). If personal photographs are
used, then it is wise to reproduce them rather than to use the originals.
Photographs can either be photocopied or scanned and printed on glossy
paper.

   Although less detailed than life storybooks, collages and storyboards,
which usually contain both text and pictures, can be laminated for protection and preservation. They provide accessible, portable summaries of people's lives. If admitted to a hospital, nursing facility, or day center, owners
can use them as passports to introduce themselves and as a bridge into the
new environment. They also assist staff in establishing relationships to
provide person-centered care and act as aids for continuing conversation in
the present.

Video and CD-ROM Diaries

Video diaries help people express significant aspects of themselves, their view of the world, and the meanings attached to life in ways that are similar to but different from how they might represent themselves in a self-portrait, a poem, or an autobiographical story. A person might script, direct, produce, and edit the video diary; however, it is more likely that the subject of the portrait will collaborate with someone else, who serves as a director/cameraperson. If this joint approach is used, then a close, trusting working relationship is essential. The role of the director/cameraperson is to draw out the views of the person being filmed and to respect and record his or her wishes concerning content, locations filmed, commentary, and soundtrack. The role is an enabling one of assisting the person to make creative observations and reflections and also to provide artistic and technical expertise. Video portraits are usually structured within a life course or chronological framework. This is achieved through the insertion of photographs of the person and significant others, past and present, and film of present home, surroundings, and possessions together with possible speech, music, and graphics. The essence of the person is primarily captured visually, so commentary is not essential—a feature that assists people with cognitive or speech impairments to participate. Such an approach demands a high degree of respect, sensitivity, spontaneity, and responsiveness on the part of the director/cameraperson, who needs to be able to encourage self-reflection and also to provide opportunities for playback and editing. Video diaries vary greatly in length and ownership, and access to the diary should be determined by the person filmed (Hargrave, 1994; Rose, 2001).

The value of such a record, a balance sheet of life, is movingly captured by Susan, an interviewee in the Mental Health Testimony Archive video (1998). This project was designed to preserve the memories of people who had been patients for many years, often for decades, in large psychiatric hospitals.

"Prior to making the film, I had been aware, now in my middle years, of an increasing need 'to make some sense' of it all. I had never really dwelt on the past, but it seemed to me that my life had felt so fragmented. Making the film gave it a substance, a cohesion that it lacked before. I felt immensely satisfied that I had said all I wanted to say. It was actually surprisingly easy for those memories to resurface—I felt that I had done justice to all that had happened to me and felt a renewed confidence in my ability to survive—whatever."

CD-ROMs are becoming increasingly popular. A family or personal history can be compiled by scanning photographs and various records (e.g., birth certificates, school reports, marriage certificates, army discharge papers), then adding video clips, text, sound recordings of speech and music, and captions or oral commentary. Archiving software can be used (see the reference to COMMA in Chapter 7) or less sophisticated approaches can give much pleasure and provide an accessible and valued sequential or thematic personal or community record.

THE PARTICIPATION OF LIBRARIES AND MUSEUMS IN REMINISCENCE WORK

The staff members of libraries and museums are uniquely well placed to contribute to reminiscence work. The role of libraries is longer established and better understood than that of museums, whose interest is more recent but growing steadily. Both libraries and museums—working alone or preferably in partnership with arts, community development, or health and social welfare organizations—have much to contribute and gain from becoming involved in the reminiscence enterprise (Gibson, 2000b). Some museums are already energetically engaged in oral history and reminiscence work. Others will require radical shifts in perspective, policy, and practice if they are to become more than interesting places for the occasional individual or group visit and become valued, respected contributors to the development of reminiscence work. For as Chapman stated, "In reminiscence programming, the emphasis is not on relaying information from the museum expert to the participant, but revealing personal history from the participant expert to the museum" (1998, p. 40).

Education and curatorial staff of museums face new challenges when reminiscence work is introduced. Their well-established historical research and teaching expertise need to be substantially augmented with enabling and group facilitation skills. They also need to develop the ability to support people who may recall painful memories. Long accustomed to working with children, museum education staff must become aware of the needs and desires of older people and to appreciate that seniors usually require more time than younger students to absorb new learning; they may also wish to cover more ground at greater depth. The reminiscence participants need to be central in the process of setting the agenda and agreeing on the program. They will have very definite ideas about how they want their memories to be represented, and they will expect their authority based on ownership to be respected. Special outreach and recruitment efforts may be required to attract nontraditional attendees, including people from ethnic minority groups who may never have felt that a museum in a second homeland was of any relevance to them.

Museums offer unequaled opportunities for handling objects, talking with others, and integrating memories stimulated by the process. Curatorial staff with a long tradition of and commitment to meticulous scholarship and guardianship of collections may at first feel deeply uneasy, if not frankly suspicious, or even sometimes bored by the domesticity and ordinariness of the discussion content in many reminiscence groups. Such attitudes reflect failure to appreciate the significance of recall for seniors who may be using the museum experience to rework and revalue their own personal past and locate it within a broader historical framework.

The museum worker's knowledge and skills can enable people to reposition themselves, not as isolated individuals, but as people with a sense of continuity at a time when they may be struggling to retain a significant place within their families and communities. In seeking to position themselves in the present in respect of the past, they are undertaking important preparation for surviving in an uncertain future because past, present, and future are all interconnected. In a quickly changing world, a museum and its collections can provide an opportunity to engage with a tangible reality. Experiencing a museum firsthand can convey a sense of community, of shared social identity in a world that increasingly stresses privacy, discontinuity, and virtual reality rather than social coherence, mutuality, and continuity.

Museums and libraries can extend their influence far beyond their own buildings through engaging in reminiscence work. Direct outreach work with people who are too frail to visit can greatly assist adult day services and residential facilities. Museum and library staff may provide reminiscence training for others and indirectly support health and social care staff members in various ways, including contributing display and exhibition competence. Museums are uniquely placed to become providers and lenders of reminiscence handling boxes. A handling box usually contains multisensory artifacts representing a broad topic or theme together with explanatory notes about the contents, their history and purpose and how they might be used to stimulate recall; a small number of cue questions is usually included to encourage discussion. Such a service has proved to be immensely useful to health and social care facilities that want to undertake reminiscence work and also to schools that use handling boxes to support teaching in history, geography, social studies, and citizenship.

It is advisable for a museum that wants to undertake reminiscence work to develop its own explicit policy about the type and extent of its involvement rather to allow reminiscence to develop in haphazard or unplanned ways. The actual handling of artifacts will challenge many curators, who will need to consider issues such as acceptable risk taking; insurance; and responsibility for damage, loss, theft, or delayed return. Policies concerning the nature and relative value of acquisitions, including the cost and storage of multiple holdings, the purchase of contemporary domestic artifacts for future use as triggers, and the logistics of establishing and managing a loan service all require attention. It may be necessary to reexamine priorities about use of staff time, use of volunteers, types of activities, age groups served, and their respective needs and sectional interests. The gains can be considerable for museums and their users. Chapman, who embraced reminiscence and reminiscence theatre as integral parts of her museum work, wrote, "Reminiscence is a doorway for building new bridges between museums and communities, not only for improving the quality of life of older adults but for all ages" (1998, p. 40).

CONCLUSION

This chapter has described only a small number of possible products to use as tangible representations of reminiscence. This is not to imply that these are more desirable than other possibilities. There are gains and losses associated with each type of representation. Books, boards, boxes, paintings, collages, and films have a static quality, perhaps erroneously suggesting a sense of immutability or completeness rather than a sense of an ongoing life that is still open to further reflection, experience, and development. Conversely, these formats have accessibility and durability that performances and temporary exhibitions lack unless publications or films accompany them. The functions of tangible products need to be carefully weighed and in keeping with the integrity and intentions of the people whose lives are to be represented; the motivation and capacity of the people involved; and the opportunities, including resources, that different contexts present.

The process of recalling and sharing memories and their transformation into some form of tangible representation is often complex and demands time, skill, and commitment. It also obliges workers and their employers to behave ethically. Making realistic plans and bringing them to fruition requires considerable versatility, perseverance, and integrity. One of the many responsibilities of a reminiscence worker is to lend a vision of what is possible; this can be very important when enabling people to see the immense possibilities inherent in the reminiscence process itself and any related representations that they may decide to pursue. The unique contribution that museums and libraries can and often do make to reminiscence work was briefly explored—in particular, their role in contributing to training, providing access to various resources and collections, undertaking community outreach, and supporting reminiscence work being done by other organizations by providing and loaning handling boxes. The value of working in partnership with people from other organizations and professional backgrounds was also stressed because it is through cooperative working that skills are shared; resources are husbanded; knowledge and experience are extended; and outcomes, both tangible and intangible, are enhanced.

Chapter 7

Promoting Social Inclusion Through Reminiscence

We differ from one another in race, in national origin, in ethnicity, in gender, in sexual orientation, in beliefs, in political loyalties, in abilities, in personal histories, and in many other ways. These differences must be acknowledged and respected. The extent to which a society is actually free and just is revealed by the extent of and the respect accorded to its diversity. But the most profound and enduring truth is what we have in common, and what we have in common is our humanity. (Lynn, 2001, p. 22)

The first six chapters have emphasized the importance of recognizing and relating to people as unique individuals. This chapter redresses this issue by considering the importance of the individual in society. It addresses the interdependence of each member of society and the necessity for each person to draw from and contribute to the common good. It is fashionable to emphasize individual rights to the neglect of mutual social obligations. We now need to reconcile the importance of individuality with the necessity of living in community. We are compelled to grapple with the anxiety aroused by freely and openly celebrating, rather than fearing, diversity in modern society. Individuality need not be divorced from community solidarity, for we are fundamentally social beings who must learn to live in relationship with others, including those who differ from us.

Photograph courtesy of Elders Share the Arts, New York, New York.

Reminiscence and its related activities are uniquely placed to address issues that both separate and unite us as members of families, groups, and communities. Although it would be wrong to expect too much from this intervention, it would be remiss to expect too little. We experience the divisiveness of personal, family, community, national, and international life on a daily basis. Our contemporary world presents itself as fragmented rather than as united or integrated. We feel threatened by differences of race, culture, religion, values, language, upbringing, education, class, and age. We are captives of our history and our heritage. No one is exempt from the threats conveyed in our perception of difference, although some will have worked harder and progressed further in developing awareness of how these threats affect their own lives, moral principles, and future hopes. At a micro level, engagement in reminiscence can contribute to our exploration of diversity and solidarity. There has never been a time when private scrutiny and public generosity were more urgently required to build stable families, congenial communities, just nations, and a peaceful world. So what, we may ask when faced with such a daunting agenda, can reminiscence possibly contribute toward welcoming and appreciating diversity while simultaneously promoting social inclusion?

THE CONTRIBUTION OF REMINISCENCE AND ORAL HISTORY

The most persuasive means for exploring different ways in which reminiscence-related activities might promote social inclusion or social integration is to describe actual projects that have been undertaken in divided communities of various kinds and to use these examples to explore possible generalizations. To do this, reminiscence is interpreted in a broad enough manner to embrace oral history, as this is the conceptual frame of reference most often used in relation to reminiscence projects that seek to achieve community change or social solidarity. Although there are many similarities between reminiscence and oral history, there are also recognized differences (see Chapter 2; see also Bornat, 2001, 2002; Martin, 1995). People undertaking reminiscence work do not expect to create utopian societies or perfect citizens, but they do aspire to contribute to the growth of greater cohesiveness within communities and enlarged magnanimity between citizens.

Reminiscence programs that are planned to assist marginalized individuals to achieve a stronger sense of their own personal identity and increased social confidence serve both personal and community objectives that may make social integration more possible. For some people, a sense of personal identity may have always been fragile. If they are then threatened by present problematic life circumstances that engender fear, hostility, and aggression, retreat into isolation rather than growth in personal confidence and social integration may result. As the case examples illustrate, reminiscence or oral history can assist individuals to find acceptance within a group, perhaps within a residential facility or a neighborhood, and it can assist marginalized groups to find a place within communities. Some people will have experienced the past as oppressive or discriminating. They may now experience present life circumstances, particularly if they are newcomers, as similarly excluding, antagonistic, and threatening. Bringing together newcomers and members of longer-established groups to share their life experiences, and to explore difference and sameness may reduce the perceived threat that each attributes to the other. This may be very relevant to people whose culture, race, religion, or gender orientation differs from the majority community around them.

For an older individual who has experienced discrimination or lacks a formal education, the sharing of stories in an oral format can facilitate the release of anger related to injustice and the sharing of the cultural norms of his or her time. It also allows for the sharing of memories not available in written form. (Soltys & Coats, 1994, p. 12)

Training skilled facilitators is crucial to success. These workers need to be assisted to become secure in their own identity, unthreatened by difference, confident in handling conflict, and able to hold people to the painful exploration of memory through the medium of reminiscence or oral history. These workers need to be able to think critically and be open to alternative perspectives. One of their major tasks is to make sure that when conflicting or multiple interpretations of past and present events emerge, all points of view are fairly represented and all stories, no matter how painful, are heard. The case studies in this chapter illustrate the special knowledge, skills, and values required and the diverse situations that facilitators face. These examples illustrate how participants are enabled to explore and reflect on the histories of their families and communities with the explicit intention or objective of encouraging consideration of existing attitudes, values, and behavior. Personal and community history is used as a vehicle for achieving realignments between individuals, groups, and communities that feel threatened or intimidated by each other. Part of this process involves efforts to explore personal and group memories, including folk memories, in attempting to extend both private and community understanding (Coleman, 2000).

Group facilitators (often called *tutors* or *adult educators* in community contexts) who undertake this kind of reminiscence work with marginalized groups need considerable confidence. They must be conscious of the impact of their own class, religion, and political affiliations and aware of the impact that the stories they hear will have on themselves and others. They need to be able to raise with the participants the implications of how stories are to be represented and the possible repercussions should the stories become more widely known or possibly disputed. They must be explicit about the agreed arrangements concerning access to materials and the ethical and legal implications of the work they are facilitating.

Workers in this arena need the courage to question the value of history and memory work and the role of history in the community because this way of "doing" history through reminiscence is relatively novel (Ritchie, 1995; Thompson, 2000). It is a means of encouraging those who participate to develop an understanding of the complexities of history, to realize that there is not just one version of history even if one particular view is dominant. It is also a means for helping people to develop sufficient confidence to question their own views, which may differ from the popularly accepted or currently fashionable view. Participants must dare to ask about what is being withheld as well as what is being told and to develop the skills to appraise their own role and the role of other interested people in setting down alternative versions. This is doing history from the bottom up, rather than from the top down, as groups not normally heard are assisted to find their voice. Workers also need to appreciate that the process that enables a composite version to emerge must find a place for the individual story, especially for dissenting views; otherwise, group or community consensus will serve only to further marginalize or suppress the discordant voice.

Using reminiscence in this instrumental way raises many complex ethical issues that although not new have assumed greater urgency as archiving and access to archives has become easier because of developments in digital technology. Stories of trauma, loss, violence, civil disorder, terrorism, collective oppression, and state-initiated oppression can now be readily placed on and accessed via the Internet. Oral accounts by victims and perpetrators produce material that is painful to hear and harder still to integrate. Reminiscence practitioners and oral historians who attempt to engage in community history to encourage processes of collective as well as individual reflection, review, and reconsideration require considerable integrity. Their understandings and representations of history are more likely to encounter direct and immediate challenge than those of conventional historians because the sources of data are living informants who customarily expect to have access to and frequently expect to approve the completed oral or written accounts.

Memory work undertaken in divided societies demands great maturity; such workers will not be perceived as neutral, nor will they remain untouched by what they hear. There can be no neutrality in reminiscence work that seeks to explore personal and public experience in which the stories and their meanings are contested and are likely to have political ramifications beyond the immediate group that has generated them. Such is the case, for example, in the ongoing preoccupation of Native Americans, first-nation Canadians, and aboriginal Australians concerning land and its ownership. In Australian courts, legal battles over land rights and native title claims are using oral accounts of personal and collective memories to establish the ownership of tribal lands appropriated by Caucasian settlers, alongside conventional ways of presenting legal evidence. Here too the "stolen generation" of aboriginal children who were forcibly removed from their parents by the state and placed with Caucasian adoptive and foster families is striving to come to terms with its pain and alienation (Pilkington, 1996). In both of these instances, oral accounts of personal memory have played an important part in seeking public acknowledgment of wrongs and restitution. The personal has become the political in deeply disturbing ways as the government and the Caucasian majority population struggle to reach a just accommodation with an ignominious past (Darian-Smith & Hamilton, 1994; Read, 1999, 2000).

Similarly, South African society has been forced to face the implications of personal memory recalled and recorded as oral testimony. These memories are being deliberately solicited through a growing number of community history projects as well as in the formal hearings of the official Truth and Reconciliation Commission as the new South Africa seeks to come to terms with its apartheid past and works to build a truly rainbow society (Nuttall & Coetzee, 1998).

Some suggest that popular history, of which oral history is the cornerstone, is nothing more than mere nostalgia, the sentimental longing for past times, places, and people, but the examples cited suggest that it serves more varied and more challenging functions. In times of personal transition, just as in times of national transition, history becomes important as a means of defining the self, the family, and the nation. The predominant functions served by oral history that draw so heavily on personal memory vary somewhat from country to country, but there are underlying similarities concerned with democratizing history and valuing the voices not often heard (Shopes, 2002). In sub-Saharan Africa, for example, development workers taped local people's memories about land use and occupation for the purpose of guiding contemporary development work (Bennett, 1995; Slim & Thompson, 1993; Thomson, 1997). In India, health practitioners have used oral history to study community attitudes to leprosy so as to inform their understanding and guide the development of leprosy treatment programs. In New Zealand, oral history is playing a pivotal role in the urgent task of seeking national self-definition. In Britain, prostitutes' life stories have been recorded and used in making a health promotion video for release to workers in the sex industry. In Alaska, oral history has contributed to the resolution of tensions concerned with disputed meanings attached to specific places that are significant because of historic loyalties and the need to preserve the cultural heritage of native-born Alaskans. A statewide project has been developed to bring indigenous people and relative newcomers together across both age and ethnic divisions to promote shared understanding and to work cooperatively on community development projects.

In Philadelphia, the Center for Intergenerational Learning at Temple University uses innovative intergenerational life experience programs to foster cooperation and exchange between generations, especially in socially and economically deprived neighborhoods. The varied projects offered within these programs include theatre groups, literacy and English language classes, drug prevention mentoring schemes, and networks linking young people with older adults or young people who have learning disabilities with frail older people, including some with Alzheimer's disease. Storytelling is one of the central processes permeating most of these varied projects based on the Center for Intergenerational Learning. These stories, which stress continuity and change over time, inevitably highlight similarities and differences in life experience across generations.

Elders Share the Arts

Elders Share the Arts (ESTA), a New York based community arts organization established by Susan Perlstein, is committed to working with ethnically diverse intergenerational groups through oral history and the arts to address a wide variety of social and community needs. ESTA works with people in impoverished communities and fearlessly addresses a wide variety of needs. It contracts with groups and organizations throughout the New York metropolitan area to undertake living history workshops that culminate in a local artistic presentation and contribute to an annual Living History Festival. It also trains artists and reminiscence workers in a national program designed to equip artists to work with community groups and to learn how to transform oral histories into theatre, storytelling, dance, performance, music, paintings, murals, poetry, and other writing. All of the projects have cultural, social, environmental, or political objectives, and participants learn new skills through working together, exploring problems, and developing shared solutions.

Many ESTA projects could be cited as examples of efforts to work through personal life history experience in order to mobilize citizens to address issues of concern in local communities. Many urban areas experience changing patterns of settlement by successive immigrant ethnic groups who, once they become more affluent, move out, leaving behind impoverished older people who find themselves living in neighborhoods now populated by people from entirely different cultures. In such circumstances, elders become increasingly isolated, alienated, and wary of the newcomers, especially the younger members of these unfamiliar groups. Such isolation encourages stereotyping, the growth of mutual suspicion, and a lack of opportunities to cross barriers created by differences in age, gender, ethnicity, and language. Before embarking on a joint project, each age group meeting separately is asked to write what they think of the other group. This exercise is repeated at the end of each project to provide a simple way to demonstrate attitude shifts, together with observed changes in behavior and relationships, that endure beyond the life of the project.

The older adults are role models and are generous in giving their time and attention to the young people, who are in turn able to practice social skills, engage in problem solving and decision making, and develop confidence for the future. Young people develop personal confidence and self-esteem through engaging in a mixed age group: "Just one person who listens to a young person's opinions, concerns, and feelings without judging can create a lifeline to self respect" (Perlstein, 1995, p. 2). ESTA's Generating Community programs provide opportunities for this kind of support, as evidenced in the Washington Heights neighborhood of Manhattan, with its reputation for violence and drug dealing. Here Dominican teenagers were trained in oral history methods and then met with frail older adults to explore their work histories and to learn how these elders had gone about seeking and keeping employment in earlier times. In Spanish Harlem, for example, seniors have become surrogate grandparents for children whose grandparents have never left Puerto Rico. In Flushing, Queens, older eastern European adults now live side by side with newer immigrants from Pacific Rim countries. Here the approach involved the seniors first interviewing each other to pinpoint changes that had occurred in their neighborhood in recent years. Many critical remarks about Korean immigrants were expressed initially, but once the seniors joined with Korean youngsters in a living history workshop and got to know them, their attitudes subtly changed. In the context of working together, they discovered that the Korean children shared the same hopes and desires as their own children and grandchildren once had. They wanted to get an education, get a job, and grow up to become responsible citizens.

Each project culminates in making a presentation in a local community venue. This helps to spread ideas because the audience readily sees itself reflected in the plays, writings, and other types of portrayals. After the 2- to 3-year-long projects end, some groups continue to meet and to carry on working together for their own and their community's benefit.

On a practical level, seniors feel safer walking home when greeted on the way by children that they know. On a deeper level, they feel needed, useful, and creative. "I like being with the children" said Mary. "I feel younger and they help keep me spry." Fanny said, "Children tell you the truth about what is happening now." Another said, "I didn't expect to get so much. We really care about each other and had a great time making the play" (Perlstein, 1995, p. 5).

Some ESTA projects pursue overtly political concerns such as in the play "Bushwick, Why vote? Why vote?" This play tackled the apathy, cynicism, and general lack of interest of young African American and Latino high school and college students in the political process (Basting, 2001). The play contrasted the determination of older African Americans to exercise their hard-won right to vote and their experiences as civil rights activists with contemporary attitudes and the ignorance of current political issues displayed by many younger people. In discussions held after each performance, audience members were encouraged to register to vote. Whatever the issue of concern that is being addressed in each project, ESTA works by means of harnessing several different strengths. These include intergenerational storytelling, oral and life history, and the creativity of the arts to raise awareness, increase understanding, develop friendships, and empower participants to achieve goals that are important to them at personal, group, and community levels.

The People's History Initiative, Northern Ireland

The Ulster People's College, founded in 1982 in Belfast, has been running a local history project since 1988. The College is a nongovernmental adult education charitable organization committed to community education, community development, and educational outreach. It seeks to provide a safe and secure environment in which learning and plurality of opinion is respected. Tutors work to strengthen the capacity of individuals and groups to combat disadvantage and discrimination, and to encourage greater participation by local people in decisions affecting their everyday lives as well as contributing toward creating a just, democratic, egalitarian, and nonsectarian society. Indigenous leaders are assisted to improve their leadership and practical skills to enable them to take effective action in order to achieve positive change and community development. The college offers occasional and regular accredited courses and staffs neighborhood outreach projects in response to identified needs and requests from local community groups, both Roman Catholic and Protestant, within the greater Belfast area and other parts of Northern Ireland.

A consortium consisting of the college and representatives of the Northern Ireland Reminiscence Network and Museums and Galleries Northern Ireland contributes to the People's History Initiative and to the management of an offshoot organization known as Community Archiving Network Northern Ireland (CANNI). The People's History Initiative undertakes work with both single identity groups consisting either of Catholics or Protestants as well as promoting exchange and shared learning across sectarian boundaries in mixed identity groups. The college identifies and involves local community activists, mostly in areas where Protestant and Catholic communities are juxtaposed and often physically separated by barriers euphemistically known as "peace walls," erected to keep the communities apart in the hope of reducing sectarian violence. It is in such socially disadvantaged, predominantly working-class areas that the greatest violence, loss of life, and economic and social hardship has occurred since the 1960s, over the period of civil unrest known locally as "The Troubles."

Nine tutor-led groups have so far worked with the Initiative. The groups consist of men and women, mostly over the age of 50, who are unemployed or in low paid part-time employment and educationally disadvantaged. Each group undertakes a 12-week accredited course that begins with an overview of Belfast and its historical, political, and geographic development. This introduction provides a context for situating and linking the history of each particular neighborhood studied. During the course, participants learn the skills required for researching local history. Sessions include introductions to oral history and reminiscence techniques; how to locate, investigate, collect, and interpret documentary and visual sources such as maps, directories, and newspapers; and how to prepare exhibitions. The Initiative is particularly noteworthy because it is using information and communication technology to enhance education, reminiscence, community development, and community relations, and in the process is building personal confidence and developing self-reflection. Participants learn to make oral and video recordings of individual and group memories of local residents and to master multimedia authoring skills in order to use a community archiving software program known as COMMA (http://www.commanet.org) to create CD-ROMs. This software enables each group to edit and produce its own archive consisting of photographs, audio and video recordings, and other personal and public records that portray its own local neighborhood.

Each course culminates in the production of either a public exhibition or a CD-ROM archive and a workshop to celebrate the outcomes of the work achieved (McCartney, 2001; McPhillips & McCartney, 2002). CANNI's function is to make all of the community archives widely accessible on a web site and to develop an Internet discussion group as a means by which local groups may access and discuss opinions about each other's representations of community history as seen in the separate archives. In these ways, the segregated nature of society in Northern Ireland and the clash of identities and political affiliations typified by religious differences will be openly represented and debated.

This approach to community relations work creates opportunities for a wealth of facilitated discussion that focuses on encouraging participants to review and evaluate both personal experience and public events, including political, security forces, and paramilitary activity within their communities. Tangible products are important outcomes from this work, but equally important are the processes of discussion and reflection. Group members bring to weekly course meetings oral and video recordings that they have completed between sessions and family photographs, documents, and other memorabilia for possible inclusion in the archive. Issues concerning how these recollections and materials are interpreted and represented are energetically debated and democratically decided with ownership of each local archive vested in the group who creates it. Joint training meetings are held between Catholic and Protestant groups to facilitate the development of greater self-confidence and to address mutual problems encountered in creating the digital archives.

It must be remembered that this initiative is taking place within the context of a society that for hundreds of years has experienced recurring violence associated with religious divisions and rampant sectarianism. Northern Ireland, with a population of approximately 1.7 million people, is characterized by increasing spatial segregation in housing; habitually contested views about many aspects of life and history; a largely segregated school system; and since the 1960s, grievous community conflict, with more than 3,700 Troubles-related deaths, some 40,000 injuries, and untold damage to property. A fragile peace process formalized in the Good Friday Belfast Agreement of 1998 struggles on despite continued paramilitary activity and lack of trust between the Protestant and Catholic communities. There is still a long way to go in the divided society of Northern Ireland before the process of truth telling, meaning making, and political and personal rapprochement command universal commitment. Only then will mutual respect, forgiveness, and genuine reconciliation— as distinct from political expediency or grudging accommodation—be achieved between the two communities long divided by history, religion, and pervasive, profound mistrust (Smyth, 2003).

A Reminiscence Group in a Hostel for Older Homeless Men

A reminiscence group was located in a hostel in London accommodating 28 homeless men age 55 years and older. Most residents had chronic alcoholism or mental health problems or both. Although many had lived in the hostel for more than 5 years, there was little interaction among residents. The hostel staff, concerned about the extreme social isolation of these men, initiated a reminiscence group whose objectives were to increase conversation and encourage the most isolated residents to mix with each other. The group was not time limited, had open membership, and met semi-weekly for 1 hour. It was co-led by a member of the hostel staff and a sessional social worker and aimed to be a nonthreatening, loosely structured, informal social event at which tea and biscuits were always provided. The men were free to leave at any time during sessions. Ground rules were minimal other than it was agreed that drinking alcohol was not permitted during group meetings, although anyone who drank beforehand would not be excluded from attending provided that he was not disruptive.

In the early months, discussions initiated by the men concerned current events, politics, and royalty. Little personal information was exchanged until the fourth and fifth months, when men began to volunteer accounts of their experience of homelessness, drinking habits, and life in the armed forces and merchant navy. These themes, especially the men's experience of homelessness, though never the reasons why they had become homeless, came to dominate the sessions. There was much conversation about homeless hostels, sleeping rough, casual work, and ways of coping with and surviving homelessness. The men seldom commented about the group either in the sessions or to the hostel staff outside the sessions. Several men became firmly attached to the group, as demonstrated by attending regularly or apologizing if unable to attend, staying for the duration of sessions, and waiting in the room well ahead of the starting time.

Eight men attended regularly. A further ten attended intermittently, including some who were the most isolated. One man who had lived in the hostel for 5 years and had never mixed with other residents or joined in any activities became a regular attendee. As the months passed, staff observed more interaction among group members than usual in the hostel, and men who seldom conversed began interacting in the group and listening to each other's contributions. Over time, the members displayed less irritation and animosity, and the group appeared to become a safe place where they could engage in conversation and develop limited relationships without having to make major commitments.

After the group had been meeting for 4 months, some photographic reminiscence triggers were introduced. Initially the men responded positively to these, but after a couple of sessions the triggers were discarded because the members preferred to decide their own topics of conversation. Some brought personal possessions to share with the group, including a naval logbook, an employee's rail pass, and a souvenir plate depicting John Wayne. Sometimes the men remained talking in the meeting room after the group had finished and then continued talking into the evening. Some sessions were preceded by excessive drinking prior to the session, which led to argumentative behavior in the group, disjointed conversation, inattentive listening, and a lot of movement in and out of sessions. The co-leaders believed these disrupted sessions coincided with and reflected more widespread periods of disruption and tension throughout the hostel, which seemed to be linked to bouts of heavy drinking by many of the residents.

Crane (1995) reported that the leaders identified modest but important social gains for this group of men who had experienced substantial, prolonged alcohol dependence, mental illness, personal isolation, and social exclusion. The group provided an acceptable forum in which the most isolated men within the hostel could socialize. It taught or renewed skills of listening, relating, and attending and became a bridge into participation in other more overt social activities in the hostel. This group took many months to form and periodically would revert to an earlier stage characterized by lack of trust, restlessness, and inattention. It provides an example of how any group must respond and adapt to the characteristics and needs of the people it seeks to serve and the context in which it meets. It illustrates how people who may be superficially considered as unlikely to join a group can benefit from such an opportunity provided that the approach used is flexible and nonthreatening. This example also shows how a reminiscence group experience can increase sociability and communication among people who are extremely isolated and marginalized.

REMINISCENCE AND RETIREMENT FROM EMPLOYMENT

If reminiscence gives meaning and coherence to life and promotes social relationships, then it could become a positive means for combating the possibility of social exclusion at the time of retirement. It is suggested that because reminiscence can make people more interesting to other people and more acceptable to themselves, it may be used as a means of preventing possible isolation at this significant point of transition.

We all need other people because we exist only in relation to other people. We require others to affirm or validate our own existence and ensure or secure our own identity in a personal and communal way. From early childhood, people learn to define themselves in terms of social relationships, I–you. Me, not in isolation, but me intimately connected to you, to another person. Although we try to develop a coherent story that gives shape to our lives, this is more readily achieved if we can locate ourselves within a broader framework in which we are assured of being connected to or in relationships with other people. Then we are not just developing our own isolated story but one that involves other people. This long developmental process begins in infancy and continues throughout life. First, an infant bonds with his or her mother or caregiver, and many writers suggest that the infant's physical and emotional growth depend on the strength and stability of these affectional bonds. The developmental challenge felt most acutely in infancy, childhood, and adolescence, yet never completely abandoned throughout the whole of life, is for individuals to differentiate themselves from others while recognizing the need to depend on others and be connected to them (Erikson, 1950). Our growth and well-being depend on our learning to look outward and to risk building close, mutually satisfying interdependent relationships with other people. Secure personal identity allows us to see ourselves as unique individuals whose uniqueness nevertheless can only be defined and affirmed in relationships with others and the broader society.

A life course developmental perspective needs to be augmented with an understanding about how we construct our identity by continually defining, interpreting, and representing ourselves to others in and through our social relationships. We are not islands but social actors. The view that we form of our past, the way we convey or interpret that view to others, and the manner in which they in turn respond all influence how we construct, deconstruct, and reconstruct our life stories (Viney, 1993). This is a complex, dynamic process that is necessary to sustain and nourish our sense of unique worth and well-being. Constructing and sharing our life story or life narrative is a way of making a positive impression on others as we gauge their reaction to how we define or present ourselves in conversation. Telling a good story makes us interesting, worth talking with, and worth keeping in a relationship. In this way, we actively confront the possibility of social exclusion associated with growing old, which retirement publicly announces and confers. Retirement heralds a process of personal and social transition that focuses attention on us and on our changing roles, responsibilities, and social relationships.

Developmentalists' concentration on the importance of reminiscence as a way of achieving personal coherence and a sense of integrity, meaning, and continuity is insufficient to explain the pervasiveness of reminiscence in the lives of many people. The social context in which the reminiscence occurs also exercises an influence. Otherwise it is difficult to understand why particular memories emerge rather than others at certain times. It seems that the memories selected and recounted tend to be those that are likely to be both socially acceptable and interesting as well as personally acceptable and coherent. These memories offer the best return in terms of living at peace with ourselves and living congenially with other people. Through the reminiscence process, we negotiate with ourselves as well as with others to secure a continuing place in the social world rather than being socially excluded while remaining physically present.

Reminiscence serves both the teller and hearer of the story. It is a mutual survival tactic that holds both parties in relationship. Threats to relationships abound in early old age, in retirement at whatever age (voluntary or involuntary), and especially in old age. Retirement brings gains and losses of many kinds. Changed economic circumstances, changed living and working arrangements, and perhaps geographic relocation have important consequences for maintaining or curtailing social networks. Longstanding, dependable associations may be severed at the time in life when they are most needed. Reduced income can mean decreased opportunities to pursue interests and sustain old friendships or to embark on new ones, although it is accepted that increased leisure and newfound freedom can also bring fresh opportunities. Our ability to make ourselves more interesting to other people at this point in our lives may ensure continuing relationships in the present and the future. This does not mean that people who fear being marginalized at the point of retirement come to use reminiscence in unethical, dishonest, or deliberately manipulative ways. On the contrary, people who are prepared to reminisce and undertake a life review at this time may be making an excellent investment in their own individual and family's well-being.

Of course reminiscing is not risk free because our stories do not unfailingly make us interesting to other people. Perhaps people will not wish to hear or will find neither the teller nor the tale absorbing. There is, however, a reasonable chance that they might. It is even possible that they may find accounts of the way we used to be, the things we did, the events we witnessed, and the lives we lived more exciting than how we now appear on first impressions as older retired people. Insofar as the reminiscence process is mutual, the well-being and survival of self and others may be ensured if everyone has sufficient courage to reach out to one another through story telling. Examples abound in the practice literature of how a seemingly uninteresting, withdrawn, or difficult person in a reminiscence group becomes the focus of attention because of his or her tales of past adventures, hardships endured, and obstacles overcome. Storytelling can attract interest, encourage relationships, and promote social inclusion.

How does reminiscence make us more acceptable to ourselves? A common theme in social gerontology and clinical and pastoral literature concerns the need for people to find consistency and meaning in life overall as well as in their own personal life. This process of meaning making becomes even more urgent when facing major transitions or personal challenges such as retirement. Total rather than gradual retirement presents exceptional challenges for some people, especially for men, whose sense of identity is often closely associated with their working achievements. Each person negotiates the transition from work to retirement in his or her own idiosyncratic way. With increasing longevity, retirement for most people now precedes death by many years, and it may be this experience rather than impending death that triggers a spontaneous life review. If this happens, then the individual will begin to construct a version of the journey to the present, including working experience that gives meaning and consistency. In this process, people seek to understand the past and to make it more acceptable to themselves. The great interest that many people develop around the time of retirement in researching and recording their life stories and family histories is symptomatic of this preoccupation.

Thinking about the past in an evaluative way allows us to attach new meanings that help to make sense of the present. The life story is reconstructed so that the person in the present retains a positive identity, although this may be exceedingly difficult to achieve if conceived wholly in personal or private terms. In seeking meaning for one's own life, most people find it necessary to locate themselves within a wider collective or larger framework. By searching for meanings that lie beyond social roles, work responsibilities, or trivial activities, it may be possible to keep at bay the stigma that becomes increasingly obvious at retirement in a society that equates worth with work and self-esteem with income. In telling our tale internally to ourselves and in sharing it with others, we reinforce our sense of personal worth and use our life experience as a source of encouragement

to others. Through reminiscence and life review, we can identify past accomplishments, thereby narrowing the gap between a present concept of
self characterized by role loss and the ideal self informed by the concept
of intrinsic human worth, regardless of role and economic or social position. As people develop an acceptable perception of themselves, they are
more likely to feel less anxious about the future and perhaps more able to
surmount pressures in old age leading toward diminished autonomy and
creeping marginalization. The revised life story that incorporates personally acceptable values becomes evidence of personal worth to the self and
to significant others.

This process, however, does not always work, either for all people or
for the same person all of the time. How else is it possible to explain the
recall of memories that fail to represent the teller in a favorable light? How
do we account for the reluctance of some people to reminisce at all? Some
people are so taken up with the present that they have no time or interest
in talking about the past. Some people's past may be so painful that they
may be unable to face it, reconstruct it, or risk sharing it with others. For
them, speaking about the unspeakable could be overwhelmingly destruc-
tive. Some people talk about the past but derive no satisfaction from doing
so (Coleman, 1986). If the teller rejects his or her own past, lacks the energy or impetus needed to reach some accommodation with it, or perceives
the hearer to be critical or lacking empathy, then the reminiscence process
can leave that person worse off.

The immediate context in which the recall takes place and the recep-
tion the teller receives influence the content and style of the recollections.
People who may be in the greatest need of acceptance and sociable company may be the least well equipped to achieve it. People who are depressed, for example, mainly recollect sad memories. They tend incorrectly
or inaccurately to generalize these negative views to the whole of life. Such
pervasive negative thinking can be effectively challenged either in individual reminiscence work or in a group and the person helped to reappraise
his or her account. If people present a view of themselves as wholly bad because of one past wrong act or bad choice, then this can be questioned and
people can be assisted to distance themselves from this single contaminat-
ing memory. As mood improves, recalled memories become more optimistic. People can be assisted to be less hard on themselves, and as they
come to feel more accepting of themselves and their life, they may also be-

come less critical and negative. As a result of becoming more positive, they are also likely to become more attractive to and accepted by others. Perlman suggested:

> At any age, our present affects our view of the past in what and how we remember. Feeling miserable and utterly useless, one person may view his whole life as having been beset with hurts and disappointments; another, still fighting to maintain self-respect and self-direction despite deterioration, may build up his sense of integrity by embellishments of his accomplishments, his place and import in the lives of others—and memory fragments will be fashioned (again only part consciously) to support this sense of selfhood.
>
> The reason for using exploration of personal memory as a means of reconciling people with themselves and each other in family, community, and national contexts is ultimately to promote applied self knowledge because only in understanding and accepting ourselves is there any likelihood of us understanding and accepting other people.
>
> "Know thyself." That is the basic condition for compassionate insight into another. One can never truly understand or accept in another person what has not been known, in some form, acknowledged, accepted, and understood, in greater or less degree, in one's self. Therein lies another reason for the unafraid exploration of the self, as it was, as it has become, and as it is becoming. (1989, pp. 166, 192)

Hongo (1995) provided an illuminating account of how personal, family, and world history are interwoven and how these three strands of influence affecting each other may serve to include or exclude people from society. Hongo wrote most eloquently of his search for belonging as a fourth-generation Japanese American.

Throughout his childhood, Hongo listened to many of his grandfather Kubota's stories. As a dutiful grandson, he recalled the old man, lonely and usually silent, periodically summoning him to join him for "talk story." One day, the story changed. "I was thirteen by then, and I suppose he thought me ready for it," said Hongo (1995, p. 303). His grandfather then told of his own unbearable shame when FBI agents arrested him in Hawaii after the Japanese attack on Pearl Harbor in 1941, the event that precipitated the United States' entry into World War II. The grandfather recounted the horror of his arrest, interrogation, internment, evacuation, and eventual relocation. This blow to his grandfather's honor was paradoxically eventually obliterated only after the man developed Alzheimer's disease. Some forgetting, Hongo suggested, seems to bring release. The grandfather's memories of degradation ultimately became part of Hongo's own life story, but this grandson's journey toward integrating the memory was remembered as a painful one.

At first Hongo thought that his grandfather was inventing the tale as a sort of horror story. So in his junior high school history class, he decided to test it out by asking questions. His teacher, a Jew, quickly silenced him, then took him aside at the back of the classroom and confirmed that the story was indeed true. So he asked his mother and then his classmates, who laughed at his ignorance. "It was the war," they said, and afterwards Japanese Americans were too busy rebuilding their lives to dwell too much on "camp." It was as if they had tried to obliterate four years of their history by not speaking about the unspeakable. But for Kubota, now an old man, the story had to be told. Unable to speak to his children, he chose Hongo, his eldest grandson, to be the recipient of his shameful story. He would or could not let it go: "In session after session, month after month . . . he pounded away at his story. . . . He gave his testimony to me and I held it at first cautiously in my conscience as if it were an heirloom too delicate to expose to strangers . . . and then his grandfather enjoined " 'you learn speak good, eh . . . ?' " Whereas other Hawaiian-American Japanese children were burdened with silence, Hongo was burdened by being chosen to be the bearer and teller of the tale, "a ritual payment the young owe their elders who have survived" (1995, p. 309).

This example echoes many other accounts that confirm there is a time to speak of the unspeakable (Hunt et al., 1997; Kaminsky, 1984; Lewis, 1992). The people who feel driven to unburden themselves, even if they pass that burden on to someone else (more often it seems to a grandchild, not an adult child), must determine that time. This may be especially true of memories of extreme trauma as in war, revolution, genocide, famine, natural disasters, or public catastrophes. The pain will be felt as keenly, if less obviously, in personal tragedies such as abuse, rape, desertion, divorce, illness, disabling accident, or bereavement. It should never be forgotten that even the most public catastrophe specifically affects private individu-als. A shared suffering, as in the case of Hongo's grandfather, too often leads to a conspiracy of silence; frequently there may be collusion in denial or the transmission of unresolved bitterness lodged in collective memory, whose corrosive influence may influence future generations.

The original tragedy may require repeated telling before its force is dissipated. For some, this point of release may never be achieved. If feeling compelled to speak and there is no one willing or able to listen or being pressured to speak before ready to do so, then the burden will be magni-fied and the opportunity for healing and for moving on will have been missed, perhaps forever. Some telling, even to a receptive hearer, may not bring release and public acknowledgment of suffering or wrong inflicted may be insufficient to make good the original harm. For some people, heal-ing and recovery may never be achieved fully or at all, for the initial wrongs can never be undone and forgiveness, recovery, and peace of mind prove to be a continuing quest, a work in progress, rather than a final resolution.

CONCLUSION

Case examples have been used to illustrate different ways in which life sto-ries, reminiscence, and oral history have been used to attempt to promote personal understanding, as a search for private and public meanings, or as a way of encouraging integration in groups and communities rather than perpetuating social exclusion and isolation. The contexts in which the ex-amples cited occurred, the specific objectives sought from the different in-terventions, and the kinds of people involved varied greatly. Yet all of the people involved were marginalized in one way or another, on the fringes rather than at the center of their family, group, neighborhood, or commu-nity. Hearing and responding to the story always makes demands. This is undoubtedly difficult work that requires much more critical exploration and many more committed courageous people willing to attempt it. For in every journey of reconciliation with marginalized, damaged people in contested communities and divided societies, there are opportunities for far-sighted people to make a difference. As Lederach suggested, "It is pos-sible to remember the past, and at the same time, choose to respond to the present on the basis of a vision for the future" (1997, p. 54).

PART III

REMINISCENCE PRACTICE IN DEMENTIA CARE

This section concentrates on a range of conditions loosely referred to as dementia and how the past can be used as a resource in the present. It adopts a positive, optimistic view and argues that much can be done to improve the circumstances and well being of people with dementia and also the many others who either live or work with them. Regardless of the type of dementia, and the growing challenge of its projected increase because of an aging population, the person who develops one or more of these disabling conditions remains first and foremost a person who is worthy of our love, concern, and respect. This understanding of the uniqueness and worth of each individual must be the foundation of all our efforts with and on behalf of people with dementia.

Two poems are used at the beginning of Chapter 8 to highlight starkly contrasting "old" and "new" understandings of dementia. The chapter then describes in more detail different understandings of dementia, the major implications of memory failure, and the constructive role of creativity in late life generally and in people with dementia at whatever age, for living and coping in the present. Chapter 9 examines reminiscence work with people who live in the community and how to encourage family members and friends to use reminiscence work in their day-to-day interactions to improve communication, and to preserve or enhance relationships. Day services have become increasingly important in dementia for providing care, social stimulation and respite for family carers so the relevance of reminiscence work in this context of care is also considered. Although there are overlapping practice issues whether a person lives in his or her own home or attends a day center, there are particular issues concerning reminiscence work when a person relinquishes domestic living and enters a residential dementia service. These implications and adaptations are explored in Chapter 10.

Chapter 8

Dementia and Creativity in Later Life

GERIATRIC

What god is proud
of this garden
of dead flowers, this underwater
grotto of humanity
in invisible
currents, faces drooping
on dry stalks, voices clawing
in a last desperate effort
to retain hold? Despite
withered petals, I recognize
the species: Charcot, Meniere,
Alzheimer. There are no gardeners
Here, caretakers only
Of reason overgrown
By confusion

–THOMAS, 1995, P. 9

Photograph courtesy of Elders Share the Arts, New York, New York.

This poem shows one view of people with dementia, how the disability affects them, and how other people regard them. It focuses only on the present, seeing valueless people—sidelined, useless, already wilted, and all but dead. Without denying the ravages of the condition, some poems celebrate the individual as once he or she was and still is. His or her present efforts to continue growing evoke respect, sympathy, and awe. The dead flowers of this poem are barely recognizable people who require only caregiving, having passed beyond the reach of cultivation. One view is described as horticultural and the other as warehousing (Miller & Gwynne, 1972). In other more contemporary terms, the one is in tune with the new culture of dementia care, whereas the other portrays the malignant social psychology of the old culture of care (Kitwood, 1997).

> The old culture is one of alienation and estrangement. Through it we are distanced from our fellow human beings, deprived of our insight, cut off from our own vitality. The old culture is one of domination, techniques, and buck-passing. To enter the new culture is like coming home. We can now draw close to other human beings, accepting all that we genuinely share. We can recover confidence in our power to

know, to discover, to give, to create, to love. And this homecoming is a cause for joy and celebration. (Kitwood & Benson, 1995, p. 11)

This chapter, it is hoped, is equally relevant to people with dementia and their family and professional caregivers, regardless of the type and cause of each person's dementia. It includes basic demographic information and the standard medical classifications of dementia and contrasts these with alternative broader understandings of this syndrome. The relevance of lifetime and social factors in influencing present behavior and the contribution of reminiscence in combating the social isolation associated with dementia are explored. The persistence of creativity in late life, even in people with dementia, is described and illustrated with case examples. When memory, activated through reminiscence, is linked with artistic, imaginative, nonverbal activities such as art, drama, and especially music, a rich resource becomes available for sustaining communication and constructive relationships with friends, relatives, and professional caregivers.

UNDERSTANDINGS OF DEMENTIA

Dementia, one of the major public health problems of our time, is described in various ways. The term refers to extensive, progressive impairment of higher mental functions, including memory, everyday problem-solving ability, the use of social skills, and altered behavior and emotional reactions. Definitions vary, but the official medical classification and definition comes from the tenth revision of the International Classification of Diseases, or ICD-10 (World Health Organization, 1992), which states

Dementia is a syndrome due to disease of the brain, usually of a chronic or progressive nature in which there is impairment of multiple higher cortical functions, including memory, thinking, orientation, comprehension, calculation, learning capacity, language, and judgment. Consciousness is not clouded. The cognitive impairments are commonly accompanied, and occasionally preceded, by deterioration in emotional control, social behavior, or motivation. This syndrome occurs in Alzheimer's disease, in cerebrovascular disease, and in other conditions primarily or secondarily affecting the brain. (Burns, Dening, & Lawlor, 2002, p. 3)

The DSM-IV (American Psychiatric Association, 1994) and DSM-IV-TR (American Psychiatric Association, 2000), with some minor text revisions, use the same codes as ICD-10. Several practice guidelines concerned with the assessment, diagnosis, and treatment of people with dementia and age-related cognitive disorders exist. The most widely used are those by Rabins, Blacker, Bland, and colleagues (1997) for the American Psychiatric Association and those of the American Psychological Association (1998). General guidelines are also available concerning current knowledge of behavioral and psychological symptoms of dementia and their implications for care and treatment (Finkel & Burns, 2000; Finkel, Cost de Silva, Cohen et al., 1996). DSM-IV refers to dementia of the Alzheimer's type as involving impairment of short- and long-term memory, impaired ability to learn new information or to recall previously learned information, and evidence of one (or more) of the following cognitive disturbances:

- Aphasia (language disturbance)

- Apraxia (impaired ability to carry out motor activities despite intact motor function)

- Agnosia (failure to recognize or identify objects despite intact sensory function)

- Disturbance in executive functioning (planning, organizing, sequencing, or abstracting)

These disturbances impair social or occupational functioning and represent a marked deterioration from previous competence. Other conditions need to be eliminated, including delirium associated with dramatic onset and physical conditions such as urinary tract or chest infections (Burns, Dening, & Lawlor, 2002, p. 8).

Many health and social care professionals believe that the biomedical model represented in these definitions does not adequately account for the complexity of the experience of dementia. Since the 1990s, a broader approach to the definition, diagnosis of, and response to dementia has gained increasing prominence (Harris, 2002). The word *dementia* is used loosely as an umbrella term to refer to a syndrome or collection of assorted symptoms that affect cognitive, emotional, and social aspects of functioning associated with various progressive organic degenerative disorders of the brain that usually spare physical health but affect thinking, behavior, and emotion. These changes include memory problems (especially short-term memory loss) and impaired reasoning, judgment, language, comprehension, and ability to learn and recall new information. Speech is affected, including difficulty in the ability to find and pronounce words, to use proper syntax, to read, to write, and to calculate. Mobility can deteriorate, and people increasingly lose their capacity to drive and to take care of themselves. They may be confused, be disoriented in time and place, behave in seemingly irrational ways if they misunderstand or are misunderstood, and become increasingly unable to recognize familiar people.

Although it is typical to talk in terms of people with dementia losing their memory, it is probably more accurate to say that people so affected are no longer able to easily retrieve memories on demand. No longer is it assumed that people with dementia lack insight into their condition or that they have changed personalities and lose all sense of self, although they are likely to experience considerable difficulty in communicating in conventional verbal ways. It is increasingly appreciated that lifelong experience, various social and psychological factors (including a sense of security), and the present environment all have considerable influence on how the underlying neurological and biological degenerative changes affect each person. How other people interact with the person with dementia is now believed to influence how well the person affected manages to retain a sense of personal identity, self-esteem, and self-confidence. It is therefore imperative that every effort is made in dementia care to sustain communication, encourage social interaction, and preserve relationships. Although memory and mental speed generally decline slightly with age, dementia is not regarded as a normal part of aging. Regardless of the causes of various types of dementia, all result in a decline in mental function, especially short-term memory.

Dementia is usually—although not invariably—irreversible, depending on the type, and it runs a progressive downward course. It appears to occur in all countries, regardless of gender, social class, income, and ethnicity, although a higher level of education appears to offer some protection. There is no universally accepted view about the nature of dementia, and we really know relatively little about how it is regarded in non-western cultures (Whitehouse, Maurer, & Ballenger, 2000). Radebaugh and Ward-Robinson (2002) wrote about dementia and cultural diversity with reference to African Americans, Latinos, Native Americans, and Native-born Alaskans. Dementia is predominately a disease of later life, although not exclusively so. Increasing numbers of people younger than 65 years of age are being identified, even though people with early onset dementia remain a small proportion of the total that is currently estimated as some 18 million people worldwide. Of this total, 66% live in developing countries and some 4 million live in the United States. As the world's population ages and the number of people being diagnosed increases, dementia is growing in visibility and making increasing demands on family caregivers and health and social welfare resources. Approximately one in ten people older than age 65 and nearly half of people older than 85 have dementia; by 2050, it is estimated that 14 million people in the United States will have Alzheimer's disease or a related disorder. There is an average life expectancy of 8 years after diagnosis, although the onset of symptoms may have first been noticed many years previously. Seven of ten people with dementia live at home, with 75% being cared for by families and friends. It is estimated that currently approximately half of all nursing facility residents have dementia or a related disorder (http://www.Alz.org). There are many different kinds of dementia. Although accounting for 50%–60% of all cases, *Alzheimer's disease* is frequently the term used generally to refer to all types of dementia. In Alzheimer's disease, there is widespread damage to brain tissue, resulting in a slow, insidious decline in memory, language, and thinking. In vascular dementia (formerly called *multi-infarct dementia*), poor blood supply to the brain results in a stepwise decline in memory, but there may be other signs of vascular disease such as strokes. People with Lewy bodies disease develop fluctuating memory problems, distressing hallucinations, stiffness, slowing of movement similar to Parkinson's disease, and falls. Damage to the frontotemporal region of the brain, such as occurs in Pick's disease, has a slow onset of memory loss, early deterioration of social behavior and personality, and early language deterioration.

More than one type of dementia may coexist. An overlap between different types of dementia is being increasingly recognized, and many different diseases can cause dementia-type symptoms. The complexity of the condition, together with the frequent presence of depressive symptoms and the lack of a definitive diagnostic test (except at postmortem examination), makes accurate differential diagnosis particularly dependent on the availability of an accurate history of deterioration.

The long-established medical approach to dementia regards dementia conditions as organic neurological diseases, mostly of unknown origin, largely untreatable, and inevitably terminal. Recent improvements in diagnostic methods are leading to earlier detection and a greater willingness to disclose the diagnosis to the person him- or herself and not just to a relative or caregiver, as was customary in the past. The development of new drug treatments is beginning to improve symptom control and feelings of well-being for a time in the early stages in some people, although it does not necessarily improve cognitive capacity. Pharmaceutical developments have produced a new range of drugs for use in the more advanced stages of dementia. Early, accurate diagnosis makes access to accurate information and constructive intervention possible. Treatment should include access to drugs if appropriate; ongoing, timely information, including legal and financial advice; support and counseling for both the person with dementia and family members; and referral for a range of psychosocial interventions and practical services. Information is constantly being updated because research into epidemiology, pathology, genetics, pharmacology, and psychosocial treatments is developing extremely rapidly. Local Alzheimer's Associations are the best source of current information (see Resources).

Although neurological deterioration undoubtedly occurs, how each individual is affected depends on a very complex interplay among organic factors, life experience (including unresolved past trauma), social interactions, and present life circumstances. A multidimensional person-centered model of care recognizes the interplay among biopsychosocial dimensions. This approach offers constructive possibilities for various types of interventions and caring arrangements to sustain functioning for as long as possible and to safeguard quality of life (Kitwood, 1997). This person-centered approach seeks to understand the individual person with all his or her richly varied, unique life experience within the context of the present.

Dementia and Depression

Depression often coexists with dementia, either as an already existing condition or as a response to a growing awareness of the implications of having dementia and the associated grief and loss, including loss of personal control that inevitably accompanies it. The clinical features of depression and dementia can be very similar and difficult to distinguish. The memory and learning impairments of dementia in many ways resemble depression. The low mood, apathy, loss of initiative, and general decline in interest, energy, and self-care often observed in depression can also be characteristic of dementia. It is crucial for people to receive a comprehensive assessment and correct differential diagnosis with appropriate treatment because many depressive conditions and some dementias do respond to various kinds of pharmacological and psychosocial treatment.

Because the diverse course of dementia cannot be adequately accounted for by neurological damage alone, contemporary writers are paying increasing attention to the influence of lifetime factors, interpersonal relationships, and the impact of present environmental circumstances on the course of the condition. The issue of selfhood, personhood, or identity and how best to assist in maintaining personhood that is threatened by dementia has become a central debate since the 1990s. Social constructionists explain selfhood in terms of each individual person having three selves that for convenience are called *Self-1, Self-2,* and *Self-3.* Self-1 involves the first-person singular pronoun. By using "I," we take responsibility for actions, feelings, and experiences as being our own. This is demonstrated in conversation or when we speak of "I" and in writing autobiographical stories. Self-2 consists of personal, mental, and physical attributes, achievements, and beliefs relating to each separate person: The color of our eyes, our height, our weight, our education, our beliefs, and our vocational attainments, for example. Many of these are lifelong attributes, whereas others are acquired or change throughout life. Self-3 consists of various social personae that we construct in different situations, each with its own distinct pattern of behavior related to various social roles. These constructions require validation by other people. If a person is viewed as defective and treated as such, as people with dementia and many other disabilities tend to be, then the only possible Self-3 personae the person can construct is also to regard themselves as defective. If others define the person with dementia solely in terms of the negative attributes arising from Self-2 characteristics that occur as a result of the dementia, then that person will suffer from excess disability. Conversely, if others honor or validate residual, intact attributes and continue to respect the individual's personhood or humanity, then the person with dementia may continue to feel positively about him- or herself (Sabat & Harre, 1992).

Such personal self-confidence is more likely to improve social interactions, sustain communication with caregivers and significant others, and preserve a sense of personal dignity, worth, and contentment. A self-fulfilling downward spiral occurs once people are labeled incompetent because lacking positive reinforcement and confidence-sustaining relationships, they soon begin to behave in the ways expected. The old idea of loss of personality, loss of self, or de-selfing is thought to be largely due to the consequences of being invalidated, of being treated as incompetent and less than a full member of the human race (Tobin, 1999). This lack of positive reinforcement is thought to result in greater difficulties than can be attributed only to the underlying organic neurological impairment (Kitwood & Bredin, 1992; Sabat, 2001a). If this view is accepted, then it can be readily appreciated that how we respect and respond to people with dementia will crucially influence the way in which they perceive themselves, which in turn will influence how they behave. The person, not the dementia, must come first. Caregivers' negativity or the provision of an inappropriate care environment should not exacerbate the impairments caused by the organic damage and other coexisting health problems.

It is helpful to remember that people with dementia also show continuity in their coping strategies. This is why knowledge of their life history is so crucial. If people habitually coped with stress by walking before developing dementia, for example, then it is highly likely they will continue to use the same stress outlet when disabled by dementia (Kitwood, 1997; Sabat, 2001b). Earlier behavior will probably be called on as a means to assist coping in the present. In these circumstances, then, any current pacing of the corridors or attempts to leave a building may reflect the reemergence of long-established behavior used when managing stress or seeking safety in the past. These lifetime patterns are reactivated, not abandoned, although it is unlikely that the person using them will be able to explain. What to a present observer may appear aimless, obsessive, and counterproductive may be the habit of a lifetime, now revived and put to use as a response to feeling under present threat.

Combating the Isolation of Dementia

Reminiscence and related activities offer an enjoyable, accessible, and effective means for combating the isolation that almost inevitably accompanies dementia. This isolation is experienced by the person with dementia as well as by his or her caregivers, who through fear of stigma, caring demands, or exhaustion are unable to sustain normal social relationships. Caring obligations become increasingly demanding as dementia progresses, friends gradually disappear, and the person with dementia and his or her primary caregiver, most often a coresiding spouse or adult child, gradually relinquish satisfying interests, activities, and social contacts. Love, duty, and obligation may sustain the caring but many caregivers pay a heavy price in terms of their own physical and mental health. Caregivers differ greatly in their coping capacity, depending on the strength of the relationship before the onset of dementia; their ability to adapt to the demands of the changing situation over an extended period of time; the amount of personal satisfaction derived from the caring role; other demands; and alternative, accessible sources of support (Cohen, Colantonio, & Vernich, 2002).

To sustain caring, it is crucially important to find creative ways of enhancing the give and take, the mutuality, and the reciprocity of relationships. Although sustaining relationships is important for paid caregivers, it is absolutely vital for old friends, spouses and partners, and adult children with caring responsibilities. Some partnerships, for example same gender partnerships, may be undermined because of other people's failure to recognize and accept them, and the caregiver's involvement and loss may remain unacknowledged. The ties that bound long-established relationships in the past may be severely eroded when assailed by the unpredictable behavior and growing dependency associated with dementia. Early in the illness, family, partners, and friends may be irritated, bewildered, impatient, and embarrassed by odd behavior, apparent self-centeredness, perceived irresponsibility or incompetence, and unreasonable demands (Kurokawa, 1998). At this time, information and advice for people with dementia and caregivers can be invaluable, but it also needs to be available throughout the entire course of the illness as circumstances and needs change.

Caregivers may also welcome assistance with other aspects of lifetime relationships affected by dementia. Grief over losses and changes in roles and responsibilities associated with the diminishing competence of the partner is inescapable. Gill stated, "The process of loss and grieving is unnaturally mixed with the humbling mechanics of maintenance" (2003,

p. 4). Often anxiety and attachment-seeking behavior overtakes many people with dementia as they try to cope with their associated distress and anxiety. The person with dementia may seek constant reassurance and be unwilling to be separated from the attachment figure who is regarded as a source of emotional security. The caregiver often finds these excessive demands, the lack of alone time, and the absence of alternative sources of satisfaction and support exceedingly stressful. Mutual engagement in reminiscence work serves two purposes in terms of recognizing the importance of attachment. It provides a reminder of the significance of the relationship in times past. This can be a source of present comfort if it has been satisfying, and it also creates the opportunity for continuing to produce a shared story about the present that openly recognizes the ongoing changing relationship (Bruce, 1998a; Sparks, 1996).

CREATIVITY IN LATE LIFE

Researchers and writers who theorize about what it is like to be old substantially agree about the gradual decline of physical health and other physical changes linked to advancing age. There is much less agreement, however, concerning the part played by emotion in late life and the preservation and expression of creative artistic capacity by engagement in various activities (Menec, 2003). Although research psychologists may study the effects of aging under artificially constructed laboratory conditions, and as a consequence make broad general pronouncements, those who encounter older people daily in real-life situations recognize great variations among individuals concerning zest, resilience, energy, mood, creativity, curiosity, well-being, and life satisfaction. Health and social care staff who daily see a skewed sample of the older population need to be vigilant lest they succumb to pessimism because of biased exposure that limits their understanding and reduces the life opportunities they provide for older people in their care. This caution applies equally to staff members who care for physically frail older people and those with dementia and depression as well as people of all ages who have various physical or cognitive disabilities.

The importance of creative approaches in gerontology was eloquently expressed by Saul (1983), a social work teacher who had worked as an educational coordinator in a New York nursing home. She said, "Creative approaches leap beyond the double stigma of aging and frailty. They are geared to meet the dependencies; to support the frailties; and, thereby, to free each person to function at the highest point of individual capability" (p. 5).

It is particularly important to understand that artistic creativity is not necessarily closely correlated with cognitive ability and that some types of existing artistic expression may come to maturity in later life or even become apparent for the first time with advancing age (Cohen, 2000). This flowering of talent in late life has been best documented in graphic artists, particularly painters and sculptors. Michelangelo, Titian, Goya, Hokusai, Monet, and Matisse, among many others, are cited as evidence (Clark, 1981; Dormandy, 1996, 2001).

There is evidence too that painters who develop dementia can successfully continue to paint. The most frequently cited example is the abstract impressionist Hans Willem de Kooning who continued to paint long after Alzheimer's disease seriously impaired his speech and cognitive abilities. The artistic quality of his late paintings, which were undertaken when he was ravaged by dementia, has been much debated. These late works display wonderful sweeping lines and softer colors with a free-flowing style that suggests inner tranquility, serenity, and freedom— utterly unlike much of his troubled, even tortured predementia work. Many people who develop dementia and who have never previously painted have also completed impressive work as demonstrated by the annual exhibitions of the Orange County Chapter of the Alzheimer's Society, described in more detail later in this chapter (Jenny & Oropeza, 1993; Rentz, 2002). The storytelling, plays, and exhibits of the Time Slips project (Basting, 1998) provide other relevant examples.

Numerous musicians continue to compose, conduct, and perform well into late life, although singing beyond late middle age and some instrumental playing are probably the exceptions. Many musicians do their best work in later years; for example, Beethoven's late quartets demonstrate profound maturity, interiority, and conditional optimism, despite his encroaching deafness, isolation, and increasing age. Some musicians, such as the pianist Rubenstein, develop compensatory techniques so they can continue to perform. Rubenstein explained that as he grew older he deliberately preceded a fast passage by slower playing than was customary so as to enhance the impression of speed and dexterity in the subsequent more demanding passage. Rostopovich, the internationally renowned cellist, felt he had recorded the first and third Beethoven cello sonatas too early, before he had the maturity to comprehend their meaning and do them justice. At age 60, he decided the time had come to record them all, and now in old age he continues to teach, perform, and record to international acclaim.

Poets and writers seem to do less well, and this may provide some clues about what kinds of nonverbal creative activities might better suit older people as they age, although here the evidence is far from clear cut. Clark (1981) suggested that the painter or sculptor in using a medium outside him- or herself is able to draw inspiration and encouragement from what he or she sees. He or she is reacting or responding to an external stimulus. Clark argued that painting is a physical act and visual experience can be vitalizing although such an argument is not entirely persuasive. Writing, conversely, requires us to dig deep within ourselves and draw from our own experience, memory, and imagination. Here memories and their imbedded emotions provide the raw material and any memories recalled must endure sufficiently long to enable them to be transformed into poetry or prose and transferred to paper, disk, or tape. Only in exceptional circumstances in which opportunities for writing or recording are denied—for example, in hostage situations such as described by Waite (1994) or in times of disabling illness—are autobiography, prose, or poetry composed in the mind and remembered for extensive periods before being committed to more durable formats.

The poet Seamus Heaney believes the quality of his work is enhanced with age and the deeper reflections that it brings. His first poems were descriptions, but later poems on the same themes were "reflections refracted by experience." He described his book *Electric Light* as a "ruminant book, full of stuff that's in the system, in the memory, that is being revisited" (Browne, 2001, p. 10). He recalled in conversation with a critic an unforgettable magical sensation when as a small child visiting his grandmother's house—he experienced electricity, an amenity his Ulster farming family did not yet have:

> The radiance of electric light. It was stronger than lamplight. . . . Then there was the magic of the switch. Years ago I may have written about that and just left it there. But, now there is something else, the outer ring of the consciousness, the part of me that is contemplating what happened to me since age six until the age of 60 (Brown, 2001, p. 10).

This example also illustrates how the seemingly ordinary for one person becomes a transforming memory for another. Maybe the original moment was enjoyed at the time or not, but it is mysteriously stored away to be revived, recalled, and reworked many years later. For everyone, it seems, lays down deposits in the memory of which we are unaware at the time, and we never know either when we are making a memory or when these memories, prompted or unprompted, will return to conscious awareness.

Given the imaginative and physical effort that writing demands, it is surprising that so many people do turn to writing in later life, even if relatively few newcomers achieve fame as first-time writers. So much of this late writing involves the reworking of our own life's narrative, the personal, family, and community value of which has already been illustrated (Krell, 1990). The physical burden of writing needs to be made as light as possible for older people so that their cognitive, imaginative, and emotional energies can be invested in recalling and reworking memories and transforming them into stories, rather than being preoccupied with the actual mechanics of transferring ideas to paper. It is here that time spent in acquiring rudimentary word processing skills can pay such handsome dividends, and not only for older people who already are able to type. Senior-Net, a nonprofit organization of some 39,000 members (see Resources) and other programs such as those run by the AARP for introducing elders to information and communication technology have a crucial role to play in this connection (Kearsley & Furlong, 1988; http://www.seniornet.org).

Creativity and Dementia

Too often it is assumed that people with dementia who are having difficulties with communication, orientation, and short-term memory are incapable of engaging in imaginative activity and creative expression. Experience suggests that the opposite is true (Basting & Killick, 2003). Creative expression is only likely to happen, however, if people have opportunities for exercising creativity within congenial, nonthreatening circumstances that emphasize what they can still do and find pleasurable, rather than what they can no longer do and find frustrating.

Creativity is the process by which we seek inner meaning, and this process needs to be nourished and supported. Because of the pervasive pessimism of many health professionals, opportunities to seek this essential nourishment may be withheld. If instead personhood is respected, then people with dementia will be less likely to be denuded of social roles and consigned to lives of monotony, inactivity, and social isolation. So many people with dementia face the double jeopardy of withdrawing into themselves because they lack rewarding social exchange and personal validation or dying from boredom through lack of creative stimulation.

Artistic creativity is not closely tied to age or to cognitive or physical ability, even though all three play a part in determining what form of expression best suits any individual. Many people with dementia who may never have engaged in creative pursuits in earlier life can derive great pleasure and show considerable talent when given the opportunity for imaginative creative expression. Dementia peels away the social veneer, acquired with considerable effort throughout the process of growing up. It strips people down to the essence of their being and frees them to be more in touch with their emotions. They communicate with greater authenticity than our customary conventional reliance on controlled emotional expression. The censoring tendencies that frequently make adults use words to obscure meaning give way in dementia to more direct spontaneous communication and imaginative metaphorical speech as Killick demonstrated with his transformation of people's speech into poetry.

In the company of accepting, empathic caregivers, people with dementia feel free to project their imaginations and expose their emotions, particularly through forms of expressiveness that do not rely on verbal communication. Many have to struggle very hard, often in the face of formidable incomprehension by other people (even highly trained professional caregivers), to express a sense of who they are and what they want, for in dementia although much is lost, much remains. Great effort is needed to prevent the erosion of their fragile identities and abilities that sometimes manage still to break through in moments of astonishing clarity, instances of acute perceptiveness, and unmistakable evidence that personhood remains. Killick and Cordonnier noted that these moments "are like a window opening and closing very quickly. . . . In dementia care we must ask ourselves: 'What exactly are people telling us?' and 'How can we create the conditions that will encourage individuals to express their ideas and opinions?' " (2000, pp. 4–5).

USING CREATIVE EXPRESSION IN REMINISCENCE

Art, music, dance, and drama therapies are long-established approaches to working creatively with people and are increasingly being undertaken with people who have dementia. There is training, accreditation, and established employment opportunities for these occupations that are explicitly psychotherapeutic in intent and undertaken in highly specialized ways (Clair, 1996). Many others are using art, music, drama, dance, poetry, storytelling, and reminiscence and life story work in less structured ways with people of all ages, including those with dementia. To label these rich, fascinating creative activities as "therapy" is doing them a disservice and undervaluing their importance in transforming care and caring relationships. It matters comparatively little what the activity is called or how the workers are described, however, provided that the people invited to participate are consulted, their wishes respected, the chosen art form is within their capacity, and the workers behave responsibly (Post & Whitehouse, 1995). Given the steadily increasing number of people with dementia, it is essential that the special skills of highly trained professionals are used to train, develop, and support other staff so that creative activities come to suffuse the entire program of adult day centers and residential facilities and are not seen as the monopoly of a small number of expert staff members.

Because reminiscence draws so much on long-term memory, it is one of the best creative psychosocial interventions for people with dementia and their caregivers. If used effectively, it will influence the well-being of people who frequently feel demeaned, ignored, and excluded. By harnessing the power of reminiscence and related interventions, people can be helped to retain a sense of personal identity and their diminishing self-esteem can be preserved. A more positive approach to care and treatment can be achieved by encouraging a person to continue to use the still healthy, intact aspects of his or her residual abilities. Two aspects of residual functioning underpin this positive approach that is often called a *strengths approach* (Fast & Chapin, 2000; Kivnick & Murray, 2001; Ronch & Goldfield, 2003). First, long-term memory, which appears to be much less affected initially by the onset of dementia than short-term memory (although in the later stages it too may be severely compromised), provides fertile ground for recall of past learning and past experience. This is especially true for procedural or nonverbal memory. When these memories are used as a bridge into linked creative activities that do not require verbal skills for their execution, the outcomes can be richly rewarding for all concerned. Needlework, woodwork, and other handicraft skills learned earlier in life are examples of other activities that with appropriate adaptation, support, and encouragement can provide some people with opportunities for pleasure and creativity, even after the onset of dementia. Knitting and sewing readily present opportunities to recall memories associated with previous use of these skills and materials. Memories of people, places, successes, and failures are recalled as people become absorbed in once again handling craft materials. Considerable concentration, emotional investment, artistic skill, and immense satisfaction have been reported in people with dementia who have demonstrated that through these and other means, they can continue to communicate and sustain warm, loving relationships far into the illness. Opportunities for continued social engagement, long thought to be a thing of the past, are opened up, and family and professional caregivers find rewarding ways of providing genuine person-centered dementia care.

Many projects are using residual long-term memory and linked creative activities, not just for diversion but also for preserving the intrinsic core identity of the person for as long as possible, notwithstanding progressive deterioration, and as sources of personal satisfaction. By sensitively using multisensory triggers that closely match the life experience of the person with dementia, it is possible and usually relatively easy to encourage communication about the past and, by doing so, to share sociable, enjoyable experiences in the present. Music, art, drama, dance, movement, and reminiscence are used both as triggers to elicit memories and as vehicles for their expression. These approaches have the potential for transforming institutional care and overcoming the limitations of impaired verbal communication and the insidious passivity so often associated with institutional living.

Creativity in a Geriatric Hospital

An impressive example of creativity in late life was demonstrated in a large geriatric hospital in France where a painter, sculptor, and musician were employed to establish artistic workshops that were strategically located in an accessible, highly visible part of the hospital. The artists were instructed not to do therapy and not to teach. This approach resembles the view of Koch (1977), who saw poetry writing with nursing facility residents as art, not some form of distracting or consoling therapy. The French artists were expressly instructed to involve themselves in the process of artistic creation and to share their art with anyone, patients or staff, who wished to join them. Faced with immediately observable creativity, patients freely and spontaneously developed the courage to join in and to project their imaginations through creative self-expression. The patients' average age was 84, and all had varying degrees of cognitive impairment and physical frailty. Most had no prior experience of the arts, nor were they well educated. Yet they were able to create original works of art, with each person demonstrating a unique individual style. The patients grew in confidence and expressed great pleasure in their impressive artistic creations, many of which were sold on a profit-sharing basis in a Paris gallery that the hospital established as an outlet. These people also recaptured or experienced for the first time respect from friends and nursing and medical staff. Voluntary engagement in creative artistic work not only filled their otherwise empty, monotonous days but also appeared to help them to transcend the physical and cognitive limitations imposed by the aging process. The instigators of the project reported,

> We conclude that an artistic workshop can create a place of freedom in a geriatric unit and show that learning and creativity persist in old age even in the mentally disabled patient; a step toward a more caring and less hopeless approach to aging and dementia. (Moullass, Laforestrie, Lizotte, & Berthaux, 1987, p. 140)

Memories in the Making:
The Alzheimer's Association of Orange County, California

Another impressive example comes from the Orange County, California, Alzheimer's Association project known as *Memories in the Making*®. Their annual exhibitions and sales of works of art have inspired many and added considerably to our understanding of the inner life and outward experience of people with dementia. An exhibition information sheet stated,

As we stand before their paintings, they call out to us in a way we cannot ignore. They tell us their stories in a language we all understand, transmitted feelings and emotions trapped inside. Slipping beyond the language of words, their paintings show us glimpses of who they were and who they still are. Listen to their poetry. When your participants lose their fear of self-expression they may find an artistic freedom that brings beauty out of disorder and confusion. We were beginning to understand that a loss of memory did not automatically signal a loss of creativity, imagination, and manual dexterity or past emotional imprints. A new technique in art expression/therapy was employed with great success from 1988. Patients found new confidence within themselves and willingly "opened up." The art sessions became enjoyable and gave credence to the belief that the patients had more memory than was once believed though not in any form that could be called-up on demand. Patients became more cooperative and gained self-confidence. The caregivers better understood the patient as they learned of his or her background. (Jenny & Oropeza, 1993)

Criteria used for selecting paintings for inclusion in *Memories in the Making*® exhibitions and working principles were identified as follows:

- A history of each artist is recorded to ensure accuracy in any biographical copy.
- Each piece of artwork is the creation of the painter alone.
- Each painting or drawing is titled and described by the artist.
- The families' wishes are respected. Each is required to sign a release. Artwork is returned to the family when requested. Requests for the artist's anonymity are honored.

The objective of the show is not to glamorize the person with Alzheimer's disease but to educate the public and caregivers about the amazing amount of information and eloquent emotion expressed. Great care is given to the reliability of the art facilitator and the locations where the classes take place.

Lutjeans, a museum scientist, described the Orange County paintings as deeply moving, clear, straightforward, and communicative. These paintings had what she described as a winsome cheerfulness:

The descriptive narrative of childhood memory, current frustrations, and unhappiness, even though unable to be communicated through verbalization or body language, are deeply rooted in their creative efforts as adults and are read as such. The disposition of line, the choice of color, the texture, space, and balance, appear to be carefully thought out. (1990, p. 7)

Cotman, a professor of psychobiology and neurology, viewed the same set of paintings and noted that despite the devastation of Alzheimer's disease, the artists clearly retained:

Some fragments of individuality, history, and feeling that they communicate to us through their art. Because AD has long been known as a progressive neurodegenerative disease that destroys the brain's centers of cognition, prevailing wisdom held that AD patients lose their ability to learn, remember, and even think. . . . patients have thus too frequently surrendered both their cognitive functions and their identity to the disease. New research findings and the art presented here prove, however, that this need not be the case. . . . the work presented here has artistic merit in its own right, but its greatest significance lies in its affirmation of the invincibility of the human spirit. That the artwork could even be created under the oppression of AD is impressive; that it is so eloquent borders on the incredible. (1990, p. 9)

There is still much to learn about the neurological basis of creativity and the optimum social context in which creativity in late life flourishes. A research project undertaken by Miller and Snyder is comparing and contrasting savants and people with dementia (Miller, 2001; Miller & Snyder, 2001). These researchers are seeking to establish neurological linkages between the type of brain damage occurring in the people with dementia who retain a capacity for creativity and the relatively rare examples of extremely creative savants. These are people who have exceptional ability to engage in mathematical calculation, meticulous drawing, painting, or music but otherwise have serious intellectual impairments. Snyder (1999) suggested that when the left anterior lobe of the cortex is damaged, compensatory activity is developed in another area of the brain. Other researchers have demonstrated that people with brain damage find it difficult to copy simple figures. People with right-sided brain damage tend to draw disorganized images with spatial errors such as locating arms and legs in the wrong place. People with left-sided damage often oversimplify their drawings, although they usually locate body parts in roughly the correct position (Crutch, Isaacs, & Rossor, 2001). The artistic work frequently contains narrative or biographical elements or suggestions, although this is not invariably so. Much remains to be understood about these creative processes and how to encourage them, but knowledge is increasingly informing efforts to widen access to appropriate creative activities for people with dementia and to increase our understanding of the nature of their achievements.

These examples illustrate how people with dementia are able to respond with great pleasure and satisfaction to opportunities to engage in creative activities. The processes of social engagement, communication, and satisfaction must be regarded as more important than the quality of any tangible artistic outcomes, although these too may be considerable. Working together in fruitful collaborative partnerships, increasing numbers of health and social care professionals and creative artists of many kinds are extending their communication skills with people with dementia and greatly enhancing the quality of the caring experience they are seeking to provide.

LIMITATIONS OF REMINISCENCE
WORK WITH PEOPLE WITH DEMENTIA

So far, a very positive view about the value of reminiscence work and related artistic activity with people with dementia has been given. For some people, however, it may not be such a successful experience. People with emerging dementia can be very conscious that all is not well with their memories and other cognitive abilities. They may be acutely anxious, depressed, and agitated as a consequence. To become involved in memory work may be more than they can tolerate. Although some people will find relief and pleasure in retrieving long-term memories and welcome cognitive exercise and opportunities for creative expression, others may be embarrassed by their short-term memory impairments and not wish to expose their problems to public view (Woods & McKiernan, 1995).

To participate in reminiscence sessions inevitably leads to new ideas about how we see our past. It is through this process of seeing, yet seeing again, that we reach fresh understanding, a kind of enlightenment. We begin to entertain long-buried thoughts as fresh understanding arises. This illumination may take place long after the actual memory has emerged because ideas triggered become the raw material for further private musing and reflection. Memories may suddenly arise again to consciousness, and we see things in a new light. As we begin to allow long-buried thoughts to be entertained, they will combine themselves with others not previously connected in our consciousness. This partially reconstructive process can be difficult for the person with dementia, but not impossible, because he or she may have considerable problems in articulating new understandings, even if the past is comprehended in new ways.

A growing body of evidence is demonstrating that when given time and encouraged by skilled listeners, people with dementia are able to rework past pain (Hunt et al., 1997; Mills & Coleman, 1994). We still have so much to learn about how to communicate with people with dementia that it would be premature to dismiss such possibilities (Allan, 2002; Killick & Allan, 2001). We need to provide a range of opportunities to encourage communication, including creative artistic means as suggested here. We must learn to listen attentively; tune in to the way each person uses verbal and body language, metaphor, and other nonverbal ways of communicating; and do our best to empathize with the feelings being expressed. In making such efforts, it is absolutely essential to observe closely and respond appropriately to any signs of distress, indications of unease, or desire to end involvement, and we must support the person in every way possible.

CONCLUSION

Research into dementia is proceeding apace within and across countries, disciplines, and professions. Old ideas are giving way to more humanistic concerns that emphasize the multidimensional nature and complexity of these various conditions. Although new pharmaceutical treatments are bringing hope for some by retarding deterioration, dementia is still regarded as mostly irreversible and terminal. Imaginative, creative psy-

chosocial interventions are also sustaining and supporting people with dementia and their caregivers in living less isolated and more fulfilling lives.
Although too many professional caregivers remain untouched by and ig-
norant of the newer more positive approaches and pessimism still persists
in too many stultifying care environments, hope and optimism are steadily
increasing. Much remains to be done to spread information, raise awareness, and disseminate ideas and skills. In the meantime, although scien-
tific breakthroughs remain elusive, much can be accomplished by applying what is already known about how to discover and use knowledge of
a person's past and his or her continuing creative capacity as tools to sustain identity, improve well-being, and enhance quality of life in the here
and now.

Chapter 9

Reminiscence at Home and in Dementia Day Centers

When dementia is viewed as a multifaceted syndrome instead of solely as an irreversible neurological condition, much can be done to assist people with dementia, their families, and professional caregivers to prolong communication, hold people in relationships, and attend constructively to sustaining quality of life. How any one person and his or her caregiver is affected by dementia depends on the extent, location, and nature of the neurological damage; lifetime social and psychological influences; present environmental circumstances; and the quality of supportive care currently available. People caring for a family member with dementia are faced with enormous physical and emotional demands that change repeatedly throughout the entire course of the illness. They are required to adjust to inevitable changes in roles and responsibilities; they experience loss of many kinds, possibly including loss of income, affection, companionship, security, sexual partnership, and friendship. Their own vulnerabilities will be exposed, and in their own right they too will need sensitive attention to their own multiple, complex needs.

Many family caregivers find it extremely difficult to continue to provide care, sometimes over many years, without their own health, quality of life, and well being becoming compromised. Just as the person with dementia comes to inhabit a shrinking world, with freedom of action curtailed, so too many caregivers' lives are changed utterly by living and coping with this disability (Mace, Rabins, Castleton, McEwan, & Meredith,

Photograph courtesy of the James Lowell Patterson family.

1999; Zarit & Zarit, 1998). Caregivers vary greatly in how they experience burden, how they cope, and what kinds of professional assistance they find helpful, whether this consists of information provision, teaching and training, access to various services, support, or counselling. Bruce stated, "Caregivers talk of being on a roller coaster of emotion, infuriated by the things that their person with dementia now does, wracked by guilt when they react angrily, protective when others are tactless or uncaring" (1998b, p. 51).

Objective burden, most often measured by the severity of dementia symptoms of the cared-for person and the amount of assistance required, is not closely associated with feelings of subjective burden as experienced and reported by caregivers. Difficulties in communication and deterioration in relationships are very common sources of stress (Teri & McCurry, 1994). Often, friends fall away, and both partners, caregiver, and cared-for experience increasing isolation, living in a contracting world (Davis, 1993).

SUPPORTING FAMILY CAREGIVERS THROUGH REMINISCENCE

Professionals are unlikely to be warmly received if they suggest to hard-pressed family caregivers that they do something differently or take on additional tasks. Many caregivers may not even describe themselves as caregivers and may feel offended to be labeled in this way. How the idea of reminiscence as a constructive, positive aid to caring at home is introduced will therefore be extremely important. Family caregivers are usually extremely sensitive to any hint of criticism or any suggestion that they are stressed or performing in a suboptimal way. The absence of satisfaction in caring is regarded as a strong predictor of the breakdown of care at home and eventual admission to a nursing facility. Caregivers are vulnerable, often stretched well beyond their physical and emotional limits at a time in their lives that is best described as a period of prolonged grief over the multiple losses that inevitably accompany dementia.

Such is the nature of dementia that family caregivers face a formidable task even if they have willingly embarked on their caring role and their relationship with the person with dementia has been a long and loving one that in the past brought mutual satisfaction. If caregivers have not freely chosen to care or when relationship difficulties predate the onset of dementia, then the inevitable strains that arise during the course of the illness will most likely be experienced as increasingly burdensome. Even if a caregiver finds satisfaction rather than burden in the caring role, it is still important for support and assistance to be available to sustain the caregiver through this extended illness. To sustain caregivers and help them to find pleasure and satisfaction in caring is an excellent investment that is likely to extend their capacity and willingness to continue to care and prevent deterioration in their own mental and physical well-being.

How to support caregivers and assist them to continue to care at home for as long as possible presents a considerable challenge to health and home care service providers. Many different forms of practical, respite, and supportive assistance will be required, as each caregiver's needs will vary and the kind of assistance required will change throughout the time that caring is required. It is centrally important that all professional and family caregivers appreciate the importance of life story and reminiscence work for people with dementia. This is because everyone's life story is an indissoluble part of the self and recalling the story is a way of owning it and a means for preserving and affirming the self. If this recall is shared with others who are willing to provide validation and affirmation, then it can become a means for promoting communication, sustaining relationships under threat, and reducing encroaching isolation.

Reminiscence work, although important, is only one kind of assistance, and workers should be equipped to provide alternative suggestions if other approaches seem to be more acceptable. Reminiscence workers may passionately believe in the utility of reminiscence, but it is unethical to impose this conviction on an already overburdened caregiver who may not share this enthusiasm. Too many caregivers already feel guilty or dissatisfied with their caring role and the increasing range of responsibilities. Depending on the nature of the needs and interests of the caregiver and the person with dementia, it is possible to use reminiscence and related activities to provide supportive social stimulation and recreation that many people in these circumstances may otherwise lack. Before embarking on reminiscence, however, it is important to make an accurate assessment of both the person with dementia and the caregiver and reach an explicit agreement about using this potentially valuable tool. Possible gains and difficulties of reminiscing with people with dementia and their family caregivers, partners, and friends are summarized next (Schweitzer, 1998).

Gains

Mutual engagement in reminiscence

- Provides a way for preserving positive interaction and enhancing communication
- Provides an opportunity to focus on positive parts of the person rather than on the illness and disability
- Rekindles a sense of unique personhood, evoking empathy and enlarging understanding
- Provides a comparison of the present mood of both the person with dementia and the caregiver in relation to earlier levels of recalled morale
- Can enhance the storytelling experience in the presence of a new audience (a trusted friend, volunteer, visitor, or worker) after the caregiver has tired of listening through repeated telling
- Allows the caregiver to become an equal participant with his or her own story to tell

Difficulties

- Caring experienced as physically exhausting and emotionally burdensome because of depleted energy and reduced motivation for undertaking any new or additional activity

- Maintaining enthusiasm when repeatedly hearing stories told as if for the first time

- Becoming defensive when stories carry implied or explicit criticism of the caregiver

- Feeling excluded or unappreciated if stories relate to a period in the person's life not shared by the present caregiver, particularly if the stories refer to an earlier partner

- Hearing a part of one's own life story told, perhaps inaccurately or repeatedly, by another person

- Viewing changes or inaccuracies in the story as proof of the teller's intellectual decline

- Being distracted from tasks felt to be more urgent

- Requiring respectful, patient, and appreciative listening that may be hard to manage

- Demanding excessive time and attention

- Presenting a challenge to long-established emotional equilibrium within relationships

- Being sufficiently disciplined not to tell the story for the person with dementia

- Wanting to tell his or her own story to someone who will demonstrate appreciation and comprehension

- Lacking genuine interest in or willingness to explore the past

- Becoming anxious to protect the family's reputation and prevent secrets being disclosed.

It must not be assumed that all caregivers will spontaneously appreciate that reminiscence offers a positive and constructive approach that they can use in their busy lives when they are already having to compensate for their loved one's failing memory by becoming his or her memory carrier. Bruce believed that considerable assistance might be necessary before a family caregiver is able to appreciate the possibilities inherent in reminiscence. She argued persuasively about the advantages of having an extra pair of ears to assist with reminiscing:

> Left alone to listen to their person's stories, caregivers often face diffi-
> cult feelings: irritation, sadness, and the frustration of hearing the same
> thing over and over again. Reminiscence easily becomes a nuisance, ir-
> relevant to the business of getting through the day. (1998b, p. 55)

She suggested that the presence of a third party, in the person of a reliable special friend or a volunteer visitor recruited for the purpose of being a willing listener, will dramatically alter a caregiver's negative perceptions of reminiscence. The primary task of listening then falls on the third person, who is likely to be less identified with the stories and less concerned about repetition, distortion, confusion, or inaccuracy. The caregiver is then free to join in, as storyteller in his or her own right, and able to participate legitimately, freely able to enjoy the experience of being heard. This raises many questions about how to recruit, prepare, introduce, and support volunteer reminiscence workers placed with people with dementia and their caregivers and at what point in the illness it may be best to do so.

Some 70% of people who develop dementia live in their own homes for many years after diagnosis. Many never receive nursing facility care except for short periods of respite to provide rest and relief for the person providing care. They manage at home, perhaps with attendance at a dementia day center and with their co-resident caregiver's assistance, frequently augmented by various home support services. Increasing numbers of people with dementia are living alone, particularly single women on low incomes (Tuokko, MacCourt, & Heath, 1999). As their condition worsens and disability levels increase, some eventually enter residential care. Others continue to live alone but require considerable assistance from nonresident friends and relatives, together with more immediate day-to-day support provided by long-term caregivers and possibly with attendance at adult day centers. If co-residing and nonresiding caregivers are to be recruited to reminiscence projects, then a supportive systematic approach is required. It needs to include careful attention to information provision, recruitment, induction, and involvement that is seen to be relevant and enjoyable and meets the needs of both the person with dementia and the major caregiver. Information giving, recruitment, and induction are discussed separately in what follows while extensive reference is made to achieving involvement and enjoyment in the description of special *Remembering Yesterday, Caring Today* projects.

Information

Introductory information about the value of reminiscence and life story work in dementia care is best provided by a professional who is already known and trusted by the person with dementia and his or her caregiver. Perhaps this person is a physician, clinical psychologist, specialist nurse, adult day center staff member, Alzheimer's Association staff member, or trained volunteer. The timing is very important as the information about reminiscence, as with all other information about dementia, may initially need to be repeated several times as well as periodically updated. It is well recognized that a single telling at a time when much bad news has to be absorbed is insufficient to influence subsequent actions. The idea of reminiscence may first be introduced briefly at the time a diagnosis is communicated because it links naturally to information being conveyed about differences in short-term and long-term memory functions. At this fraught time, the information may go unheeded, but it can be repeated again later on. Whether awareness of dementia comes in a flash or only gradually, the impact of the diagnosis can be devastating for all concerned. Emily Dickinson's poem, although probably not written with dementia in mind, captures the pain endured when processing bad news such as this.

1667

I watched her face to see which way
She took the awful news—
Whether she died before she heard
Or in protracted bruise
Remained a few slow years with us—
Each heavier than the last—
A further afternoon to fail,
As Flower at fall of Frost.

–DICKINSON, 1914, P. 681

Once the initial import of the diagnosis has been absorbed, it is a good time for a trusted professional to follow-up with further simple information about the desirability of continuing engagement in social life for both partners and how this might be achieved. Other information about aspects of dementia, medical treatment, service provision, appropriate activities, early stage support groups for people with dementia (Yale, 1995) and caregivers' support groups are necessary (Herbert, Levesque, Versina, et al., 2003). Any information conveyed verbally needs to be realistic and constructive and supplemented by simple written leaflets or other ways that account for differences in ethnicity, language, and communication skills, including hearing and visual impairments. Information about the value of reminiscing can also be introduced at this time.

Recruitment

It can be extraordinarily difficult to recruit family caregivers to support programs in the early stages of their dementia caring experience. Denial may be strong, there is likely to be a powerful determination to manage alone, and informal help from other family members and friends will not yet have evaporated. At this time, caregivers are determined to work hard to keep everything as normal as possible and to carry on as usual. As symptoms of dementia are usually already affecting behavior long before a diagnosis is sought or obtained, increasing, social isolation may already have occurred without being acknowledged as such.

A period of dawning recognition may follow this early denial. Both the people with dementia and their caregivers may experience relief once the problem is openly recognized, a diagnosis is made, and the initial deterioration becomes understandable. At this point, help needs to be focused on constructive ways of assisting in the preservation of retained abilities and efforts to sustain communication and relationships. It is important to mobilize every available resource so that ordinary life may continue while preparations are begun for meeting the inevitable changes in roles and responsibilities that will eventually follow. The person with dementia is likely to experience considerable anxiety and anticipatory grief as well as the caregiver, who will begin to realize that new demands are being made and life is changing. As with crises of many kinds, this can also be a time for positive engagement on a number of different emotional and practical levels.

Most of all, this is a time when the person with dementia will need to have his or her identity confirmed, self-esteem bolstered, and humanity affirmed by the maintenance of positive responses from other people. Opportunities to revisit the past through conversation, perhaps by visiting places of past significance and becoming involved in various life story activities can play a vital part in achieving these desirable outcomes. The needs of the person with dementia and the caregiver differ, yet both can begin to be met if mutual engagement in enjoyable activities can be sustained. Reminiscence can assist because it can bring to mind good times and past achievements as well as give opportunities for rehearsing long-established knowledge and skills. Early intervention, rather than the more customary relative neglect by professionals in these early days after diagnosis, can also reduce potential isolation and assist in preserving social functioning.

One of the most effective ways to recruit family caregivers into a reminiscence project or group is to involve other family caregivers who can speak with conviction about how reminiscence has helped them cope. They speak with more persuasive conviction than professional caregivers may be able to do. Some caregivers realize for themselves how important memory work can be, whereas others will need considerable persuasion about its relevance. A younger brother, age 82, who was caring for his much older sister discovered its value for himself:

> We are going on as usual but the years are beginning to tell more and more. Elizabeth's memory is not what it was. I have only recently begun to appreciate the value of reminiscing. For example, as Elizabeth's short-term memory fades, I realize the need to allow her to dwell on her earlier life and to recount, maybe for the umpteenth time, experiences she enjoyed in the past.

Some people with emerging dementia work out for themselves how best to cope with their failing memory and how to use reminiscence, whereas others can be helped through sensitive training, example, and encouragement:

My husband had ceased beginning discussions with, "Do you remember . . ." and now talked to me about experiences we had shared
as though advising me for the first time. Indeed, sometimes his reminiscences were lost from my memory. Other times, however, his
words would spark a memory still alive and retrievable within my
brain, giving me a chance to expand, "Yes, and that was also
when..." It was a kind way of determining whether I had recall of
that particular occurrence, without humiliation. Asking if I could remember a particular event was demeaning, regardless of whether I
could remember it or not. I felt much more comfortable when he
simply recounted an event, as it left the door open for me to either
listen to this "new" old memory or to join in his remembrance. (Friel
McGowin, 1993, p. 109)

Sometimes the best way to reach people with dementia is through the
immediate present rather than the past. Babies, small children, and domestic animals rarely fail to interest and to stimulate, as Roberts found:

[My baby son Iain] provided the best link with my mother as dementia progressed. He met her with no preconceptions, no expectations, no demands, and she saved her most lucid moments for him—
snapshots of her inner self. . . . She could sing and recite nursery
rhymes and poems learned by rote in lessons at school. Iain would sit
on her knee and be gently bounced to strains of "Daisy Daisy," in-
terspersed with tales of Jack and Jill going up the hill.
    As a 2-year-old Iain's exuberance enabled us to break down bar-
riers. . . . The natural, unrestricted affection of this toddler and his
wonderful enthusiasm to explore, prod, and poke made him the ideal
vehicle for tactile contact with mum. . . . He shared rubber blocks,
sticky sweets, and even his favorite teddy. Iain was content to take
whatever mum had to offer him and we learnt to do the same. We
stopped looking at what she couldn't do and concentrated on the
here and now. Every response was an occasion for celebration. (2002,
p. 3)

Chapters 4 and 5 are relevant to planning and beginning reminiscence work with people with dementia and their caregivers. The dementia-
specific information given here builds on these general foundations. If re-

cruitment to a group project is being undertaken, then some resistance may be anticipated. It may arise from the caregiver's anxiety and physical limitations, possible opposition from the person with dementia, and practical difficulties such as transport. If the couple is already socially isolated either because of lifelong or dementia-related factors, then it will be even more difficult to overcome any such initial obstacles to achieve participation in a group. Some caregivers fear embarrassment or ostracism. Perhaps other family members are discouraging or pessimistic. The hope–fear or optimism–pessimism balance needs to be addressed because unless caregivers believe they may gain more than they lose by the effort required to participate, they are unlikely to make the effort to do so. Similar apprehensions may also apply to the person with dementia, who must be consulted and agree to participate. A recommendation or prescription given without unethical pressure by a trusted or respected person, especially a health care professional, can tip the balance. An invitation couched in terms of "come and see for yourself" is liable to be well received and is frequently effective in overcoming initial hesitation.

Induction

As in all reminiscence group work, beginnings are crucial; first impressions are all important (Coyne, 1999). People need to be warmly received without being overwhelmed. If a person has a paid home caregiver or a volunteer visitor, then it is suggested that this person, in addition to any family caregiver, also attend whenever possible to learn how to use reminiscence outside the group at home. Embarrassment or early exposure of memory problems or other failures must be avoided. Do not expect people to introduce themselves in front of other group members or to remember other people's names. Some carefully designed, straightforward adult warm-up exercise can be used to advantage at the beginning of the first session and at each subsequent session. Pattern, repetition, and ritual are important to people with dementia so that a regular routine at the opening and closing of each session helps to establish a sense of security, familiarity, and continuity. Some groups rely effectively on using opening and closing songs or special forms of greeting and farewell as regular rituals. Whatever format is used, it should convey hope, decrease anxiety, and help people to feel relaxed and comfortable. There are countless ways this can be achieved. One of the most successful involves placing a small number of objects, memorabilia, or old photographs of the immediate neighborhood on small tables and encouraging people to circulate freely while examining them. Spontaneous, enjoyable conversation invariably occurs, and after this, people can be invited to choose an object that attracts them, sit down, and show their chosen object to another couple sitting near them. This can easily lead on to discussion in the whole group and to introductions. The facilitator can then explain the purpose of the project in straightforward general terms, reach for feedback, and establish a preliminary contract with those present about how to proceed. Refreshments turn the meeting into a social occasion, and the timing of their presentation needs careful thought: "It was after we had turned off the projector (the group had been using artifacts and 35mm photographic slides of the neighborhood in earlier days), put down the things we were passing around and the tea arrived that the real chat began." Given the effort that many couples will likely have expended in coming to this and subsequent group meetings, it is vital that feelings of pleasure, curiosity, and personal satisfaction predominate. People need to go home feeling that interesting things happen during reminiscence, that it was worth making the effort to come, and that they would like to come again.

REMINISCENCE IN ADULT DAY SERVICES

Reminiscence activities are well suited to adult day services, where it is easy to use various approaches to link the person with dementia, his or her family caregiver, and day center staff and volunteers. Work may be undertaken with individuals, couples, or groups. Reminiscence groups consisting solely of people with dementia need to be very small with a higher ratio of helpers to members than in conventional reminiscence groups. A ratio of one to one or one and a half to one is desirable. Sessions may also need to be shorter and held more frequently. Background knowledge is essential so that highly specific triggers can be used, as the more closely they relate to member's backgrounds, the more evocative they are likely to be. Vague, open-ended questions may achieve little response compared with focused, relevant discussion situated in familiar reassuring territory. Questions should not be asked in ways that resemble a test, and the person with dementia must not be made to feel he or she is being subjected to an in-quisition. Once interest is aroused and the worker succeeds in making what Kunz (2002a, p. 27; 2002b) referred to as a *reminiscence match* (defined as "a stimulation of one or all senses"), interest can be sustained long be-yond the expectations of most caregivers as conversation flows backward and forward between the present and the past.

Whether working with an individual, a couple, or a group, access to detailed life history information is essential. It is not sufficient just to col-lect biographical information. It has to be accessible and used to inform present care practice. Bell and Troxel (2001) identified different ways this can be achieved. They suggested that although detailed histories may be kept in people's medical files, it is advisable to keep summary sheets in a ring binder in the staff break room.

> Short summaries on bullet cards are another way that life stories can get off the charts and into the hands of staff who need them. Facts about persons are highlighted by bullets and can work wonders for students and volunteers or new staff who may not have had a chance to read and review the longer life stories. (2001, p. 137)

Bell and Troxel (2001, p. 136) summarized the ways in which life story information can be used in day centers and nursing facilities:

- Greet the person and improve recognition
- Introduce and reintroduce people
- Reminisce about the person's life
- Provide one-to-one comforting care
- Improve communication through clues and cues
- Use the knowledge to fill in conversational gaps
- Use the life story to improve activities
- Identify continuing constructive roles
- Point out accomplishments
- Prevent challenging behaviors
- Respect lifelong habits and idiosyncrasies

- Encourage the continuation of rituals
- Broaden the caregiving network with volunteers
- Provide material for celebration at life's end

The following case study illustrates many of these applications and shows how detailed knowledge of a person's life story can assist in establishing or reestablishing contact with someone with dementia who, unable to cope with the present, retreats into a private world. An experimental, open-minded approach is essential. The life story may suggest possibilities, some of which may work, others not, but in the process of trying, the worker comes to appreciate the uniqueness of the individual and works imaginatively to build a caring relationship with him or her.

Andy and his wife Anna were both in their mid-sixties when Andy developed dementia and began attending a day center twice per week. Anna needed relief from the constant supervision that her husband required because of his rapidly deteriorating condition and his increasingly bizarre behavior. They had been next-door neighbors as children, becoming childhood sweethearts and marrying when Anna was 16. Andy had been a merchant seaman, but once the couple had children, he took a shore job as a factory operative and was a devoted husband and father. Their three married adult children all lived close by. Throughout his life, Andy had been quiet and placid. He always enjoyed a joke and loved to play the guitar. Anna was well known for being the life and soul of any gathering, and her very close and loving relationship with Andy remained throughout his 2-year illness. When first diagnosed, he talked freely to his social worker about his family, telling stories and joking, but within a year he had stopped talking completely, even to Anna. He became increasingly restless and agitated, which, together with his total silence, greatly distressed his devoted wife.

In an effort to stave off their growing isolation, Anna agreed to compile a comprehensive diary based on careful observation of Andy's behavior. Over several days, she chartered his restlessness and agitation that revealed a consistent pattern of regular early afternoon distress. In parallel with her careful observations, Anna worked with the social worker for several weeks to compile a systematic, detailed, chronological account of her husband's life history, including information about major family events, employment history, hobbies, interests, and significant people in Andy's life. A well-ordered collection of family photographs simplified the task of compiling the life story, and Anna was delighted to make a positive contribution to her husband's care.

The day center staff then used the photographs and the detailed information several times each day to cue Andy into recognition, recall, and conversation about family members, trips, and significant family occasions. Having identified his lifelong love of classical guitar music, this precise information was used at home after lunch (his most restless period) to encourage Andy to lie back in his favorite chair, relax, and listen to recorded guitar music for an hour or more most days of the week. Because such detailed knowledge was available from the life history, it became possible to locate all conversation within familiar territory. Andy no longer needed to fear being confronted with strange general questions or made to feel a failure, and he started to talk again despite his continued rapid general deterioration. For a time, this combination of current observation matched with detailed knowledge of his life story enabled Andy to reengage with his wife, children, social worker, and day center staff. It was the specificity of the information about the past that guided this constructive intervention in the present and assisted both Andy and his wife to cope better in the time that was left than they were managing to do before using this approach. (Gibson, Marley, & McVicker, 2000)

Remembering Yesterday, Caring Today

The European Reminiscence Network has established a project known as *Remembering Yesterday, Caring Today* (RYCT) to explore new ways of jointly supporting community-residing people with dementia and their family caregivers. The RYCT project was first pioneered in 10 countries and aims to reach out to isolated people by means of reminiscence and related activities. RYCT emphasizes the positive aspects of people's lives and relationships while not ignoring pain, loss, and stress. By means of involvement in reminiscence, RYCT aims to reduce social isolation, enhance communication, and develop partnerships among people with dementia, family caregivers, volunteers, and dementia care professionals. Each separate RYCT group seeks to provide failure-free social opportunities through the medium of reminiscence within a warm accepting sociable ethos that values and respects everyone involved as being of equal worth. The pilot projects demonstrated that this multidimensional, multidisciplinary, psychosocial approach enabled family caregivers to increase their understanding of dementia, and learn new ways of listening and attending to the cared-for person and decreased the sense of burden and isolation (Bruce & Gibson, 1999a, 1999b).

Each RYCT project involves the person with dementia together with his or her family caregiver in reminiscing at home and in a series of group social events with a reminiscence activity focus. The joint group meetings especially seek to create an ambience akin to a party where everyone becomes involved in having fun together. The approach, however, does not need to be restricted to couples living together at home. It is possible to involve long-term home care staff, nonresident family caregivers, other partners, or friends, even if the person with dementia lives alone or in a nursing facility. Caregivers may be spouses, partners, adult children, paid home caregivers, residential or day center staff, contemporary friends, or "best friends." In this latter connection, the work of Bell and Troxel (1997, 2001) is highly relevant. RYCT projects encourage couples to rediscover shared fun, best described as a togetherness of jokes, rooted in the resources of a common past that can hold people together when dementia may be driving them apart. The importance of continuing to have fun together in the present should never be underestimated in efforts to preserve relationships and provide high-quality dementia care. Still being able to share fun can be the cement that holds long-established relationships together through bleak times. Bayley, the husband of Iris Murdoch, the novelist and philosopher who developed Alzheimer's disease, stressed the importance of shared jokes, accumulated over a lifetime together: "Humor seems to survive anything. A burst of laughter, snatches of doggerel, song, teasing nonsense rituals once lovingly exchanged, awake an abruptly happy response, and a sudden beaming smile" (1998, p. 43).

Characteristics

Projects usually comprise a series of approximately 18 weekly meetings used to introduce caregivers to reminiscence work and to provide opportunities for them and the people with dementia for whom they care to participate jointly in reminiscing at home and in group meetings. Each project begins by forming a multiprofessional group of dementia care professionals and arts workers, often drawn from varied professional backgrounds and service agencies, and recruiting and training volunteers. Home visits are used to explain the approach to referred couples and to collect basic background life history information. The first meeting enables caregivers and people with dementia to sample reminiscence, meet other participants, and settle in. Three subsequent weekly meetings follow in which people with dementia and caregivers spend time working in separate groups but in close proximity to each other to allay separation anxiety and to avoid the need for alternate care arrangements.

In these separate meetings, the people with dementia undertake reminiscence activities that are led by a facilitator and volunteers. The caregivers undertake relaxed, informal training in communication, including attentive listening skills and experiential reminiscence activities. Caregivers are encouraged to reminiscence themselves; to learn about incomplete, coded, and unconventional communication; and to try out different reminiscence activities. The remaining 14 meetings alternate between planning upcoming joint sessions in which people with dementia and their caregivers engage together in shared reminiscence and alternate sessions when the caregivers and people with dementia meet separately. In the ongoing separate sessions, caregivers review and plan the joint sessions, engage in their own reminiscing and life story work, and discuss caring issues. Whenever possible throughout the project, a volunteer visits each dyad at home to engage in reminiscence and to encourage the caregiver to consolidate basic reminiscing and communication skills. Toward the end of the project, future plans are made that usually include arrangements for continuing informal social contact among caregivers, volunteers, and people with dementia, such as outings or monthly drop-in reminiscence sessions.

RYCT is based on the assumption that by training the caregivers and providing them with opportunities to relate their own life stories in alternate weeks, they will be more able to encourage reminiscence both at home and in subsequent group sessions, especially if supported by a trusted volunteer. Reminiscence has the potential for assisting the dyad to recall positive aspects of their relationship before the onset of dementia. It reminds caregivers of the origins and foundations of their attachment to the person for whom they are now caring. They are helped to rediscover enjoyable, satisfying aspects, all too easily obliterated by the day-to-day demands of the situation created by the disability of dementia. Professional caregivers discover that reminiscing is enjoyable and that it reveals aspects of the person with dementia—his or her personality, residual abilities, and interests—that are not always easily visible in conventional professional relationships. This approach seeks to achieve greater caregiver satisfaction by involving them in supported reminiscence training that uses a combination of experiential exercises, group discussion, participation, modeling, and observation of other caregivers' behavior. At the same time, caregivers have their own life experience validated and their needs as caregivers addressed within a social rather than a clinical context. Key features of RYCT projects include

- People with dementia and their caregivers participate together
- Caregivers have some time separate from the people they care for
- Involvement of volunteers makes the group sessions feel like normal social occasions, and volunteers also provide additional personal attention and friendship between meetings
- Failure-free friendly groups to utilize people's strengths
- Arts-based activities to broaden and extend nonverbal communication

Customary Themes

The reminiscence themes used in the joint group meetings vary according to the interests of any particular group, but the following themes and topics, taken from the RYCT Handbook, have proved very fruitful (Bruce, Hodgson, & Schweitzer, 1999, pp. 68–103):

1. My childhood, home, and family
    - Family members
    - Favorite foods and mealtimes
    - Games and toys
    - Bedtimes
    - Being naughty and being punished
    - Childhood illnesses
    - Household chores
    - Bath times
2. My neighborhood
    - My street

- Running errands
- Childhood friendships
- Street games
- Songs and rhymes

3. School days
- The classroom
- Poems and multiplication tables
- Writing and drawing
- Talking in class
- The playground
- Favorite and least favorite teachers
- Missing school
- Special school days

4. The world of work
- Remembered dreams and fantasies
- My first paycheck
- Remembering old skills
- The working day
- A woman's work

5. Dressing up, looking good, and going out
- In my bag
- Fashions of the time
- A favorite outfit
- Watching films and talking about them
- Dancing the night away

6. Courtship and marriage
- Back by ten
- The bottom drawer or hope chest
- The wedding list
- Something borrowed, something blue
- Wartime weddings
- Photographs and honeymoons

7. Outings and holidays
- Ready for time off
- A picture postcard
- Mapping the route

- I can hear it now
- Working holidays
- The holiday of a lifetime

8. Special days and festivals
   - Many happy returns
   - Special food for special days
   - Party pieces
   - Where were you when
   - Rites of passage

The group meetings utilize many different creative approaches. These include much music, spontaneous drama, and making simple tangible products involving writing, recording, painting, and drawing. Sometimes caregivers and volunteers work as executive assistants to help an individual participant to create a personal record. A combination of intensive one-to-one attention and small- and larger-group activities utilizes everyone's talents. In one group, for example, a 90-year-old woman described the village in which she grew up to a young talented volunteer, who drew a map. The volunteer illustrated various events as these were enthusiastically recounted. This map then provided a focus for further reminiscing at home. The woman's daughter, who worried a great deal about her mother's disorientation in time and place, reported the following week at the caregivers' session that her mother "had been in her village all week," and that she had now decided that "this doesn't matter as long as mother is content" (Bruce & Gibson, 1998).

Often in joint sessions, a caregiver will partner with another person with dementia, extending the social contacts of both. Sometimes as many as 20 people may participate in a session. This may seem like an extremely large group for a person with dementia to cope with. The availability of a high ratio of helpers to people with dementia and a mixture of activities undertaken with individuals, pairs, and the whole group, however, enables substantial crucial individual attention to be provided. In RYCT joint sessions, it frequently becomes impossible to distinguish who has dementia and who does not or to distinguish between professional or family caregivers. It is as if participants are simply enjoying a sociable event and having fun.

The projects have been replicated several times in various European countries. This has enabled continuing refinement of the initial training program for caregivers and the scope of suggested activities to be increased. The training materials contained in the handbook (Bruce, Hodgson, & Schweitzer, 1999) have been translated into Catalan, Danish, Dutch, French, German, Italian, Spanish, and Swedish. The results continue to support the initial findings that this novel approach to reminiscence and caregiver training and support, including volunteer home visiting, offers substantial and consistent transnational dividends. These include prolonging pleasurable aspects of relationships with existing family members, partners, and friends; sustaining communication; and decreasing social isolation (Thorgrimsen, Schweitzer, & Orrell, 2002).

These RYCT projects have identified several consistent needs of caregivers and people with dementia that appear to transcend national boundaries. Family caregivers rarely have an opportunity to observe how other caregivers behave in the company of the person for whom they are caring. Reminiscence groups provide a rare opportunity to observe and compare how other couples conduct their changing relationships. In the early meetings, most caregivers seem very burdened and need substantial time to share their worries with other caregivers before they are able to attend to reminiscing. Facilitators have learned to provide firm direction within a trusting relationship or a whole session can be totally consumed with problem-centered talk. Once started on telling about their own life experience, however, caregivers then find it hard to stop. Separate time for caregivers to do their own talking about problems and to tell their own life stories is therefore crucial. Discussion about dysfunctional communication is very practical, and there is ample opportunity for illustrating alternative positive approaches. When in the company of the person with dementia, for example, many anxious caregivers are liable to take over and, in trying to protect the person who has dementia, speak for the person. When this happens, any possibility of the person speaking for him- or herself is quickly destroyed and fragile confidence is undermined. There are, of course, some naturally gifted and relaxed caregivers who seem able to go with the flow, take whatever comes, and demand very little in return. Without knowing, these caregivers become models and mentors. Other caregivers learn from them how not to be embarrassed by odd behavior, not to correct, and not to be concerned if the stories told are not factually correct. Caregivers slowly learn to attend to what is important to the people with dementia; to join their time frame; and to give up insisting that they conform to the caregivers' own needs, demands, and expectations.

The Importance of Volunteers

Volunteers are pivotal in such work. They augment the amount of personal attention that it is possible to give to individuals, and they bring local knowledge to a project as well as many social and artistic skills. If they can be attached to co-residing couples and visit regularly to continue to stimulate reminiscence at home, then there is a greater likelihood that new patterns of communication will be learned and consolidated. The volunteer's visit is a gentle reminder about reminiscing and the good times shared. In this way, reminiscence becomes embedded in the relationship, not to the exclusion of talk about the here and now, but as a bridge into congenial conversation, whether about the past, the present, or the future.

Projects that focus on reminiscence activities do not just teach about creative approaches but actually demonstrate and model enjoyable sociability and having a good time. They contribute toward overcoming the double stigma of aging and dementia. They are able to encourage caregivers and professionals working with them "to find the speaking touch that tells what language cannot say" (Fallding, 2001), and they encourage caregivers to find strength in sharing experience with others whose lives are becoming similarly confined.

Brief Guidelines for Reminiscence Work with People with Dementia

- Select people with care and only after making an initial assessment.
- Plan work carefully, but be prepared to be flexible, experimental, and responsive.
- Learn the person's life story in detail and use it as a working tool.
- Provide consistency of approach and take time to establish trust.
- Avoid setting people up for failure.
- Stress mutual pleasure and enjoyment.

- Slow down and allow time for responses to be made and conveyed.

- Take the initiative in reaching out and in making and sustaining contact.

- Read and respond to changes in mood, energy, and interest.

- Be flexible about timing, pace, frequency, and duration of sessions.

- Match triggers to the known life experience and past interests of the person.

- Introduce talk about familiar people, places, and experiences.

- Stress nonverbal activities.

- Utilize preferred, familiar music whenever possible.

- Believe rather than disbelieve the story being told—suspend judgment.

- Try to decode symbolic conversation.

- Avoid challenging the truthfulness of the story.

- Respond to the emotional content of what is being said.

- Be prepared to enter the world of the person with dementia and to validate his or her experience.

- Be flexible and prepared to vary your approach.

- Use reminiscence in its own right and as a passport to creative artistic activities.

- Always seek consent and convey respect.

CONCLUSION

Although reminiscence is not the answer to all caregivers' problems, for some caregivers it undoubtedly provides a very useful set of tools for enhancing communication and sustaining relationships. It can help couples and families retain or rediscover a sense of shared fun and mutual pleasure in each other's company. If professional health and social care staff participate in either formal or informal reminiscence, then they will learn much useful detailed information that illuminates the present needs and behavior of people with dementia and the concerns of their partners. Such life story knowledge contains much more than mere facts. To be a useful tool, it needs to contain information about how the person feels about the facts. If used sensitively and carefully, then the life story will inform caring activities and transform caring relationships. Group projects such as RYCT have much to commend them, but work with individuals and couples can be equally fruitful, as the case history of Andy and Anna illustrates. Whether working with an individual, a couple, or a group, common principles and a considerable number of activities can be readily adapted for reminiscing with people who are at home, away from home in day centers and community groups, or living in substitute homes.

A home care support worker aptly summed up the value of using a reminiscence and life story approach. She compiled an illustrated detailed life storybook that remained in the home of an exceptionally withdrawn, suspicious, isolated woman who lived alone. The support worker and the visiting psychiatric nurse frequently used the book to assist them in making contact with the woman. The support worker found this working tool invaluable and aptly declared that "in learning to talk about the past, we learned to talk and to listen."

Chapter 10

Reminiscence in Dementia Residential Facilities

There are many different reasons why people with dementia enter facilities but seldom are such admissions a welcome life event. (In this chapter, the term *facility* refers to nursing facilities and board and care homes for the long-term residential care of people with dementia.) Dementing conditions affect individuals in diverse ways, as does the ability of families, partners, friends, and formal health and welfare services to provide sufficient support to sustain care at home. Deteriorating health, loss of a long-term partner, or other major change in a support network can precipitate a breakdown in living arrangements. Frequently the seriousness of a person's cognitive deterioration is not recognized until the illness or death of a partner reveals the extent to which the partner had assumed major responsibilities for maintaining the person at home, often for many years. Increasing deterioration in the self-care capacity of people living alone may eventually lead to admission to a facility because of unacceptable risks to the person or to other people, or because the costs incurred in providing extended home care services overtake nursing facility fees.

Transfers to long-term care facilities frequently follow admissions to acute hospitals because of accidents or trauma such as a fractured bone or an episode of acute illness or infection. At this time, professionals may recognize the presence of dementia and recommend long-term placement. Whatever the reasons leading to admission to a care facility, the move is usually experienced as a major life transition. The move, either from home

249

Photograph courtesy of Elders Share the Arts, New York, New York.

or hospital, and the circumstances that have precipitated it can lead to secondary deterioration superimposed on the underlying dementia. It is therefore a major challenge to families and health professionals to lessen the negative impact of transitions to institutional living. This chapter explores how reminiscence, life review, and linked activities can lessen the damaging impact of admission to care and contribute toward improving the quality of life for residents, a large number of whom have either depression or dementia and a substantial proportion of whom have both dementia and depression.

ADMISSION TO CARE FACILITIES

If an older person has been living with a family, usually a daughter (approximately three times as many women as men provide care for older adults or people with disabilities), and the parent then moves into care, then the admission is usually charged with considerable emotion. Whatever the prior living arrangements were, either at home, in a substitute home, or in a hospital, admission to long-term care is invariably associated with feelings of loss, grief, and bereavement for the older person. If a family member—

who may be a spouse, partner, adult son or daughter, friend, or elderly sibling—has tried to care but failed and given up, then he or she will also have very mixed feelings. Admission arouses ambivalence at the best and incapacitating guilt at the worst (Matthiesen, 1989). At first relief may predominate as the burden of care is exported to others. The principal caregiver may have long since exhausted him- or herself, possibly having jeopardized personal health and well-being or compromised relationships with a spouse, a partner, or children. Under the circumstances, overwhelming relief may be a very natural response. Long-relinquished opportunities for rest, relaxation, and renewal of friendships and time for other members of the family or even reentry to the labor market may bring some temporary satisfaction. Caregivers who have cared single-handedly or in great isolation or who have held complex care packages together for many years will be relieved to know that their relative is assured of basic physical care, warmth, and security. If skilled help is available at the point of admission, however, then relatives may be enabled to contribute to the older person's continuing need for love, belonging, spiritual development, and self-fulfillment.

Relief is much more likely to be tinged, if not overtaken, by feelings of failure and guilt, for many caregivers have absorbed a strong moral imperative that decrees that "families should take care of their own." Even if the unreasonableness or impracticality of this imperative is intellectually accepted, it is still hard for many people to escape its long shadow. Admission to residential care from a family base is a public declaration that a caregiver has failed in a job, either willingly or reluctantly attempted. The failure is acutely felt by the caregiver and is all too often reinforced not only by other relatives but also by human services professionals. Frequently the care of a physically or mentally frail person falls disproportionately on one member of a family even when others live nearby. Notions of life space, personal territory, adult children's perceptions of how they were parented as children, unresolved sibling rivalries, real or imagined parental favoritism, personal gain, and inheritance ambitions may all be implicated, quite apart from the demands and resources of the caregiver's own family circumstances.

Making sense of the transition into care is exceedingly important because if admission is associated with chronic, unresolved depression, then quality of life and life satisfaction are both severely affected. Reminiscence and formal life review can positively influence this admission process and affect eventual outcomes in terms of morbidity, survival, acceptance, morale, well-being, and life satisfaction (Tabourne, 1995a). Haight, Michael, and Hendrix (1998, 2000) presented persuasive evidence of the effectiveness of structured life review (see Chapter 5) for elderly people recently admitted to nursing facilities. They undertook life reviews with 256 newly relocated nursing facility residents who were allocated either to a control group whose members received a friendly visit only or to an experimental group whose members engaged in life review. They used psychological well-being, life satisfaction, self-esteem, despair and hopelessness, and suicidal ideation as outcome measures.

When applying these measures 8 weeks after admission, the results showed that life review was effective in preventing clinical depression. When participants were reassessed at 1 year, there were significant differences between the control and experimental groups. People who had undertaken life review continued to show improvement and had significant decreases in depression and hopelessness and measurable increases in life satisfaction. At 1 year, Haight et al. (2000) concluded that life review prevented despair and depression and reduced suicide in older people who had been newly admitted to nursing facilities. When again followed up at 3 years, the 52 remaining survivors who had undertaken life review on admission had scores indicating increased integrity and decreased despair on 5 of the 6 outcome measures used (the exception concerned ideas about suicide). The control group who had not undergone a life review on admission showed decreased scores, especially on the life satisfaction scale. At 3 years, the authors concluded that life review improved quality of life and made long-term nursing facility residents more accepting of their anticipated death.

Cappeliez (1999, 2002) was concerned with integrative and instrumental types and functions of reminiscence and combined reminiscence group work with cognitive therapy for depressed older people in day hospitals and long-term care facilities. In 10 weekly group sessions, he focused on four themes to encourage reflection on family origins, life turning points, personal accomplishments, and knowledge of personal strengths. He demonstrated the effectiveness of using reminiscence to elicit thoughts and beliefs drawn from across the life span that influence depression and are available for exploration, reappraisal, and adaptation by means of cognitive therapy linked to reminiscence.

When families are nurtured and sustained in a timely way while caring for relatives with dementia at home, admission to care facilities may be postponed or, for some, avoided altogether. If and when admission becomes necessary, then families need to feel that the information that they can provide is welcomed and used to turn the admission into a positive experience for all concerned (Hansebo & Kihlgren, 2000; Pillemer, Hegeman, Albright, & Henderson, 1998). An example from Ingersoll-Dayton, Schroefer, Pryce, and Waarala illustrated this point.

A woman, who was born and raised on a farm where she continued to live until too frail to live independently, was admitted to a nursing facility. At meal times she consistently became aggressive, causing consternation, and attracting attention by throwing food on the floor. Her daughter was able to explain that this socially unacceptable behavior arose from her mother's lifelong frugal habit of feeding the chickens on the farm. Staff members were asked to provide a container into which the woman put scraps of food with the assurance that the chickens would be well fed. (2003, p. 420)

Involvement in reminiscence and life review can play a central role during times of transition. As in periods of national transition when history becomes important as a means of defining the nation, so in personal transitions, history defines the self, the family, and the residential community. If you are frail and facing moving from your own home and into care, then it becomes urgent to rework and represent to others an acceptable view of yourself. This task is difficult to accomplish at any time and is even harder when the person is assailed by dementia. Supportive assistance from other people will be essential at this time.

Some adult day centers and long-term facilities require the compilation of a life storybook as a condition of acceptance for admission. Bell and Troxel (2001) believed that staff members need as much information about a newcomer's life story as they do about the person's medical history. They believed this information is vital and requiring it before admission demonstrates to the family that staff members are serious about getting to know and to respond to each person as a unique individual. Few could doubt that this is desirable, but it is also necessary to consider how best to involve family members in the process so that they too may benefit. Life story and life review work undertaken in anticipation of a major change in the living arrangements of a family member can assist both the individual and the family in the process of taking stock and attending to unfinished business.

Such stocktaking provides a vehicle for making positive decisions about the dispersal or disposal of possessions and making choices about what cherished objects should accompany the person to his or her new place of residence. Objects are important because they provide familiarity, homeliness, comfort, and tangible reminders of the past and can become a focus for conversation in the new environment. Like a life storybook, cherished objects become a bridge, used to assist their owners and others who will share in the next phase of life, now to be lived in a new location. Far too often admission to a care facility is accompanied by the loss of tangible reminders of personal identity, when home and belongings are disposed of and loss of familiar people, places, and possessions exacerbates regret and inevitable anxiety about the future. Tidying things up usually means putting away, discarding, or shedding possessions. People moving into a facility are likely to feel as if they too are being tidied away. Admission to long-term care can precipitate a crisis of identity. If properly managed, however, then it can become an opportunity to confirm identity and value what is important by recognizing how the person is to be represented in his or her new context. It can be an opportunity for personal growth and development as well as for grief and regret. Retaining some cherished tangible possessions can be immensely important at this highly significant time of change (Sherman, 1991b).

Because admission to a nursing facility can have such extensive repercussions for the health and well-being of residents, any intervention that can lessen the negative impact and provide constructive assistance toward integration into the new surroundings and lifestyle is very important. Tabourne (1995b) showed that people with Alzheimer's disease who were newly admitted to a nursing facility and engaged in a life review program were able to decrease their disorientation and achieve improved social interaction and increased self-esteem. There was also suggestive evidence that somehow the improvements were stored in memory and triggered when the life review program was later repeated. The extent to which any person with dementia is able to complete a structured life review varies, but there is no doubt that by means of reminiscence many people can undertake it to some extent and it is almost always worth attempting with cooperative people. At this stage, reminiscence and life review can provide a sense of continuity, a means for promoting sociability and establishing new relationships with other residents and influencing the perceptions of staff members. Its contribution to the formulation of care plans and the choice of activities will also be very important as new patterns of daily life are established (Taft & Nehrke, 1990).

At the time of admission, engagement with others in reminiscence groups can serve many constructive functions. Webster's taxonomy, discussed in Chapter 2, provides justification for why engagement in reminiscence can be so crucial in the early days following admission. All of Webster's eight functions can be relevant at this significant time. Whether in one-to-one work or, preferably, involvement in a very small group, reminiscence is a natural, accessible means for assisting newcomers to begin to feel included. At its simplest and most immediate level, reminiscence and life story work can provide conversation to invoke the past as a means of connecting with others and obtaining social support. It can be used for intimacy maintenance at a time when personally significant people are not present but can nevertheless be remembered in the imagination. Uncertainty and change may trigger anxiety about death. In new surroundings, when role change and role relinquishment inevitably occur, reinforcement of a sense of personal identity becomes urgent. Threats to present security will be precipitated by the need to adjust to a new lifestyle and new people, yet these demands may activate old problem-solving skills successfully used in the past. The person with dementia is probably not well equipped to cope with present problems, but reminders of effective coping strategies from the past may reinforce a fragile sense of ability to cope in the present. Reminiscence can also reduce boredom by providing a constructive, enjoyable activity when other interests and occupations have been relinquished.

In addition to endemic depression among nursing facility residents, other complex behavior is frequently reported. Some individuals, for example, seriously misrepresent their former social status, wealth, and general life circumstances, possibly as a defense against their current surroundings and unrewarding lives. An example is the misrepresentation of military service by men posing as war veterans. This may be done either consciously or unconsciously in the hope of acquiring status, entitlement, respect, and attention from staff members and other residents when faced with present threats to personhood and fears about the future. It could also be a manifestation of a lifetime personality disorder, a symptom of mental illness, or a more recent defense triggered by profound anxiety associated with failing health and lost independence necessitating admission to a care facility. It is important to try to assess the significance of such claims and the purposes they serve. It may be wise not to challenge these misrepresentations, especially in front of other residents, but to seek to provide substitute forms of current satisfaction and reassurance.

TYPES OF REMINISCENCE WORK IN CARE FACILITIES

Bornat, Chamberlayne, Chant, and Pavey (1998) identified five different types of reminiscence work undertaken in residential health and social care contexts: 1) Formal Group, 2) Formal Individual, 3) Informal (intimate) Individual, 4) Informal Ad hoc, and 5) Reminiscence-Related Activities (see Figure 10.1). They distinguish between the nature of the reminiscence encounter in terms of the level of formality or informality that equates to the terms planned or unplanned and the number of people involved. Informal individual reminiscence described as *intimate* refers to the content of and circumstances in which the reminiscence occurs—situations in which personal care is being undertaken in private. These circumstances tend to precipitate reminiscences with more intimate content than is customary in informal or ad hoc group or individual reminiscence that occurs spontaneously in passing and is usually associated with other activities such as meals. This type of talk is commonly described as just chatting or gossiping (McKee, Wilson, & Elford, et al., 2003). An additional type refers to reminiscence-related activities such as entertainments, trips, singsongs, and quizzes in which reminiscence of a general collective kind occurs alongside or in association with another major activity. Bornat et al. suggested that all these types could occur together or separately. They believed that if successful outcomes are to be achieved, reminiscence work of whatever type must be integrated and imbedded in the policies, care plans, and care practices of the residential facility. Otherwise residents feel that their life stories, although encouraged by some staff, are actually disregarded by senior staff and care staff colleagues; this indifference makes people feel demeaned as a consequence of becoming involved in reminisc-

1. **Formal group:**   Most readily recognized form of reminiscence work, arranged and regular, staff time set aside, use of props, volunteers, or designated members of staff as facilitators, individuals as well as collective memories encouraged.

2. **Formal individual:**   As above but with one individual client; individual memories stimulated.

3. **Informal (intimate) individual:**   Carried out at impromptu level on a one-to-one basis at times when physical care is being provided (e.g., bath or bed times, getting dressed, meal times, feeding, toileting, medication), usually carried out by care assistant, individual memories possibly of a more intimate nature discussed.

4. **Informal ad hoc (groups and individual):**   Usually described as "chatting" when staff are "passing through" serving tea or coffee, also opportunities arise when clients are gathered watching television or at meal times, all members of staff involved (usually care assistants), some individual but usually collective memories discussed.

5. **Reminiscence-related activites:**   Any activity that is not specifically described as reminiscence (usually a form of entertainment), but from which reminiscence often arises (e.g., barge trip, making items for a bazaar, singsongs, quizzes), designated member of staff or volunteers, mainly collective memories.

Figure 10.1.   Five types of reminiscence work. (From Bornat, J., Chamberlyne, P., Chant L., & Pavey, S. [1998]. *Redefining reminiscence in care settings* [p. 17]. London: Open University and University of East London; reprinted by permission.)

ing. These authors stressed the need for care staff to feel adequately trained and supported because if staff lack sufficient confidence to engage residents in exploration of the painful memories that inevitably arise during all types of reminiscence work, people will be left feeling their pain has been ignored or avoided.

Depression is more common in people of equivalent age who reside in nursing facilities compared with those who live in the community or in assisted living facilities (Grayson, Lubin, & Whitlock, 1995; Manton, Cornelius, & Woodbury, 1995). Once again life history details and life stories can contribute invaluable information to a comprehensive assessment. Too often depression remains an unrecognized and untreated burden that affects residents and relationships with staff. It is imperative that depression is accurately diagnosed because positive responses to treatment by medication and psychosocial interventions including life review, reminiscence, counseling, and engagement in constructive creative activities can be achieved (Ashida, 2000; Coleman & Mills, 1997; Fleming, 2001; Mosher-Ashley & Barrett, 1997).

UNDERSTANDING DIFFERENT
PEOPLE AND THEIR STYLES OF REMINISCING

Different styles of reminiscing have been observed, and these may persist in some fragmentary ways even when a person develops dementia. A lifelong style may wrongly be attributed to the impact of dementia, recently acquired depression, or to present circumstances when it may more accurately represent how the person has always been. Fry (1995) identified three styles: affirmative, negative, and despairing. People with an affirmative style of reminiscing have accepted both positive and negative aspects of life. They have habitually faced conflicts or problems with reasonable optimism and continue to feel confident that they can resolve present or future problems. Overall they have a sense of wholeness or cohesion about their lives. People with a negative style suggest their life has been pleasant and gentle, they minimize or ignore painful or problematic experience and tend to recount public rather than personal experiences. People with a despairing style are painfully aware of conflicts and distressing experiences and consistently exhibit lack of fulfillment, pain, and disappointment. They seem to be captives of the past for although believing that the past intrudes and contaminates the present, they seem unable to leave it behind or grow beyond it.

Other lifelong characteristics are also relevant. Some people who wish to preserve a sense of self as they age actually resist engaging in any process that is likely to lead to substantial change of self-image, even in the face of major life transitions or traumas. Such people do not desire change, growth, or development; their sense of personal security is vested in managing to remain just as they always have understood themselves to be. They strenuously avoid life review or any other approach aimed at promoting reflection, growth, and personal development. Life review in old age may be more favored by people who feel less secure in the present, more adrift as they face various life crises such as admission to a care facility (Parker, 1999). The context of present living—as much as personality and lifelong experience, together with broader historical or cultural trends—also influences whether reminiscence and life review are appropriate for and acceptable to each person. How far these lifetime styles persist when people develop dementia is not always easy to identify. Core characteristics do persist in recognizable fragments, and talking in global terms of people with dementia becoming changed personalities is usually misleading. If we can learn enough about people in earlier periods of life through life histories, then we may be able to untangle how much of any present negativity is attributable to changed circumstances and how much reflects lifelong characteristics. Indifferent health and diminished strength coupled with increasing loneliness because of the death of friends and contemporaries sap resilience and can result in a litany of complaints and unfavorable comments about families, other residents, or staff. It is never easy to tolerate such negativity, particularly when staff members may feel the person's relatives are trying hard to sustain a loving relationship with the older person. Such negativism is very counterproductive because it alienates the very people that are most needed to fend off the encroaching isolation. Under these circumstances, it is vital for staff members to appreciate the implications of negativity and despair and to encourage the maintenance of personal relationships by every available means. Staff members need to model and demonstrate to family members and residents respect, reliability, and dependability in ways that each relative and resident can recognize. It is not sufficient for staff members to think they show respect. They must be able to convey this in ways that will be appreciated by each person. Davis, in describing his journey into Alzheimer's, put it this way:

> There is still a part of that vital person living inside that sometimes helpless looking body—a person who deserves to be treated with dignity. Just because a person is incontinent or requires feeding doesn't give some eighteen year old twit the right to call them dearie or sweetie. (1993, p. 114)

MUSIC-MAKING AND THE PROVISION OF PHYSICAL CARE

Music is one of the most important, if not the most important, means available for reaching or connecting with people who have dementia. Although much has been written about how readily so many people with dementia respond to music and how naturally music and reminiscence augment each other, many caregivers still neglect to use these natural but important means of communication in the course of providing everyday care. There are many well-documented, impressive, sophisticated accounts of how music improves dementia care (Aldridge, 2000; Clair, 1996; Rose & Schlingensiepen, 2001), but so often these accounts refer to special events or short-term projects, not to daily encounters in the ordinary business of living. Rose and Schlingensiepen have developed an approach called *Music for Life* that uses improvised music-making in residential facilities as a vehicle for relating to people with dementia and care staff. Professional musicians and care staff share, cherish, and learn through music from intensely moving encounters with people with dementia. Profound if momentary emotional links among musicians, residents, and staff members become catalysts for changed communication and more positive reciprocal ways of relating between staff and residents.

Swedish studies show how individual music-making by care staff dramatically transform daily care routines, which so frequently become sources of considerable stress for both residents and caregivers. This work, undertaken with nursing facility residents with severe advanced dementia, demonstrates the importance of using lifetime musical preferences to influence or ameliorate present problem behavior. Gotell, Brown, and Ekman (2002) based their study on the work of Clair (1996, 2000), who suggested that familiar and preferred music is more effective than unfamiliar music in caregiving situations. This view is confirmed by the experience of Whall (2002). When she played recorded bird songs en route to the bathroom and during showering routines, she achieved the cooperation of rural women living in a dementia care facility who were resisting bathing.

Because of its wide appeal and potential for easy application in many caregiving situations, the work of Gotell et al. (2002) is described here in some detail. It shows how care staff improved communication, reduced troubling behavior, and achieved compliance in tasks of daily care by singing simple, familiar folk songs and lullabies. So called "challenging behavior" or "noncompliant behavior," more accurately redefined as behavior that challenges caregivers (e.g., screaming; shouting; wandering; expressing agitation, aggression, and general confusion), was greatly reduced or eliminated through the simple device of singing by caregivers during the course of undertaking their everyday caring duties. The controlled study involved ten women ages 80–90 who had an average age of 84 years. The women averaged three years' residence in the nursing facility and scored between 0 and 12 points on the Mini Mental State Examination (MMSE; Folstein, Folstein, & McHugh, 1975). They and their five experienced, familiar, regular caregivers, ages 20–39 years, were all native Swedish speakers. The study focused on the daily morning care routines that were undertaken in a private bathroom and lasted 6–22 minutes.

The behaviors of paired patients and caregivers when involved in three different interventions were compared. The first control condition consisted of the usual daily care situation with no music. This was compared with the same care routine accompanied by background music, typically popular songs from the 1920s to the 1960s. This second condition was called *suggested music,* which was identified by means of interviews with relatives who indicated each woman's lifetime musical preferences, as the women were too impaired to convey this information verbally themselves. The interviews with relatives also established that five of the ten residents had customarily sung to their own children, one had undertaken vocal training, and another had sung in a choir. Preference for or rejection of this suggested music was tested by means of observing nonverbal and facial responses when it was played on a CD before being used in the care situation. The third condition involved the same care routines carried out while the caregiver sang folk or popular songs dating from the early part of the 20th century, including children's songs and drinking songs. The caregivers chose these songs from their own personal repertoires. On average, the second routine using suggested music took place three days after the first trial, in which no music was used, and the third trial took place nine days after the second.

Under the third condition, the caregivers sang to or with the women while performing the same routine care tasks of assisting with washing, toileting, hair combing, and teeth cleaning. None of the caregivers were trained in singing. although one did sing in a choir and the other four sang only occasionally at informal social events. None had used either background music or singing in their caring work before taking part in this study. Under this third condition, most caregivers sang songs with words but some only hummed the tunes. All of the care sessions were videotaped and after each care session, debriefing interviews with the caregivers were audiotaped. All of these recordings were subjected to careful detailed analysis.

Although in condition two (involving suggested background music) and condition three (with caregiver singing) the caregivers gave fewer verbal instructions than in condition one, and the amount of verbal communication substantially decreased, the participant's understanding seemed to increase. This was especially obvious in the third caregiver singing intervention. The analysis showed that in trial one without any music, staff worked exceedingly hard at trying to make the care tasks comprehensible to the person with dementia, who nonetheless responded to instructions and demonstrations with confusion, muteness, incoherent or ungrammatical speech, and disruptive noises. All of these responses interrupted and prolonged the care routine and required greater effort from the caregivers. The women displayed pushing, hitting, resistance, and muteness together with abusiveness and inability to name the common objects being used such as a comb or toothbrush. The women failed to understand instructions and were actively resistant, despite the caregivers frequently using the person's name and displaying a genuinely nurturing and encouraging approach.

Analysis of the second trial using suggested familiar recorded background music showed that there was increased understanding and cooperation, as if the participants comprehended what tasks needed to be accomplished. Because of the increased understanding and compliance, the caregivers reduced their amount of verbal instruction, explanation, and exhortation. In the third trial using direct caregiver singing or humming, participants seemed to know intuitively what to do. They spontaneously used the various items to initiate and complete many of the tasks themselves. Otherwise they cooperated while the caregiver completed the tasks, or else they completed a task already initiated by the caregiver without further instruction or assistance. Some of the women joined in the singing, and verbal instructions and explanations ceased almost entirely. Give-and-take was displayed, and the women expressed personal preferences and desires together with successful task completion. The singing and the words of the songs also frequently led to coherent reminiscence conversations about home, families, and past personal life experience.

This study confirmed what is already widely documented in dementia care literature about how dementia impairs verbal capacity, memory, and other cognitive abilities and frequently causes emotional disturbance, including aggression, resistance, and difficulty in achieving effective cooperation. The positive benefits of background music on mood, behavior, and communication have also been well documented. The study demonstrated the immense value achieved by direct, simple singing of familiar songs, long ago laid down in early memory and utilized as a resource in the present. Instructions were not sung as is sometimes done to achieve compliance with people who have experienced cognitive impairment due to strokes. The effective songs referred to common or universal themes of love, play, and nature, but humming without words achieved similar results. This active music-making or "music therapeutic caregiving" (Brown, Gotell, & Ekman, 2001) was the simple tool used, one that is well within the existing competence of all care staff. The researchers suggested that minimal training is desirable so as to increase staff confidence and alert them to the need to seek out information about, and be sensitive to individual differences and personal lifetime musical preferences.

The tradition of folk music and folk singing is very strong in Sweden, and these results need to be tested further both with participants whose childhood is well rooted in communal music-making by means of singing and those who lack this early musical experience. Although further replication studies are necessary, this approach is nevertheless very encouraging. It is simply founded on the need to understand people's earlier life experiences and musical preferences. Reminiscence with people with dementia and their contemporary friends and family could obviously assist with gathering this information. Even if the approach does not prove to be universally effective, if most people respond positively, it shows what can be achieved by caregivers using simple, culturally relevant, economical singing (or humming) to reach out to nurture, support, and communicate with people who are contending with profound disabilities. Herein lies hope that the authoritarian phrase "managing challenging behavior" and the directive, authoritarian attitudes implied will soon disappear from caregivers' vocabularies.

Just as mothers have always sung to soothe their tired, irascible, or unhappy children, so caregivers too, through using simple direct singing, might reach out in truly person-centered caring encounters. Any ethical intervention that succeeds in replacing incomprehension, anxiety, and resistance with comprehension, cooperation, and task accomplishment must be worth attempting. This simple, inexpensive approach could be applied immediately in all dementia care contexts, including day centers, hospitals, long-term care facilities, hospices, and people's own homes. Professional and nonprofessional caregivers might be able to dramatically change care and caring relationships by directly singing familiar, time-appropriate songs. Such a transformation is bound to decrease stress and enhance satisfaction for everyone involved.

VISITING FRIENDS AND FAMILY
MEMBERS IN HOSPITALS AND CARE FACILITIES

Continuing to visit a person with dementia who has relinquished living independently and moved, or been forced to move, into a care facility presents complex challenges and arouses many mixed emotions. Sustaining rewarding, regular visiting over many months or years can be exceedingly arduous. Success is likely to depend on the strength of relationships before admission to care, the circumstances surrounding the admission, and the degree of mutual acceptance of the changed arrangements. Small, contemporary nuclear families, competing intergenerational demands, increased longevity (especially of older women), old age poverty, labor mobility, and geographic distance can all become obstacles to maintaining close contact and regular visiting. There are other less obvious impediments that residents and family members may need assistance to overcome if regular, fulfilling visiting is to be established and sustained. A person entering a care facility brings to this major life event a whole long history of family relationships that can be neither ignored nor easily undone. Possibly, if these relationships have been problematic, admission to care presents a new opportunity for fresh work to be undertaken in the hope of achieving better understanding and mutual acceptance. Such opportunities are frequently lost; past pain and present guilt persist and continue to contaminate all attempts to establish satisfying visits.

Professional caregivers sometimes share hostile myths about the families of residents: "Young ones don't care," "Families don't visit when they think there is no money (or property) to get," "Families won't take the time these days." All of these sentiments betray attitudes quickly absorbed by a sensitive relative who is already feeling ambivalent, guilty, unappreciated, or misunderstood. Abandonment does happen, particularly following hospitalization of an older person, especially one with dementia. The space at home seems to close over in his or her absence, family life improves, newfound freedom is enjoyed, and intergenerational tensions may decrease. Families who are ignored by service providers or forced to persevere in caring until an irreversible crisis occurs may have persisted longer if help had been forthcoming sooner, when first required. In the long run, withholding flexible and timely help usually results in much more costly health and social care provision being required.

Families and the relationships within them can be very complex. Many families manage to continue visiting relatives in the hospital even if they have no intention of taking them back home because hospitals, including geriatric and psychogeriatric hospitals, command public respect in subtle ways denied to many alternative forms of care. The wonder is that so many families, with so little help, still persist in visiting, for they face a triple jeopardy: the older person's pain, the hostility of some professionals, and their own guilt. If relatives (and friends and neighbors) can be helped to establish a pattern of constructive visiting from the time of admission, then everyone is likely to gain. The foundation is best laid, if possible, during the initial process of assessment and referral. It then needs to be carried through at the time of admission and continued until a well-established pattern of visiting is achieved and the newcomer is well settled in the new facility.

There will be many variations on how this is accomplished and which members of staff are best equipped to assist with the process. However it is managed, life review and reminiscence should play a central part. The person moving into the facility and family and friends all need to be encouraged to undertake reminiscence or life story work. Many of the ideas already discussed in this and other chapters are relevant. How this work is facilitated and by whom will depend on the context of care, the people concerned, and the defined objectives. Although as always it is important to begin with the people and to respect their wishes, work on some tangible product is usually desirable in these circumstances. It becomes a proof of mutual engagement, a mark of work achieved, a stimulus for further conversation, an incentive for continuing visits, and a reassuring permanent record for the family to keep after the death of their relative.

Good practice suggests that in all facilities there needs to be an honest acknowledgment that families have a right to visit, regardless of how well or badly they have conducted their past relationships with the resident. The only possible exception might be where there is evidence of past abuse, neglect, or exploitation and even then current visiting arrangements should depend on individual circumstances and needs. If past abuse or exploitation, including domestic violence, is suspected, then the wishes of the resident, as best as can be established, must be respected without compromising personal safety or well-being.

Families should be encouraged to visit regularly and helped to manage the duration of their visits in ways they can tolerate and that are neither too demanding nor too inhibiting for all concerned. Generally some privacy on these occasions is highly desirable. To visit one person who is sick or has disabilities may be demanding enough. To visit in the full glare of a room full of frail people may be more than many relatives, particularly men and self-conscious adolescents, wish to face. Well-informed staff members will also need to be readily available to give relatives information, if requested, and respond to their anxieties.

New approaches to nursing facility care provision such as those developed by the Eden Alternative (Hamilton & Tesh, 2002) are succeeding in making nursing facilities attractive places in which to spend time and are achieving more frequent and longer visits by family members. The Eden philosophy, for example, is committed to transforming institutions previously based on a medical model of care into "human habitats." These facilities create decentralized organizational structures and a warmly welcoming lively environment in which companionship, variety, and spontaneity flourish; residents thrive; and small pets, plants, children, and activities, particularly gardening, abound. On-site child care arrangements provide assistance for staff, after-school care brings many young people into the home and promotes intergenerational friendships, and a variety of clubs and community organizations meet on site. This range of provision enables these facilities to achieve local relevance—to be at the center, not the periphery, of their neighborhoods.

Environments such as these can help to assuage the inevitable grief caused by cumulative losses of many different kinds, keenly felt by older people obliged to relinquish so many significant aspects of their lives. A poet in residence in a dementia facility captured this mixture of grief and nostalgia when he wrote down the words of a resident and returned them to her, edited but with nothing added in this poem:

GRASS

A young fella carried me
  In here, it were a long way
  And a long time ago,
  I were lying on grass …
I don't want to stay, no
  There's nothing for me
  They're all very kind
  But I don't want to be
Inside anywhere at all
  It's much too bright
  It just don't feel right
  I've not been used
  I need the fresh air
  I keep calling out:
  Nurse, nurse, carry me
  Outside to where
I were lying on grass.

–KILLICK, 1997, P. 39

LIFE STORY WORK IN RESIDENTIAL FACILITIES

Relatives' support groups can also be immensely valuable for both residents and family caregivers because they assist relatives and friends to identify with and share in the life of the facility. These groups provide a forum for information sharing and emotional support and can provide a safe place for acknowledging relief, grief, guilt, continuing anxieties, and disquiet when seeing staff coping more successfully with relatives' needs and demands. Such groups develop understanding of the ethos and philosophy of the facility and its staff. As regular visitors come to terms with their own feelings about having a relative in care, they may have emotional energy to spare for other residents who are isolated, lonely, and unvisited with whom they gradually become acquainted. A friends and relatives group can provide support when inevitable bereavement comes and may also assist its members to accept their own inescapable aging and mortality. Rather than a relative's support group being perceived by staff as a forum for airing complaints or for fund raising, it can become a valued resource that is used to equip staff and caregivers to share the care of the residents in genuine partnership (Ejaz, Noelker, & Schurr, 2002).

What residents in long-term facilities most lack is quality time spent constructively with personally significant people. Too many residents still spend their days doing nothing. Support groups for relatives can be used to develop interest in reminiscence life story work and to assist relatives and friends to acquire the rudimentary skills needed to undertake it. Life story work is not the only way to enrich visiting. Involving relatives in shared activities within the facility or in outings and excursions outside it provides mutual engagement and a focus for further conversation. Activities can be enjoyed on their own account but also should be used as vehicles for communication that assist people to make sense of their lives. Painting, music, dancing, exercise, cooking, carpentry, needlework, and gardening are just a few of these activities. Likewise, writing groups, worship services, concerts, and other events can all be shared to advantage (Everett, 1996). Knowing whatever occupation, interests, and recreation the resident once enjoyed is likely to provide the best clues to what the person might still enjoy. In addition to doing something together with the resident (engaging in a medium congenial to the other), relatives may be helped to extend their capacity for visiting silent, withdrawn, depressed, agitated, or very ill people by doing needlework, tapestry, embroidery, or knitting while sitting with them. Talking is not always necessary for a successful visit, but companionship is. Being with each other and spending time together in a quiet, accepting, relaxed, natural way can bring great mutual satisfaction if it can be achieved.

There are a number of different ways in which a visitor might seek to use reminiscence work to transform visits to a resident in a care facility. Depending on the residual abilities and level of concentration, time may need to be seized in small fragments if the details of the family history and life story of the informant are to be captured and recorded. A timeline or lifeline might be used to plot the major significant personal events or milestones in a person's lifetime. A parallel timeline can easily be added, on which are noted major national and international events to help place the personal or family events within a wider historic framework. A timeline is closely related to a family tree that draws a more extensive picture of the interrelationships within a family across several generations. All of these devices encourage discussion of the people, places, and events as the information is being entered, and the slowly accumulating record provides endless opportunities for future conversation.

Family trees can be tedious to draw but are easy to present if readily available computer software packages are used to enter the information, draw the diagram, and print the family tree, which can then be easily incorporated into a life storybook. Not all genealogical computer programs permit multiple and unconventional relationships to be readily entered. A timeline or family tree could be enlarged and placed in a person's bedroom as a device to assist staff to locate the resident within the context of the extended family and as a conversation starter. Consent is essential, as some residents and their families may not wish any unacknowledged or unconventional family relationships to be so publicly displayed. Life maps, genograms, and network diagrams are similar to family trees except that more information, where it is known, is added about places of origin, strength of emotional ties, work histories, personal achievements, and important events.

Any of these activities, including annotating photograph collections (best done in loose-leaf binders to allow for easy rearrangement if necessary), can be constructively shared during visiting times providing the older person sets the pace. Each person's capacity to recognize and identify people in photographs will be enormously varied, as will be their ability to provide information for a lifeline or family tree. So the earlier these records are begun, the more complete they are likely to become. If they can be commenced in anticipation of a person entering care, then they can serve a number of different objectives already discussed in connection with transitions and admission to care. Chapter 6 contains additional ideas about recording, presenting, and preserving family history.

Special Celebrations

Care facilities are usually well tuned to celebrating seasonal, cultural, and religious festivals and holidays. Changing seasons and specific holidays bring opportunities for special celebrations that can readily involve a reminiscence element. Although different from the kind of individual and small-group work previously described, these large-group events, which need to be sensitive to minority as well as majority cultural needs and interests, can be used as springboards for much related reminiscence work. They can also lead to more personal activities with individuals, couples, or small groups. Entertainment, music, food, and related activities serve as here-and-now celebrations, but they can also be exploited to utilize long-term memory to encourage conversation and planned or unplanned spontaneous reminiscence. Regular theme days spaced throughout the year have proved very popular with some staff members, families, friends, and residents. These are days when everyone dresses up, the facility is appropriately decorated, and food, individual and group activities, and entertainment are all linked to the chosen theme, which is intended to provide a multisensory, multifaceted experience. Associated quizzes and games, cooking, dancing, music, and neighborhood involvement is also possible. Another approach uses single events such as fashion parades, mock weddings, cookery demonstrations, dances, movies, plays, exhibitions, and concerts to involve many people. Although the primary purpose may be entertainment, there will be many opportunities for conversation about comparisons between now and then. Large events help to achieve a feeling of camaraderie and shared pleasure among residents and staff, and the families of both. They are as relevant to people who do not have dementia as to those who do. These opportunities demonstrate that people, wherever they live, can still participate in social life, behave in socially appropriate ways, and respond with pleasure to sociable occasions. They provide rare opportunities to get dressed up, put on jewelry and makeup, wear a favorite tie, and escape, at least for a time, from the usual daily routines. Special occasions can also evoke special behavior, meaning that such occasions can successfully evoke ordinary behavior. This kind of social learning is deeply embedded in people's long-term memories. When placed in appropriate contexts and given the right cues, the requisite behavior resurfaces. People with considerable cognitive impairment behave as if nothing is wrong because the old learning and behavior associated with particular social events and places are temporarily reactivated.

Residential facilities can sometimes rightly be accused of demanding too little, of having low expectations of residents, and as a consequence get too little response in return. When taken to pubs, restaurants, family parties, weddings, religious services, and social events, many people with dementia become indistinguishable, at least for a time, from everyone else. Provided that the person feels secure in the presence of a trusted attachment figure, the occasion rekindles appropriate behavior. If too much is demanded in too complex a social situation, then anxiety may develop and behavior deteriorates. Families need encouragement to take these risks, to deal with their own anxieties around issues of embarrassment and stigma and not to limit the life opportunities available to people with dementia. Such people who need long-term care require a prosthetic environment that assists them to make the most of their failing mental powers and gives them opportunities to continue to exercise their cognitive, social, and creative abilities. Residual abilities need to be encouraged and practiced within a supportive, safe environment based on good dementia design principles, within which anxiety will be replaced with laughter and panic with pleasure (Calkins, 1997, 2002). In an environment such as this, reminiscence will play a part in ensuring familiarity, in assisting communication, and, above all, in enriching relationships.

ALTERNATIVES TO REMINISCENCE

In addition to reminiscence work, caregivers use a variety of other techniques when working with people with dementia. It is important that caregivers are aware of multiple approaches because each person is different and may respond to and benefit from alternative methods.

Validation Therapy

Validation therapy is used with people in advanced old age with advanced dementia who are experiencing considerable pain from the resurgence of memories of loss or grief associated with events in their past lives. Reality as perceived by the person with dementia in the present is respected, and the underlying feelings associated with that reality are accepted or validated. The validation approach does not attempt to dissuade the person with dementia from strongly held views or recurring preoccupations; instead, it focuses on present emotional needs. Disturbances in emotion, thinking, and behavior often seem to be concerned with agitated searching and seeking for deceased parents, spouses, or absent children long since grown to adulthood. Some writers use attachment theory to account for this disturbed behavior (Miesen, 1992). Feil (2002), however, suggested that this behavior represents the struggle of the person with dementia to restore the past as a way of surviving in the bleakness of the present, which is dominated by feelings of loneliness and despair. Staff and family caregivers practicing validation therapy acknowledge this struggle; they seek to empathize and provide accepting, loving relationships and respectful reassurance.

Reality Orientation

Throughout the 1980s the intervention known as *reality orientation (RO)*, which originated with the work of Folstein, Folstein, and McHugh (1975) with older people in long-stay psychiatric hospitals, was very popular. These writers stressed the individuality and humanity of people, and from this RO developed the hope of assisting people with dementia to remain in touch with the present. RO classes or groups stressed here-and-now orientation through discussion and instruction. Twenty-four hour RO sought to involve all staff in contact with the people with dementia in providing consistent orientation reminders. Memory joggers, large clocks, information boards, calendars, color-coding, and labels were used as reminders. The approach mostly fell into disrepute because of its insensitivity; irrelevance to the people with dementia; erroneous, outdated orienting information; and minimal benefits achieved despite the effort invested. It also stressed the values and preoccupations of staff rather than the concerns of the person with dementia. It tended to encourage confrontational, demeaning, and depersonalizing practice that drew attention to people's impairments and failures, whereas reminiscence (Gibson, 1998a), validation therapy (Feil, 2002), and person-centered care (Kitwood, 1997) offer more respectful, constructive approaches that try to view the world through the eyes of the person with dementia and to appreciate an alternative time perspective.

Except for some highly specific selective applications, RO was largely abandoned until recent effective work on cognitive stimulation and mental exercise training programs for selected people with cognitive impairment revived interest. Current work that combines cognitive stimulation with reminiscence and validation within a humanistic value framework is producing promising results (Spector, Orrell, Davies, & Woods, 2001; Spector, Thorgrimsen, & Orrell, 2001; Tappen, 1997). Cognitive rehabilitation approaches that concentrate on achieving specific, focused goals that are important to the individual are now using various memory aids and simple intensive learning techniques to assist coping with identified difficulties. Woods suggested that

> The person's reaction and adjustment to their cognitive impairment may well emerge as an important factor in cognitive stimulation and rehabilitation work; those who deny difficulties entirely may be impossible to engage, and a certain level of awareness may be a therapeutic requirement. (2002, p. 156)

This implies that too much anxiety will inhibit new learning whereas too little is equally unhelpful because of reduced motivation. Again it seems that careful selection of participants is important and that a general approach that ignores individual differences is bound to be ineffective. The confrontational approach of old-fashioned RO has proved neither effective nor acceptable. If the new enthusiasm for person-centered cognitive rehabilitation is to prove helpful for some people with dementia, then it too will need to pay attention to the emotional, behavioral, social, and prosthetic environmental dimensions of each individual person's past and present life.

CONCLUSION

The importance of timely help with the transition when people need to relinquish their own home and move into a long-term care facility is now widely recognized; reminiscence and life review work undertaken at this significant life branching point can contribute enduring benefits for life satisfaction and well-being. Life review is now recognized as an effective intervention for adults with depression or those at risk of depression associated with nursing facility admission, although the evidence of effectiveness when dementia is also implicated is less clear-cut. The needs of families who have relatives living in long-term facilities also require attention, and different ways have been suggested about how they also may benefit from involvement in various kinds of support groups and reminiscence and life review activities, particularly those involving the preparation of tangible representations of individual's lives and family histories.

Much remains to be learned about how best to engage people with dementia and their families in these various processes. Increasingly, however, we understand more about the importance of verbal and nonverbal communication in continually constructing and reconstructing the life story. We are becoming more skilled in using details from this life story to inform and assist in unraveling complex linguistic communication, reading body language and interpreting behavior, then using this understanding to inform our responses. People with dementia can be assisted to communicate through many ways that mobilize their long-term memory, do not make excessive verbal demands, and utilize residual abilities. Creative artistic means, most of all music, continue to provide pathways and opportunities for many people with dementia to engage in expressive forms of artistic communication that help sustain relationships, preserve communication, and prevent deterioration in quality of life. Much still remains to be discovered about how best to harness such creativity in ways that make possible continued participation in everyday life for people who have dementia and those who live or work with them.

Several recurring themes have permeated this book. Memory and reminiscence, although appearing simple and straightforward, are complex processes that exercise important influences on our perceptions of the past, present, and future. Memory is an active, reconstructive process, not a passive, fixed repository of changeless recollections. Interactions among people recounting the stories of their lives and people hearing these stories influence what is told and how it is told. Reminiscence and recall fulfill many different functions that change over time and are influenced by present circumstances. Reminiscence and life story work along with their evaluative counterpart of life review have considerable potential for building bridges between people of all ages and diverse backgrounds. They provide pathways into imaginative, creative artistic activities that stretch our imaginations and enhance the quality of our lives, and our commitment to each other as members of families, groups, and communities. When facing the uncertainties and vicissitudes of life at any age, and especially in old age, our memories can serve as an invaluable resource that gives hope, affirmation, and satisfaction or as a millstone that impedes, depresses, and disturbs us. We are only beginning to understand why this is so, although increasingly we know how to work with people to structure reminiscence and related activities to increase the likelihood of achieving positive outcomes.

Reminiscence can transform relationships within health and social care environments and substantially extend the understanding and enhance the skills of caregivers. In education, library, and museum services as well as in many community service and arts organizations, involvement in reminiscence and oral history work extends the uptake of services, adds fresh interest to established programs, and opens up new opportunities. Talking about the past and capturing aspects of it in tangible forms becomes a gateway to constructive engagement in the present and a means of encouraging people to value themselves and in this process to value others.

APPENDIX A

Personal History Form

Personal history of: _____

Source of information: _____

Date: _____ Compiled by: _____

Preferred language: _____

Preferred form of address: _____

Date of birth: _____

Place of birth: _____

Present marital status: _____

Maiden name: _____

Spouse's name: _____

No. of children: _____ No. of grandchildren: _____

No. of great grandchildren: _____

Name of children: _____

_____

_____

Name of children's spouse: _____

_____

Name of grandchildren: _____

_____

_____

BEREAVED

Mother's name: _____

Birthplace: _____

Occupation: _____

Father's name: _____

Birthplace: _____

Occupation: _____

Brothers/sisters: _____

_____

_____

Spouse: _____

Children: _____

_____

EARLY EDUCATION

School:_____

Significant teachers: _____

_____

Friends: _____

_____

Hobbies: _____

_____

Attainments/honors/awards: _____

_____

_____

HIGH SCHOOL EDUCATION

School:_____

Significant teachers: _____

_____

Friends: _____

_____

Hobbies: _____

_____

Attainments/honors/awards: _____

_____

_____

COLLEGE EDUCATION

School:_____

Significant teachers: _____

_____

Friends: _____

_____

Hobbies: _____

_____

Attainments/honors/awards: _____

_____

_____

Courtship and marriage _____

_____

_____

_____

_____

_____

Employment _____

_____

_____

_____

Last position before retirement: _____

_____

Places of special significance: _____

_____

Reasons why significant: _____

_____

_____

_____

Special memories about children/grandchildren/great grandchildren: _____

_____

_____

_____

Special medical conditions: _____

_____

_____

Sensory impairments: _____

_____

_____

Musical preferences at different times throughout life: _____

_____

_____

Travel, trips, and holidays: _____

_____

_____

Pets: _____

_____

_____

Religion: _____

Church/synagogue/mosque attended: _____

_____

_____

Personal values: _____

_____

_____

Likes: _____

_____

_____

Dislikes: _____

_____

_____

Additional information: _____

_____

_____

APPENDIX B

Sessional Group Attendance Form

Session Number:_____ Date: _____

Leaders and volunteers:_____
_____
_____

Members' present: _____ Members' absent: _____
_____   _____
_____   _____
_____   _____
_____   _____
_____   _____
_____   _____

Reasons for absence: _____
_____
_____
_____

Objectives of the session: _____
_____
_____

Main topics discussed and materials used: _____
_____
_____

Activities and participation by individuals: _____
_____
_____

Overall assessment of session: _____
_____
_____

The Past in the Present: Using Reminiscence in Health and Social Care by Faith Gibson
© 2004 by Health Professions Press, Inc. All rights reserved.

APPENDIX C

Group Activity Form

GROUP: _____ SESSION: _____ DATE: _____

LEADERS:

COMMENTS/OBSERVATIONS: (Note absentees and reason)	GROUP MEMBERS			
1. WILLINGNESS TO JOIN GROUP				
0. Too ill (i) or absent (a)				
1. Refused to join group				
2. Needed persuading				
3. Needed reminding				
4. Came along without prompting				
2. CONFUSION/INAPPROPRIATE CONTRIBUTIONS *Rating based on answering the question appropriately. The number of comments is irrelevant: only rate the content.*				
0. Did not contribute anything/ all contributions inappropriate				
1. Almost all contributions confused/inappropriate				
2. Some contributions inappropriate				
3. Most contributions appropriate				
4. All contributions appropriate				
3. ENERGY LEVEL				
0. Doziness frequent				
1. Persistent restlessness				
2. Intermittent doziness				
3. Intermittent restlessness				
4. Appeared appropriately calm				

GROUP MEMBERS

4. TYPE OF REMINISCENCE *Positive/negative/neutral = emotion expressed by member, not content's emotion. Member must elaborate the memory to be scored as "reminiscing." "Yes/No" answers to prompts score as "No reminiscence."*				
0. No reminiscence				
1. Recalled neutral-tone events				
2. Recalled positive-tone events				
3. Recalled negative-tone events				
4. Recalled positive and negative events				
5. INTERACTION/RELATIONSHIPS *Check all appropriate boxes.*				
0a. Rude/inconsiderate				
0b. Monopolized the session				
0c. Disruptive				
0d. Said nothing				
1. Spoke only to leaders or members when prompted				
2. Made spontaneous comments to no one in particular				
2a. Made spontaneous comments to staff				
2b. Made spontaneous comments to one other member				
3. Made spontaneous comments to other members				
4. Helped others take part				
6. INTEREST/PARTICIPATION IN THE GROUP *Need not be verbal. Check all appropriate boxes.*				
0. Little response/uncooperative				
1. Active participation when prompted				
2. Active participation without prompting some of the time				
3. Active participation without prompting most of the time				
4. Active participation without prompting all of the time				

GROUP MEMBERS

7. ENJOYMENT/SATISFACTION				
0. Showed no signs of enjoyment/satisfaction				
1a. Occasionally showed pleasure/satisfaction				
1. Showed some enjoyment/satisfaction most of the time				
2. Enjoyed/satisfied with majority of sessions				
3. Thoroughly enjoyed/satisfied with session				

From Thorgrimsen, L., Kennedy, L., Douglas, C., Garcia, C. and Bender, M. (2002). The group activity form. *Journal of Occupational Therapy,* 65, 6, 283–287; reprinted by permission.

APPENDIX D

Clearance Form

Name: _____

Your contribution of _____
will form part of the collection of materials relating to the past and the
present. This form has been drawn up to ensure that your contribution is
used only in accordance with your wishes.

1. May we use your contribution
   1.1. *for public reference?*   Yes/No
   1.2. *for research purposes?*   Yes/No
   1.3. *for educational purposes?*   Yes/No
   1.4. *for broadcasting purposes by Internet, radio, or TV?*   Yes/No
   1.5. *as a source of information that may be published?* Yes/No
   1.6. *in a public performance, display, or exhibition?*   Yes/No

2. May we mention your name?   Yes/No

3. Are there any further restrictions
   you wish to place on this material?   Yes/No
   Please specify.

   _____
   _____
   _____

Signature:_____ Date: _____

Signature of principal family caregiver: _____ Date: _____

Signature of reminiscence worker: _____ Date: _____

Signature of professional caregiver: ____ _____ Date: _____

APPENDIX E

Timeline

1900
- Re-election of **WILLIAM MCKINLEY**
- Second modern Olympic Games in Paris, France; U.S. dominates field events
- The American Can Company is created as a merger of 175 can manufacturers

1901
- **THEODORE ROOSEVELT**
- U.S. acquires Oklahoma Territory from Native Americans, thousands of settlers stake their claims
- President McKinley assassinated
- The first "instant" coffee is developed

1902
- U.S. Army discovers that mosquitoes carry yellow fever
- American Automobile Association (AAA) formed in Chicago
- Barnum's Animal Crackers are introduced
- Pepsi-Cola Co. is founded in North Carolina

1903
- Immigrants forced to pay a $2 tax to enter the country
- First World Series played in Boston
- Orville and Wilbur Wright make first flight in heavier-than-air machine
- Milton Hershey breaks ground for a chocolate factory 13 miles east of Harrisburg, PA
- Canned tuna fish is introduced

1904
- New York City subway opens
- The Thermos bottle is introduced
- The hamburger is introduced at the St. Louis Exposition
- The banana split is created in Pennsylvania

1905
- Number of immigrants being admitted into the U.S. reached 1 million annually
- Rules changed in football to decrease violence
- Ovaltine is introduced

1906
- San Francisco earthquake and fire kills thousands
- Pure Food and Drug Act made law, prohibits mislabeling of all food and drugs manufactured and shipped within U.S.
- The term "hot dog" is first used for frankfurters when a cartoonist depicts a dachshund inside of one

1907
- Roosevelt announces the voyage of Great White Fleet
- Hershey milk chocolate Kisses are introduced

1908
- First Model T automobile produced in Detroit
- Tea bags are introduced in New York
- Jack Johnson becomes first African American to win the boxing heavyweight championship

1909
- **WILLIAM H. TAFT**
- Steel worker strikes in Pittsburgh
- Farmers reap unprecedented profits as corn becomes the nation's most valuable product
- U.S. ice cream sales reach 30 million gallons

1910 — Thomas Edison introduces first "talking pictures"
— Boy Scouts of America founded
— National 4-H Clubs are founded, the organization adopts a clover
  as its symbol

1911 — Rockefeller company Standard Oil found guilty of restraint of
  trade and forced by Supreme Court to dissolve within 6
  months
— Stainless steel is introduced

1912 — Titanic sunk on maiden voyage from England to New York
— Woodrow Wilson elected President by minority vote

1913 — **WOODROW WILSON**
— Woodrow Wilson gives first State of the Union address
— Henry Ford establishes assembly line in Michigan
— Federal Reserve System created

1914 — Panama Canal opened
— World War I begins in Europe
— Clarence Birdseye develops fish freezing

1915 — German submarines sink Lusitania killing 124 Americans
— Einstein develops new theory of relativity in Germany
— Telephone service between New York and San Francisco begins

1916 — Ford builds less expensive automobile, millions of Americans
  abandon horse and buggy travel
— The first mechanical refrigerators are advertised for homeowners
— The fortune cookie is developed in Los Angeles

1917 — U.S. declares war on Germany, enters World War I
— Selective Draft Act signed into law, all men between 21 and 30
  years of age must register for possible military service

1918 — Woodrow Wilson presents 14 points for post-war settlement
— One million U.S. women reportedly working in factories to aid
  war effort
— World War I ends with Germany signing armistice
— The first automatic pop-up toaster is introduced

1919 — League of Nations created in Versailles
— Charlie Chaplin, D.W. Griffith, Mary Pickford, and Douglas
  Fairbanks, Sr., form United Artists film company
— Sir Barton becomes the first thoroughbred to win the Triple Crown

1920 — Prohibition goes into effect
— Women win the right to vote
— Eight baseball players from the Chicago White Sox indicted on
  charges of conspiring with gamblers to fix the 1919 World
  Series

1921 — **WILLIAM G. HARDING**
— Congress institutes act to limit immigration
— *The Four Horsemen of the Apocalypse* is released in theaters

1922 — First issue of Reader's Digest published
— King Tut's tomb found in Egypt

1923 — **CALVIN COOLIDGE**
— President William G. Harding dies suddenly
— The Popsicle is introduced
— The Yoo-Hoo chocolate drink is introduced

1924 — Woodrow Wilson dies
— Metro Pictures, Goldwyn Pictures, and the Louis B. Mayer
  Company merge to form MGM studios
1925 — The tri-state tornado strikes Missouri, Illinois, and Indiana,
  destroying 164 square miles in 3.5 hours
— Chrysler Motor Company founded
— "The Charleston" dance craze begins in South Carolina
— Clarence Birdseye develops a freezing process for cooked foods
1926 — Secretary of Commerce reports that Americans are enjoying the
  highest standard of living in history
1927 — Charles Lindberg makes first transatlantic flight
— Babe Ruth hits 60th home run, setting the major league record
— Wonder Bread is introduced
— Kool-Aid is introduced
1928 — Alexander Fleming discovers germ-killing properties of penicillin
— Mickey Mouse makes his film debut
— Legendary gunman Wyatt Earp dies
— Sliced bread is introduced
1929 — **HERBERT HOOVER**
— "Black Thursday" stock market crash; start of Great Depression
  in U.S.
— First Academy Awards ceremony held
1930 — Great Depression spreads worldwide
— Mob wars erupt in Chicago
— The first supermarket opens
— Robert T. Jones, Jr., wins golf's Grand Slam
1931 — Empire State Building opens becoming the world's tallest
  building
— Thomas Edison dies in New Jersey
1932 — U.S. dominates Los Angeles Olympic games
1933 — **FRANKLIN D. ROOSEVELT**
— Franklin D. Roosevelt makes inaugural speech including the
  words "the only thing we have to fear is fear itself"
— The 18th Amendment is repealed ending Prohibition
— *King Kong* is released in theaters
— Ritz crackers are introduced
1934 — Civilian Conservation Corps (CCC) employs thousands of young
  people to help rebuild and maintain the nation's outdoors
— President Roosevelt signs treaty ending U.S. involvement in
  Cuban affairs
— Famous gangster John Dillinger is killed outside a Chicago
  movie theater
1935 — Severe dust storms ravage the Midwestern United States
  causing breathing difficulty, livestock death, and staggering
  crop damage
— The most powerful hurricane (Category 5) of the 20th century
  hits the Florida Keys killing 256 people
— National Labor Relations Act is signed into law, supporting the
  rights of employees to join labor organizations

Social Security Act is signed into law, providing care for older adults, people with disabilities, and the unemployed

The Jolly Green Giant first appears in advertisements

1936 Swing dancing is defined at a meeting in New York as the craze sweeps the nation

The Joy of Cooking is published

1937 Amelia Earhart vanishes while attempting to circle the globe in an airplane

Snow White and the Seven Dwarves is released in theaters

Kraft Macaroni and Cheese dinner is introduced

1938 The census shows that more than 7 million Americans are unemployed

President Roosevelt signs Fair Labor Standards Act, setting a minimum wage of 40¢ an hour

Orson Welles directs a radio broadcast of the H.G. Wells novel *The War of the Worlds* causing a panic as many Americans believe the performance to be a live news broadcast

1939 The New York World's Fair opens

World War II erupts in Europe

Gone With the Wind is released in theaters

1940 The first peace time military draft lottery is held

President Roosevelt calls the U.S. the "arsenal of democracy" in one of his famous "fireside chats" broadcast across the country

Fantasia is released in theaters

McDonald's hamburger stand opens in California

1941 Japanese bomb Pearl Harbor military base

The United States declares war on Japan, entering World War II

1942 The United States interns people of Japanese ancestry

General Dwight D. Eisenhower assumes command of U.S. troops in Europe

Enrico Fermi succeeds in creating the first controlled nuclear chain reaction

Bambi is released in theaters

1943 U.S. troops invade Italy as World War II rages on

1944 U.S. troops begin attacks on Pacific islands under the command of General Douglas MacArthur

More than 160,000 troops land on the beaches of Normandy in what will be called D-Day

Roosevelt wins fourth term in office

1945 **HARRY S. TRUMAN**

President Roosevelt dies

Nazi death camps opened by U.S. soldiers, revealing the atrocities that had occurred

Germans surrender unconditionally, ending the war in Europe

United Nations formed in San Francisco

U.S. planes drop atomic bombs on Hiroshima and Nagasaki; Japanese surrender unconditionally

Tupperware Corp. is founded

1946 — United Nations holds first session
— International Business Machines (IBM) develops fast electronic
  calculator

1947 — Motion Picture Association decides to refuse work to Communists
— The first commercial microwave oven is introduced
— Jackie Robinson breaks baseball's color barrier and begins
  playing for the Brooklyn Dodgers

1948 — President Truman asks Congress to outlaw lynching and to
  establish a federal commission on civil rights
— U.S. recognizes the state of Israel
— The House Un-American Activities Committee begins
  investigating espionage rings within the government
— Citation wins horse racing's Triple Crown

1949 — The North Atlantic Treaty Organization (NATO) is organized,
  allying the U.S. and western Europe
— The U.S. learns that Russia has atomic weapons
— Prepared cake mixes hit supermarket shelves

1950 — Korean War begins

1951 — President Truman strips General MacArthur of his command
  duties in Korea
— Government actively testing Hydrogen bomb in the Pacific

1952 — "Don't Walk" signs are first installed in New York City
— President Truman signs peace treaty giving Japan sovereignty

1953 — **DWIGHT D. EISENHOWER**
— Korean armistice begins
— Senator Joseph McCarthy accuses President Truman of Assisting
  communists, beginning of McCarthylsm
— The first "TV Dinners" are introduced

1954 — The Nautilus, the first submarine powered by atomic energy,
  is launched
— The Boeing 707, the first four-engine airliner, takes flight in
  Seattle
— The first Burger King hamburger stand opens in Florida

1955 — African Americans in Montgomery Alabama boycott the city's
  bus service in protest of bus segregation laws

1956 — Supreme Court rules that it is unconstitutional to segregate buses
— Elvis Presley performs on Ed Sullivan's "Toast of the Town" as a
  record 54 million people tune in
— The Ten Commandments is released in theaters

1957 — African Americans allowed to attend a segregated high school
  after a court ruling and presidential order
— The Soviet Union launches Sputnik, the world's first manmade
  satellite, beginning the "space race"

1958 — U.S launches Explorer I, its first space satellite

1959 — Two monkeys make successful space flight as a prelude to the
  first manned space flight
— Alaska and Hawaii made 49th and 50th states respectively
— Ben Hur is released in theaters

1960 African Americans begin lunch counter sit-ins across the South to protest segregation in food service establishments
Presidential candidates Kennedy and Nixon participate in first televised debate
Kennedy elected, becomes youngest President ever
Nondairy creamer is introduced

1961 **JOHN F. KENNEDY**
Berlin Wall erected in Germany, marking the peak of the Cold War between the U.S. and Russia
101 Dalmatians is released in theaters

1962 John Glenn becomes the first American to orbit the Earth
The Supreme Court bans official prayer in schools
Cuban Missile Crisis

1963 **LYNDON B. JOHNSON**
John F. Kennedy assassinated in Dallas
Lee Harvey Oswald killed
Martin Luther King, Jr., leads mass demonstrations

1964 President Johnson signs the Civil Rights Act of 1964 into law, granting equal rights to Negroes
The Vietnam War begins
The second-largest earthquake in recorded history hits Alaska's Prince William Sound
The Beatles arrive in the U.S.
Goldfinger is released in theaters

1965 President Johnson signs Medicare bill into law
Malcolm X is assassinated
The Sound of Music is released in theaters
Tang is introduced

1966 Unmanned U.S. space ship Surveyor I photographs moon surface
Edward W. Brooke becomes the first African American Senator elected by popular vote

1967 First successful heart transplant
Muhammad Ali is prosecuted for draft dodging and has his boxing license revoked
Tennis player Billie Jean King is selected as "Outstanding Female Athlete of the World"
The Graduate is released in theaters

1968 Martin Luther King, Jr., assassinated in Memphis
Robert Kennedy assassinated in Los Angeles

1969 **RICHARD NIXON**
Armstrong and Aldrin walk on the moon
Woodstock Music and Arts Fair held in New York
Hurricane Camille strikes Mississippi and the Gulf Coast becoming the second strongest storm of the 20th century to strike U.S. shores

1970 Two war protesters are killed by National Guardsmen at Kent State University
The National Football League and the American Football League merge to become the NFL
Hamburger Helper is introduced

1971 — *The New York Times* prints the "Pentagon Papers" after a Supreme Court ruling upholds their rights to do so

1972 — Seven individuals indicted on charges of conspiring to break into the Democratic national headquarters; this marks the beginning of the Watergate scandal
— Last Apollo moon mission completed
— *The Godfather* is released in theaters
— Soft frozen yogurt is introduced

1973 — Vietnam War ends
— The World Trade Center is completed in Manhattan, making it the second largest structure in the world
— *The Exorcist* is released in theaters

1974 — **GERALD FORD**
— Nixon becomes first U.S. President to resign after Watergate controversy implicates him

1975 — The Apollo-Soyuz space mission has Soviet and U.S. astronauts meeting in space and docking spacecraft together
— *Jaws* is released in theaters

1976 — The nation celebrates its Bicentennial (200th) birthday
— Dexatrim one-a-day diet pills introduced

1977 — **JAMES CARTER**
— Television miniseries "Roots" draws largest-ever television audience at 80 million viewers
— Elvis Presley dies in his Memphis home
— *Star Wars* is released in theaters

1978 — First "test tube baby" conceived outside the human body in London
— In the Jonestown massacre, more than 900 American cultists commit suicide in Guyana as part of a planned suicide ritual
— *Grease* is released in theaters

1979 — Three Mile Island nuclear generating plant begins emitting radiation
— The Pope makes first visit to U.S.
— First *Zagat Restaurant Survey* is published

1980 — Mount St. Helens erupts in Washington state emitting steam and tons of ash
— Olympics held in Moscow, U.S. among nations boycotting the games

1981 — **RONALD REAGAN**
— President Reagan is shot and wounded in Washington, DC
— Columbia, the world's first reusable spacecraft, successfully orbits the Earth 36 times before landing safely at Edwards Air Force Base in California
— *Raiders of the Lost Ark* is released in theaters
— Artificial sweetener Aspartame gains FDA approval

1982 — First human recipient of an artificial heart
— *ET: The Extra Terrestrial* is released in theaters

1983 — President Reagan proposes "Star Wars" defense plan
— Terrorists bomb the U.S. Embassy in Beirut
— Sally K. Ride becomes the first American woman to go into space

1984 — Olympic games in Los Angeles
— *Ghostbusters* is released in theaters

1985 — President Reagan and Soviet leader Gorbachev meet in Geneva,
    longest U.S./Soviet meeting in history
— The compact disk is introduced
— *Back to the Future* is released in theaters

1986 — The space shuttle Challenger explodes shortly after takeoff
— Microwave popcorn is introduced

1987 — The stock market drops 508 points, far worse than crash of 1929
— U.S. and U.S.S.R. sign pact to reduce nuclear arms
— "Hole" in the ozone layer found over Antarctica

1988 — U.S. indicts Manuel Noriega for bribery in an attempt to remove
    him from power in Panama

1989 — **GEORGE BUSH**
— U.S. invades Panama and arrests Noriega
— *Exxon Valdez* runs aground, dumping more than 10 million
    gallons of oil into Alaskan waters

1990 — Space shuttle Discovery is launched carrying the Hubble Space
    Telescope
— The U.S. sends troops to Saudi Arabia after Iraq annexes Kuwait
— The Berlin Wall is torn down, uniting East and West Germany for
    the first time since World War II

1991 — The Persian Gulf War begins as the U.S. begins bombing Iraq and
    Kuwait
— The U.S. and Soviet Union agree to cut back long-range nuclear
    weapons 30% by 1999

1992 — The Internet Society is chartered and 1,000,000 computers are
    connected
— Riots occur in Los Angeles after local police are acquitted of
    beating Rodney King

1993 — **WILLIAM J. CLINTON**
— The World Trade Center in New York is bombed, killing six and
    injuring more than 1,000
— Federal Alcohol, Tobacco, and Firearms (ATF) agents storm the
    Branch Davidian complex in Waco, Texas, beginning a 51-day
    standoff
— Twelve American soldiers are killed and more missing when they
    come under attack in Somalia
— Researchers at The George Washington University successfully
    clone nonviable human embryos
— *Jurassic Park* is released in theaters

1994 — Figure skater Nancy Kerrigan is assaulted in an attempt to
    prevent her competition in the Olympics
— Statistics show that approximately 56% of men and 52% of
    women living in the U.S. are married

1995 — The Murrah Federal Building in Oklahoma City is bombed,
    killing 168 people
— No-smoking rules take effect in New York restaurants seating
    more than 35 people

1996 — During the 100th anniversary of the Olympics in Atlanta, a bomb explodes in Centennial Park, killing one and injuring 111 more

1997 — The NASA probe *Pathfinder* lands on Mars and live shots are sent back to Earth from the rover *Sojourner*

— America Online announces that its membership has reached 10 million people

— *Titanic* is released in theaters

1998 — Two U.S. Embassies are bombed, killing 258 people; Islamic radical Osama bin Laden claims responsibility

— President Clinton denies having an affair with White House intern Monica Lewinsky; becomes the second U.S. president to be impeached

1999 — President Clinton is acquitted of impeachment charges

— Two teenage students kill 15 and wound 23 in a Littleton, Colorado, high school

— Businesses and individuals alike prepare for the anticipated problems associated with Y2K

2000 — The Human Genome Project completely maps the genetic code of a human chromosome

— George W. Bush is declared the president after votes are recounted in Florida; the Supreme Court ruled the recount unconstitutional

2001 — **GEORGE W. BUSH**

— Two airliners are flown into the World Trade Center "Twin Towers" in New York City, one airliner is flown into the Pentagon, and a fourth crash lands in Pennsylvania in a coordinated terrorist attack; thousands of lives are lost

— President Bush outlines his plans for a "War on Terror" in response to the growing threat around the world

— U.S. special forces overthrow the Taliban government in Afghanistan

2002 — Weapons inspectors are sent to Iraq to uncover weapons of mass destruction believed to be held by Iraqi leader Saddam Hussein

— The Odyssey space probe on Mars finds large pockets of ice below the planet's surface, raising once again the question of life on Mars

2003 — U.S. military invades Iraq, the Iraqi leadership under Saddam Hussein is overthrown

— Space shuttle Columbia breaks apart during its descent, the shuttle and all of its crew are lost

— Major power outage affects most of the northeastern U.S., power is restored after 24 hours

— California holds first-ever recall election; Governor Gray Davis is defeated by Arnold Schwarzenegger

The Past in the Present: Using Reminiscence in Health and Social Care by Faith Gibson
© 2004 by Health Professions Press, Inc. All rights reserved.

APPENDIX F

Quick Reference Age Grid

Age by	1900	1910	1920	1930	1940	1950	1960	1970	1980	1990	2000	2005
Born												
1900		10	20	30	40	50	60	70	80	90	100	105
1905		5	15	25	35	45	55	65	75	85	95	100
1910			10	20	30	40	50	60	70	80	90	95
1915			5	15	25	35	45	55	65	75	85	90
1920				10	20	30	40	50	60	70	80	85
1925				5	15	25	35	45	55	65	75	80
1930					10	20	30	40	50	60	70	75
1935					5	15	25	35	45	55	65	70
1940						10	20	30	40	50	60	65
1945						5	15	25	35	45	55	60
1950							10	20	30	40	50	55
1955							5	15	25	35	45	50
1960								10	20	30	40	45
1965									15	25	35	40
1970									10	20	30	35
1975										15	25	30
1980										10	20	25
1985										5	15	20
1990											10	15
1995											5	10
2000												5

APPENDIX G

Haight's Life Review and Experiencing Form (LREF)

Protocol for One-to-One Life Review

The life review is divided into six visits; however, the entire process takes eight visits: a primary get-acquainted and assessment visit, six visits for the life review, and a closing evaluation visit. This eight-week time span, used repeatedly in research projects, is suggested as an average satisfactory span of time. However, as in all protocols, the length of time should be individualized to the client's needs. The linchpins of a therapeutic life review are individuality (one-to-one technique), structure (life span), and evaluation (summary).

The Life Review and Experiencing Form (LREF) guides the process of life review. The LREF contains questions that were validated and added to by more than 350 participants who took part in life review sessions in a variety of research projects. The questions cover: 1) death, 2) grief, 3) fear, 4) religion, 5) school, 6) hardships, 7) sex, 8) work, and 9) relationships over the entire life span. The reviewer need not ask every question on the LREF; the questions serve as guidelines. However, what is important is to cover the entire life span and to evaluate the life as it was lived. Before implementing a life review interview, the reviewer needs to undertake certain tasks.

I. Set up a preliminary interview and begin to establish trust (people will not share their life histories without first establishing trust).
   A. Find a quiet place that provides privacy and few interruptions.
   B. Assess the individual's mental status by asking questions about orientation (person, place, time, and other).
   C. Establish a contract for six visits, 1 hour per week for 6 weeks continuously.
   D. Assure the individual of strict confidentiality.
   E. Obtain permission to tape the life review and code the tapes for confidentiality. Explain the coding process (i.e., Jane Smith = C1). The tape is helpful to the person conducting the life review to re-listen and note the individual's responses and feelings. However, if the individual is against taping or will not feel comfortable being taped, respect that decision.
   F. Assess psychological status using tools for depression and life satisfaction to determine status both before and after the 6-week life review process.
   G. Share LREF with the individual so he or she will be prepared for the questions to be asked.

H. Make adjustments for the individual's comfort and sensory problems (hearing and seeing) as stated in the directions for one-to-one reminiscence (I–VIII).

II. Visit 1 week later to begin a review of the past.

  A. As the review progresses, address childhood, family, and home for two weeks using the questions and probes on the LREF.

  B. Remember the session is not an interrogation, but a listening process, and that questions and probes are the only guidelines.

  C. Help the person to evaluate his or her life by gentle probing, for example: How did you feel about that? Would you do the same thing again? Though the process employs many psychotherapeutic skills, untrained people who care can be reviewers.

  D. Following are tested questions to guide the life review for the first two weeks. However, if the client prefers to follow a personal agenda, the client's lead should be followed until the client has exhausted the subject to his or her satisfaction.

Haight's Life Review and Experiencing Form (LREF)

Begin Sessions 1 & 2, which cover the childhood and adolescent years (after a pre-intervention session).

  A. Childhood

    1. What is the very first thing you can remember in your life? Go as far back as you can.
    2. What other things can you remember about when you were very young?
    3. What was life like for you as a child?
    4. What were your parents like? What were their weaknesses, strengths?
    5. Did you have any brothers or sisters?
    6. Did someone close to you die when you were growing up?
    7. Did someone important to you go away?
    8. Do you ever remember being very sick?
    9. Do you remember having an accident?
    10. Do you remember being in a very dangerous situation?
    11. Was there anything that was important to you that was lost or destroyed?
    12. Was church a large part of your life?
    13. Did you enjoy being a child?

B. Adolescence

    1. When you think about yourself and your life as a teenager, what is the first thing you can remember about that time?

    2. What other things stand out in your mind about being a teenager?

    3. Who were the important people for you? Tell me about them. Tell me about parents, brothers, sisters, friends, teachers, those you were especially close to, those you admired, those you wanted to be like.

    4. Did you attend church and youth groups?

    5. Did you go to school? What was the meaning for you?

    6. Did you work during these years?

    7. Tell me of any hardships you experienced at this time.

    8. Do you remember feeling that there wasn't enough food or necessities of life as a child or adolescent?

    9. Do you remember feeling left alone, abandoned, not having enough love or care as a child or adolescent?

    10. What were the pleasant things about your adolescence?

    11. What was the most unpleasant thing about your adolescence?

    12. All things considered, would you say you were happy or unhappy as a teenager?

    13. Do you remember your first attraction to another person?

    14. How did you feel about sexual activities and your own sexual identity?

C. Family and Home

    1. How did your parents get along?

    2. How did other people in your house get along?

    3. What was the atmosphere in your home?

    4. Were you punished as a child? For what? Who did the punishing? Who was "the boss"?

    5. When you wanted something from your parents, how did you go about getting it?

    6. What kind of person did your parents like the most? The least?

    7. Who were you closest to in your family?

    8. Who in your family were you most like? In what way(s)?

III. Sessions 3 & 4 cover the adult years. The individual may want to spend more than 2 weeks discussing the adult years. This may be because this is the time of life when the individual made the most life decisions (and possibly the most mistakes). In such a case, the reviewer can be flexible about the amount of time spent, but it is wise to keep it to a minimum of two hours.

A. Adulthood

1. Now let's move to your life as an adult, starting when you were in your twenties up until today. Tell me of the most important events that happened in your adulthood.

2. What place did religion play in your life?

3. What was life like in your twenties and thirties?

4. What kind of person were you? What did you enjoy?

5. Tell me about your work. Did you enjoy your work? Did you earn an adequate living? Did you work hard during these years? Were you appreciated?

6. Did you form significant relationships with other people?

7. Did you marry?

(yes)   What kind of person was your spouse?

(no)   Why not?

8. Do you think marriages get better or worse over time? Were you married more than once?

9. On the whole, would you say you had a happy or unhappy marriage?

10. Was sexual intimacy important to you?

11. Did you want children? Tell me your thoughts about raising a child.

12. What were the main difficulties you encountered during your adult years?

a. Did someone close to you die? Go away?

b. Were you ever sick? Have an accident?

c. Did you move often? Change jobs?

d. Did you ever feel alone? Abandoned?

e. Did you ever feel need?

IV. Sessions 5 covers the summary portion of the life review and furthers the evaluation of life. During this portion of the life review, the individual integrates his or her life and puts life events in their proper place. A summing up of life events occurs and the individual achieves a balance and integration of those events that were troublesome before the life review. There is a freeing quality in completing a life review that allows the individual to move on to live more fully.

A.   Summary and Evaluation by the Individual

    1.   On the whole, what kind of life do you think you've had?

    2.   If everything was the same, would you live your life over again?

    3.   If you were going to live your life over again, what would you change? Leave unchanged?

    4.   We've been talking about your life for quite some time now. Let's discuss your overall feelings and ideas about your life. What would you say the main satisfactions in your life have been? Try for three. Why were they satisfying?

    5.   Everyone has disappointments. What have been the main disappointments in your life?

    6.   What was the hardest thing you had to face in your life? Please describe it.

    7.   What was the happiest period of your life?

    8.   What was the unhappiest period of your life? Why is your life more happy now?

    9.   What was the proudest moment in your life?

    10.   If you could stay the same age all your life, what age would you choose? Why?

    11.   How do you think you've made out in life?

    12.   Let's talk a little about you as you are now. What are the best things about the age you are now?

    13.   What are the worst things about being the age you are now?

    14.   What are the most important things in your life today?

    15.   What do you hope will happen as you grow older?

    16.   What do you fear will happen as you grow older?

    17.   Have you enjoyed participating in this review of your life?

V.   The eighth visit is the termination and the purpose is a final interview evaluation by the reviewer.

A.   Tests of depression and well being such as the Geriatric Depression Scale (GDS) and the Life Satisfaction Index (LSIA) serve as valuable evaluation tools, particularly if they were given before and after the life review. When given as pre- and post-tests, the reviewer can state the outcomes and evaluate how the life review has changed the individual. Outcomes are of prime importance in evaluating individual care and interventions.

B.   The reviewer and the individual terminate; usually both will have grown in the 8-week period.

C.   To date, research has shown that the positive effects of a life review last for approximately one year. There is no known data as yet that directs one to repeat a life review or perhaps investigate a session that will in itself recall the benefits of a life review. That remains a question for future research.

From Haight, B.K. (1991). Reminiscing: The state of the art as a basis for practice. International *Journal of Aging and Human Development,* 33(1), 1–32; reproduced by permission.

References

Aday, R.A., & Aday, K.L. (1997). *Group work with the elderly: An annotated bibliography.* West Port, CT: Greenwood Publishing Group Inc.

Aldridge, D. (2000). *Music therapy in dementia cares.* London: Jessica Kingsley Publishers.

Allan, K. (2002). *Finding your way: Explorations in communication.* Stirling, Scotland: University of Stirling, Dementia Development Centre.

American Association of Retired People. (1993). *Inter-generational projects ideas book.* Washington, DC: Author.

American Psychiatric Association. (1994). *Diagnostic and statistical manual of mental disorders (DSM-IV).* Washington, DC: Author.

American Psychiatric Association. (2000). *Diagnostic and statistical manual of mental disorders (DSM-IV-TR).* Washington, DC: Author

American Psychological Association. (1998). Guidelines for the evaluation of dementia and age-related cognitive decline. *American Psychologist, 53,* 1298–1303.

Ashida, S. (2000). The effect of reminiscence music therapy sessions on changes in depressive symptoms in elderly persons with dementia. *Journal of Music Therapy, 37*(3), 170–182.

Atkinson, D. (1994). "I got put away": Group-based reminiscence with people with learning difficulties. In J. Bornat (Ed.), *Reminiscence reviewed: Perspectives, evaluations and achievements* (105–115). Birkshire Buckingham, England: Open University Press.

Atkinson, D., Kim, A., Ruelas, S., & Lin, A. (1999). Ethnicity and attitudes toward facilitated reminiscence. *Journal of Mental Health Counseling, 21*(1), 66–81.

Badderley, A., Wilson, B., & Watts, F. (1995). *Handbook of memory disorders.* New York: John Wiley & Sons.

Ballinger, S. (2001). *The recovered memory debate.* Australian Psychological Society, unpublished conference paper.

Basting, A.D. (1998). *Time slips project.* Retrieved November 2002, from http://www.timeslips.org

Basting, A.D. (2001). *The stages of age.* Ann Arbor, MI: University of Michigan Press.

Basting, A., & Killick, J. (2003). *The arts and dementia care: A resource guide.* New York: Center for Creative Aging.

Bayley, J. (1998). *Iris: A memoir of Iris Murdoch.* London: Gerald Duckworth & Co.

Beck, C. (1999). Enabling and empowering certified nursing assistants for quality dementia care. *International Journal of Geriatric Society, 14,* 197–212.

Beecham, M.H., Anthony, C., & Kurtz, J. (1998). A life review interview guide: A structured systems approach to information gathering. *International Journal of Aging and Human Development, 46*(1), 25–44.

Bell, V., & Troxel, D. (1997). *The best friends approach to Alzheimer's care.* Baltimore: Health Professions Press.

Bell, V., & Troxel, D. (2001). *The best friends staff: Building a culture of care in Alzheimer's programs.* Baltimore: Health Professions Press.

Bender, M. (1994). An interesting confusion: What can we do with reminiscence groupwork? In J. Bornat (Ed.), *Reminiscence reviewed: Evaluation, achievements and perspectives* (32–45). Birkshire Buckingham, England: Open University Press.

Bender, M. (2002). In L. Thorgrimsen, L. Kennedy, C. Douglas, C. Garcia, & M. Bender (Eds.). The group activity form—Is it valid and reliable? *Journal of Occupational Therapy, 65*(6), 283–287.

Bender, M., Baukham, P., & Norris, A. (1999). *The therapeutic purposes of reminiscence.* London: Sage Publications Ltd.

Bennett, O. (1995). Oral history as a tool for overseas development. *Oral history, 23*(1), 89–92.

Berman-Rossi. (Ed.). (1994). *The collected writings of William Schwartz.* Itasca, Illinois: F.E. Peacock Publishers Inc.

Betjamin, J. (1963). Summoned by bells. *Oxford book of quotations.* Oxford, England: Oxford University Press.

Beverly, J. (1996). *Treating traumatized children: New insights and creative interventions.* New York: Free Press.

Birren, J.E. (1993). Understanding life backwards: Reminiscing for a better old age. In R.N. Butler & K. Kiikuni, (Eds.). Who is responsible for my old age? (18–29). New York: Springer-Verlag.

Birren, J.E., & Birren, B.A. (1996). Autobiography: Exploring the self and encouraging development. In J.E. Birren, G.M. Kenyon, J.E. Ruth, J. Schroots, & T. Svensson. (Eds.), *Aging and biography* (283–300). New York: Springer-Verlag.

Birren, J.E., & Cochran, K.N. (2001). *Telling the stories of life through guided autobiography groups.* Baltimore: The Johns Hopkins University Press.

Birren, J.E., & Deutchman, D.E. (1991). *Guiding autobiography groups for older adults: Exploring the fabric of life.* Baltimore: The Johns Hopkins University Press.

Bishop, E. (1991). The art of losing. In S. Heaney, *The redress of poetry.* London: Faber & Faber Ltd.

Bluck, S., & Levine, L.J. (1998). Reminiscence as autobiographical memory. *Ageing and Society, 18*(2), 185–208.

Boal, A. (1995). *The rainbows of desire: The Boal method of theatre and therapy.* New York: Routledge.

Bornat, J. (Ed.). (1994). *Reminiscence reviewed: Perspectives, evaluations and achievements.* Birkshire, England: Open University Press.

Bornat, J. (1998). Reminiscence reviewed. In P. Schweitzer, (Ed.), *Reminiscence in dementia care* (43–49). London: Age Exchange.

Bornat, J. (2001). Reminiscence and oral history: Parallel universes or shared endeavours. *Ageing and Society, 21*(2), 32–35.

Bornat, J. (2002). Reminiscence and oral history: Comparisons across parallel universes. In J.D. Webster, & B.K. Haight (Eds.), *Critical advances in reminiscence work: From theory to applications* (33–43). New York: Springer-Verlag.

Bornat, J., Chamberlayne, P., Chant, L., & Pavey, S. (1998). *Redefining reminiscence in care settings.* London: University of East London, Centre for Biography in Social Policy.

Browne, V. (2001). Seamus Heaney: Still finding himself in his poetry. *Irish Times, News features, 31,* (p.10).

Brooker, D.J.R., & Duce, L. (2000). Well-being and activity in dementia: A comparison of group reminiscence therapy, structured goal-directed activity and unstructured time. *Aging and Mental Health, 4,* 356–360.

Brown, S., Gotell, E., & Ekman, S. (2001). Music-therapeutic caregiving: The necessity of active music-making in clinical care. *Arts and Psychotherapy, 28,* 125–135.

Bruce, E. (1998a). Holding on to the story: Older people, narrative, and dementia. In G. Roberts, & J. Holmes (Eds.), *Healing stories* (181–205). Oxford, England: Oxford University Press.

Bruce, E. (1998b). Reminiscence and family carers. In P. Schweitzer, (Ed.), *Reminiscence in dementia care* (50–57). London, England: Age Exchange.

Bruce, E., & Gibson, F. (1998). Remembering yesterday, caring today: Evaluators' report. *Conference Papers.* London: Age Exchange.

Bruce, E., & Gibson, F. (1999a). Stimulating communication: Project evaluation part 1. *Journal of Dementia Care, 7*(2), 18–19.

Bruce, E., & Gibson, F. (1999b). Remembering yesterday: Having fun, making friends: Project evaluation part 2. *Journal of Dementia Care, 7*(3), 28–29.

Bruce, E. Hodgson, S., & Schweitzer, (1999). *Reminiscing with people with dementia; A handbook for carers.* London, England: Age Exchange. (Catalan, Danish, Dutch, French, German, Italian, Spanish and Swedish translations available)

Buchanan, K., & Middleton, D. (1995). Voices of experience: Talk, identity and membership in reminiscence groups. *Ageing and Society, 15*(4), 457–491.

Buhler, C. (1968). The course of life as a psychological problem. *Human Development, 11,* 184–200.

Burns, A., Dening, T., & Lawlor, B. (2002). *Clinical guidelines in old age psychiatry.* London, England: Martin Dunitz Ltd.

Burnside, I. (1984). *Working with the elderly: Group process and techniques.* Boston: Jones and Bartlett Publishers Inc.

Burnside, I. (1990). Reminiscence: An independent nursing intervention for the elderly. *Issues in Mental Health Nursing, 11,* 33–48.

Burnside, I. (1996). Life review and reminiscence in nursing practice. In J.E. Birren, G.M. Kenyon, J.E. Ruth, J. Schroots, & T. Svensson, (Eds.), *Aging and biography* (283–300). New York: Springer-Verlag.

Burnside, I. & Schmidt, M. G. (1994). *Working with the elderly: Group process and techniques.* Boston: Jones and Bartlett Publishers Inc.

Butler, R.N. (1963). The life review: An interpretation of reminiscence in the aged. *Psychiatry, 26,* 65–76.

Butler, R.N. (1995). The life review. In B.K. Haight & J.D. Webster (Eds.), *The art and science of reminiscence* (xvii–xxii). Washington, DC: Taylor & Francis Inc.

Butler, R.N. (1996). Life review. In J.E. Birren (Ed.). *Encyclopedia of gerontology: Age, aging and the aged* (53–58). New York: Springer-Verlag.

Butler, R.N. (1999). Thoughts on the life review. Pioneers in reminiscence and life review panel presentation. *Reminiscence and life review conference papers, (36).* Superior, WI: University of Wisconsin–Superior.

Calkins, M. (1997). Home is more than carpeting and chintz. *Nursing Homes, 44*(6), 20–25.

Calkins, M.P. (Ed.). (2002). *Creating successful dementia care settings.* Baltimore: Health Professions Press.

Cappeliez, P. (1999). Cognitive-reminiscence therapy for depressed older adults. *Reminiscence and life review conference papers,* (37–39). Superior, WI: University of Wisconsin–Superior.

Cappeliez, P. (2002). Cognitive-reminiscence therapy for depressed older adults in day hospital and long-term care. In J.D. Webster, & B.K. Haight, (Eds.), *Critical advances in reminiscence work: From theory to applications* (300–313). New York: Springer-Verlag.

Chamberlain, M. (1997). *Narratives of exile and return.* London: Macmillan Publishers Ltd.

Chandler, S., & Ray, R. (2002). New meanings for old tales: A discourse-based study of reminiscence and development in late life. In. J.D. Webster, & B.K. Haight (Eds.), *Critical advances in reminiscence work: From theory to applications* (76–93). New York: Springer-Verlag.

Chapman, S.A. (1998). The power of reminiscence. *Alberta Museums Review, 24*(2), 40–44.

Clair, A.A. (1996). *Therapeutic uses of music with older adults.* Baltimore: Health Professions Press.

Clair, A.A. (2000). The importance of singing with elderly patients. In D. Aldridge (Ed.), *Music therapy in dementia care: More new voices* (81–101). London: Jessica Kingsley Publishers.

Clark, K. (1981). *Moments of vision.* London: John Murray Ltd.

Clark, M.M. (2002). *Oral History, 30*(1), 26.

Clarke, A., Hanson, E.J., & Ross, H. (2003). Seeing the person behind the patient: Enhancing the care of older people using a biographical approach. *Journal of Clinical Nursing, 12,* 697–706.

Clements, J. (1975). *Chronology of the United States.* New York: McGraw-Hill.

Cohen, C.A., Colantonio, A., & Vernich, L. (2002). Positive aspects of caregiving: Rounding out the caregiver experience. *International Journal of Geriatric Psychiatry, 17*(2), 184–188.

Cohen, G. (2000). *The creative age: Awakening human potential in the second half of life.* New York: HarperCollins.

Cohen, G., & Taylor, S. (1998). Reminiscence and ageing. *Ageing and Society, 18*(5), 601–610.

Cole, D.B. (1968). *Handbook of American history.* San Diego: Harcourt Brace Jovanovich.

Coleman, P. (2000). *Village elders.* Champaign, IL: University of Illinois Press.

Coleman, P.G. (1974). Measuring reminiscence characteristics from conversation as adaptive features of old age. *International Journal of Aging and Human Development, 5,* 281–294.

Coleman, P. (1986). *Ageing and reminiscence processes.* New York: John Wiley and Sons.

Coleman, P.G. (1999). Creating a life story: The task of reconciliation. *Gerontologist,* 133–139.

Coleman, P.G., Hautamaki, A., & Podolskij, A. (2002). Trauma, reconciliation, and generativity: Stories told by European war veterans. In J.D. Webster, & B.K. Haight (Eds.). *Critical advances in reminiscence work: From theory to applications* (218–232). New York: Springer-Verlag.

Coleman, P.G. and Mills, M.A. (1997). Listening to the story. Life review and the painful past in day and residential care settings. In L. Hunt, M.M. Marshall, & C. Rowlings (Eds.), *Past trauma in late life: European perspectives on therapeutic work with older people* (171–183). London: Jessica Kingsley Publishers.

Conway, M.A. (1996). Autobiographical knowledge and autobiographical memories. In D.C. Rubin (Ed.), *Remembering our past: Studies in autobiographical memory* (67–93). Cambridge, England: Cambridge University Press.

Cook E. (1998). Effects of reminiscence on life satisfaction of elderly female nursing home residents. *Health Care for Women's International, 19,* 109–118.

Cooley, R.N. (1999). Spiritual life review with medically challenged elders. *Reminiscence and life review conference papers,* 41–44. Superior, WI: University of Wisconsin–Superior.

Cotman, C. (1990). A personal view from a researcher. *Memories in the making '90.* Orange County, CA: Alzheimer's Association.

Coyne, R.K. (1999). *Failures in group work: How we can learn from our mistakes.* Thousand Oaks, CA: Sage Publications.

Crane, M. (1995). A reminiscence group for older homeless men. *PSIGE Newsletter, 54,* 39–40 London: British Psychological Society.

Cross, K.P. (1991). *Adults as learners.* San Francisco: Jossey-Bass.

Crutch, S., Isaacs, R., & Rossor, M. (2001). Art and the brain. *Alzheimer's Newsletter,* 4–5.

Darian-Smith, K., & Hamilton, P. (1994). *Memory and history in twentieth century Australia.* Melbourne: Oxford University Press.

Davis, R. (1993). *My journey into Alzheimer's Disease.* Carol Stream, IL: Tyndale House.

De Baggio, T. (2002). Losing my mind: An intimate look at life with Alzheimer's. New York: Free Press.

De Botton, A. (1997). *How Proust can change your life.* London: Picador.

De Medeiros, M. (2000 February 9). Turning to autobiography for emotional growth in old age. The share your life story group, Galveston Texas. *New York Times,* A14.

Denis, P. & Makiwane, N. (2003). Stories of love, pain and courage: AIDS orphans and memory boxes. *Oral History, 31*(2), 66–74.

De Souza, E.M. (1995). Generation to generation: A Brazilian experience. *Reminiscence, 10,* 4–5.

De Souza, E.M. (2003). An intergenerational reminiscence research programme in Brazil. *Reminiscence Exchange, 2,* 17.

De Vries, B., & Watt, D. (1996). A lifetime of events: Age and gender variations in the life story. *International Journal of Aging and Human Development, 42*(2), 81–102.

Dickinson, E. (1970). 1667. In T. Johnson, (Ed.), *The complete poems of Emily Dickinson.* London: Faber & Faber Ltd.

Dobrof, R. (1984). Introduction: A time for reclaiming the past. In M. Kaminsky (Ed.), *The uses of reminiscence: New ways of working with older adults.* New York: Haworth Press.

Dormandy, T. (1996). Creative genius in old age. In J.M. Allen, Y.A. Barnett, F. Gibson, & P.G. McKenna (Eds.), *Celebrating age* (47–55). Hants, England: Avebury Publishing Ltd.

Dormandy, T. (2001). *Old masters: Great artists in old age.* London: The Hambledon Press.

Droes, R.M. (1997). Psychosocial treatment for demented patients: An overview of methods and effects. In B.M.L. Miesen and G.M.M. Jones (Eds.), *Care-giving in dementia: Research and applications* (127–148). London: Routledge.

Dunn, P.H., Haight, B.K. (2002). Power dynamics in the interpersonal life review dyad. *Journal of Geriatric Psychiatry, 35*(1), 77–92.

Ejaz, F.K., Noelker, L.S., & Schurr, D. (2002). Family satisfaction with nursing home care for relatives with dementia. *Journal of Applied Gerontology, 21*(3), 368–384.

Elders Share the Arts. (1994). *Intergenerational training manual.* Brooklyn: Author.

Eliot, T.S. (1969). Four quartets. In Norton, *The complete poems and plays.* London: Faber & Faber Ltd.

Erdelyi, M.H. (1996). *The recovery of unconscious memories.* Chicago: University of Chicago Press.

Erikson, E. (1950). *Childhood and society.* New York: W.W. Norton & Company Inc.

Erikson, E.H. (1982). *The life cycle completed.* New York: W.W. Norton & Company Inc.

Erikson, E.H., Erikson, J.M., & Kivnick, H.Q. (1986). *Vital involvement in old age.* New York: Norton.

Everett, D. (1996). *Forget me not: The spiritual care of people with Alzheimer's.* Edmonton: Inkwell Press.

Fallding, H. (2001). *To a wife with Alzheimer's disease.* (unpublished).

Fast, B., & Chapin, R. (2000). *Strengths-based care management for older adults.* Baltimore: Health Professions Press.

Feil, N. (2002). *The validation breakthrough: Simple techniques for communicating with people with Alzheimer's-type dementia.* Baltimore: Health Professions Press.

Feinberg, R.I. (1996). The use of reminiscence groups to facilitate the telling of life stories by elderly Russian Jewish immigrants. *Smith College Studies in Social Work, 67*(1), 39–51.

Ferguson, M. (2000). Memory lane: Setting up a reminiscence group. *Museum Ireland, 10,* 36–38.

Finkel, I., & Burns, A. (2000). Behavioral and psychological symptoms of dementia: A clinical research update. *International Psychogeriatrics, 12* (Supplement 1).

Finkel, S.I., Cost de Silva, J., Cohen, G.D., et al. (1996). Behavioral and psychological signs and symptoms of dementia: A consensus statement on current knowledge and implications for research and treatment. *International Psychogeriatrics, 8* (Supplement 3), 497–500.

Fischer, L. (1994). Qualitative research as art and science. In J.F. Gubrium and A. Sanker (Eds.), *Qualitative methods in aging research.* Thousand Oaks, CA: Sage Publications.

Fisher, B.J. (1995). Successful aging, life satisfaction, and generativity in later life. *International Journal of Aging and Human Development, 41*(3), 329–350.

Fivush, R., & Reese, E. (2002). Reminiscing and relating: The development of parent-child talk about the past. In J.D. Webster, & B.K. Haight (Eds.), *Critical advances in reminiscence work: From theory to application* (109–122). New York: Springer-Verlag.

Fleming, R. (2001). *Challenge depression: A manual to help staff identify and reduce depression in aged care facilities.* Canberra, Australia: Commonwealth Department of Health and Ageing.

Folstein, M.F., Folstein, S.E., & McHugh, P. (1975). 'Mini mental state': A practical method for grading the cognitive state of patients for the clinician. *Journal of Psychiatric Research, 12,* 189–198.

Forster, S. (1998). Kingston Center reminiscence program for older people. In P. Schweitzer (Ed.), *Reminiscence in dementia care* (54–63). London: Age Exchange.

Freeman, M. (1993). *Re-writing the self: History, memory, narrative.* London: Routledge.

Frenkel-Brunswick, E. (1963). Adjustments and re-orientation in the course of the life span. In R.G. Kuhlen and G.G. Thompson (Eds.), *Psychological studies of human development.* New York: Appleton.

Friel McGowin, D. (1993). *Living in the labyrinth: A personal journey through the maze of Alzheimer's.* San Francisco: Elder Books.

Fry, P.S. (1995). A conceptual model of socialization and agentic trait factors that mediate the development of reminiscence styles and their health outcomes. In B.K. Haight and J.D. Webster (Eds.), *The art and science of reminiscing: Theory, research, methods and applications* (49–60). Washington, DC: Taylor and Francis Inc.

Fry, P.S., & Barker, L.A. (2002). Female survivors of abuse and violence: The influence of storytelling reminiscence on perceptions of self-efficacy, ego strength, and self-esteem. In J.D. Webster, & B.K. Haight (Eds.), *Critical advances in reminiscence work: From theory to applications* (197–217). New York: Springer-Verlag.

Funder, D., Parke, R., Tomlinson-Keasey, C., & Widerman, K. (1993). *Studying lives through time: Personality and development.* Washington, DC: American Psychological Association.

Garland, J. & Garland, C. (2001). *Life review in health and social care: A practitioner's guide.* New York: Routledge.

Gearing, B., & Coleman, P. G. (1996). Biographical assessment in community care. In J. Birren, G.M. Kenyon, J.E. Ruth, J.J. Schroots, & T. Svensson (Eds.), *Aging and biography: Explorations in adult development.* New York: Springer-Verlag.

Gibson, F. (1987). *Report on the reminiscence project in the Coleraine, Ballymoney and Moyle Unit of Management of the Northern Health and Social Services Board.* Coleraine, Northern Ireland: University of Ulster.

Gibson, F. (1994). What can reminiscence contribute to people with dementia? In J. Bornat (Ed.), *Reminiscence reviewed perspectives, evaluations and achievements* (46–60). Buckingham: Open University Press.

Gibson, F. (1998a). *Reminiscence and recall: A guide to good practice.* London: Age Concern.

Gibson, F. (1998b). Reflections on the contribution of reminiscence work to staff development. In J. Bornat, P. Chamberlayne, & L. Chant (Eds.), *Reminiscence: practice, skills and settings* (10–14). London: Centre for Biography in Social Policy, University of East London.

Gibson, F. (2000a). *The Reminiscence Trainer's Pack.* London: Age Concern.

Gibson, F. (2000b). Reminiscence and museums. *Museum Ireland, 10,* 26–35.

Gibson, F., Marley, J., & McVicker, H. (2000). Through the past to the person, In S. Benson (Ed.). *Person-centred care: Creative approaches to individualized care for people with dementia (11–12).* London: Hawker Publications Ltd. 18–19.

Gill, A.A. (2003). My father's got Alzheimer's. *Sunday Times Magazine, 5,* 6–7 Magazine.

Golden, S., & Perlstein, S. (2003). *Legacy works: Transforming memory into visual art.* New York: Elders Share the Arts.

Goldwasser, A., & Auerbach, S. (1996). Audience-based reminiscence therapy intervention: Effects on the morale and attitudes of nursing home residents and staff. *Journal of Mental Health and Aging, 2*(2), 101–104.

Gotell, E., Brown, S., & Ekman, S. (2002). Caregiver singing and background music in dementia care. *Western Journal of Nursing Research, 24*(2), 195–216.

Grayson, P., Lubin, B., & Whitlock, R.V. (1995). Comparison of depression in the community-dwelling and assisted-living elderly. *Journal of Clinical Psychology, 51*(1), 18–21.

Greenspan, H. (1999). *On listening to Holocaust survivors: Recounting and life history.* Westport, CT: Praeger Publishers.

Habermas, T., & Bluck, S. (2000). Getting a life: The emergence of life story in adolescence. *Psychological Bulletin, 126*(5), 749–769.

Haight, B.K. (1991). Reminiscing: The state of the art as a basis for practice. *International Journal of Aging and Human Development, 33*(1), 1–32.

Haight, B.K. (1998). Use of the life review/life storybooks in families with Alzheimer's disease. In P. Schweitzer (Ed.), *Reminiscence in dementia care* (85–90). London: Age Exchange.

Haight, B.K., & Burnside, I. (1993). Reminiscence and life review: Explaining the differences. *Archives of Psychiatric Nursing, 7*(2), 91–98.

Haight, B.K., Coleman, P. and Lord, K. (1995). The linchpins of a successful life review: Structure, evaluation and individuality. In B. Haight, & J. Webster, (Eds.), *The art and science of reminiscence* (179–192). Washington, DC: Taylor and Francis.

Haight, B.K., & Hendrix, S. (1995). An integrated review of reminiscence. In B.K. Haight & J.D. Webster (Eds.). *The art and science of reminiscence* (3–21). Washington, DC: Taylor and Francis.

Haight, B.K., & Hendrix, S. (1998). Suicidal intent/life satisfaction: Comparing the life stories of older women. *Suicide and Life Threatening Behavior, 28*(3), 272–284.

Haight, B.K., Michel, Y., & Hendrix, S. (1998). Life review. Preventing despair in newly relocated nursing home residents short and long-term effects. *International Journal of Aging and Human Development, 47*(2), 119–142.

Haight, B.K., Michael, Y., & Hendrix, S. (2000). The extended effects of the life review in nursing home residents. *International Journal of Aging and Human Development, 50*(2), 151–168.

Haight, B.K., & Webster, J.D. (Eds.), (1995). *The art and science of reminiscing: Theory, research, methods, and applications.* Washington, DC: Taylor and Francis.

Hamilton, N., & Tesh, A.S. (2002). The North Carolina Eden alternative coalition: Facilitating environmental transformation. *Journal of Gerontological Nursing, 28*(3), 14–22.

Hansebo, G., & Kihlgren, M. (2000). Patient life stories and current situations as told by carers in nursing home wards. *Clinical Nursing Research, 9*(3), 260–279.

Hargrave, T. (1994). Using video life reviews with older adults. *Journal of Family Therapy, 16*(3), 259–268.

Harris, P.B. (2002). (Ed.). *The person with Alzheimer's disease. Pathways to understanding and experience.* Baltimore: The Johns Hopkins University Press.

Heaney, S. (2001). *Electric light.* London: Faber & Faber Ltd.

Help the Aged. (1981). *Recall.* London: Author.

Henderson, C.S. & Andrews, N. (1998). Partial views: An Alzheimer's journal. Dallas: Southern Methodist University Press.

Hendricks, T. (1995). (Ed.) *The meaning of reminiscence and life review.* New York: Baywood Publishing Co.

Hendrix, S., & Haight, B.K. (2002). A continued review of reminiscence. In J.D. Webster, & B.K. Haight (Eds.), *Critical advances in reminiscence work: From theory to applications* (3–29). New York: Springer-Verlag.

Herbert, R., Levesque, L., Versina, J., et al. (2003). Efficacy of a psychoeducational group program for caregivers of demented persons living at home: A randomized controlled trial. *Journal of Gerontology, 58B*(1), 558–567.

Hirsch, C., & Mouratoglou, V. (1999). Life review of an older adult with memory difficulties. *International Journal of Geriatric psychiatry, 14*(4), 261–265.

Holland, C.A., & Rabbitt, P.M.A. (1991). Ageing memory: Use versus impairment. *British Journal of Psychology, 82,* 29–38.

Hongo, G. (1995). Volcano. In J. McConkey (Ed.), *Anatomy of memory* (299–309). New York: Oxford University Press.

Hoover, R.C. Healing gardens and Alzheimer's disease. *Journal of Alzheimer's Disease, March/April,* 1–9.

Hossack, A., & Standidge, K. (1993). Using an imaginary scrapbook for neurolinguistic programming in the aftermath of a clinical depression: A case history. *Gerontologist, 33*(2), 265–268.

Hunt, L., Marshall, M.T., & Rowlings, C. (Eds.). (1997). Past trauma in late life. In *European perspectives on therapeutic work with older people.* London: Jessica Kingsley Publishers.

Hunt, L. & Robbins, I. (2001). The long-term consequences of war: The experiences of World War II. *Aging and Mental Health, 5*(20), 183–190.

Hussain, F., & Raczka, R. (1997). Life story work for people with learning disabilities. *British Journal of Learning Disabilities, 25*(2), 73–76.

Ingersoll-Dayton, B., Schroefer, T., Pryce, J., & Waarala, C. (2003). Enhancing relationships in nursing homes through empowerment. *Social Work, 48*(3), 420–423.

Innes, A. (2003). *Dementia care mapping: Applications across cultures.* Baltimore: Health Professions Press.

Ives, E.D. (1995). *The tape-recorded interview: A manual for fieldworkers in folklore and oral history.* Knoxville, TN: University of Tennessee Press.

Jenny, S., & Oropeza, M. (1993). *Memories in the making: A program of creative art expression for Alzheimer's patients.* Orange County, CA: Alzheimer's Association.

Kadushin, A. (1972). *The social work interview.* New York: Columbia.

Kadushin, A., & Harkness, D. (2002). *Supervision in social work.* New York: Columbia University Press.

Kaminsky, M. (1988). All that our eyes have witnessed: Memories of a living history workshop in South Bronx. *Journal of Gerontological Social Work, 12*(3–4), 101–109.

Kearsley, G., & Furlong, M. (1988). *Computers for kids over sixty: Opening new windows on the world.* La Jolla, CA: Park Row.

Kent, R. (1999). *The wisdom tree: A new way to write the past for the future.* Clarkesville, GA: Wisdom Keeper.

Kenyon, G.M. (1996). Ethical issues in ageing and biography. *Ageing and Society, 16,* 659–675.

Kenyon, G.M., De Vries, B., & Clark, P. (2001). *Narrative gerontology: Theory, research and practice.* New York: Springer-Verlag.

Killick, J. (1994). There's so much to hear when you stop and listen to individual voices. *Journal of Dementia Care, 2*(5), 16–17.

Killick, J. (1997). *You are words.* London: Journal of Dementia Care.

Killick, J., & Allan, K. (2001). *Communication and the care of people with dementia.* Philadelphia: Open University Press.

Killick, J., & Cordonnier, C. (2000). *Openings.* London: Journal of Dementia Care.

Kimble, M.A., McFadden, S.H., Ellor, J.W., & Seeber, J.J. (Eds.). (1995). *Aging, spirituality and religion: A handbook.* Minneapolis, MN: Augsburg Fortress Press.

Kitwood, T. (1997). *Dementia reconsidered.* Buckingham: Open University Press.

Kitwood, T., & Benson, S. (Eds.). (1995). *The new culture of dementia care.* London: Hawker Publications Ltd.

Kitwood, T., & Bredin, K. (1992). Towards a theory of dementia care: Personhood and well being. *Ageing and Society, 12,* 269–287.

Kivnick, H., & Murray, S. (2001). Life strengths interview guide. *Journal of Gerontological Social Work, 34*(4), 7–32.

Koch, K. (1977). *I never told anybody: Teaching poetry writing in a nursing home.* New York: Random House.

Koffman, S. (2000). *Structured life reminiscence and gestalt life review: Group treatment of older adults for later life adjustment.* Washington, DC: Taylor and Francis.

Kotre, J. (1995). *White gloves: How we create ourselves through memory.* New York: Simon & Schuster.

Krell, F.F. (1990). *Of memory, reminiscence and writing.* Indianapolis, IN: Indianna University Press.

Kropf, N., & Tandy, C. (1998). Narrative therapy with older clients: The use of a "meaning-making" approach. *Clinical Gerontologist, 18*(4), 3–16.

Kunz, J. (2002a). Targeted reminiscence interventions for older adults with dementia. *Journal of Geriatric Psychiatry, 35*(1), 25–49.

Kunz, J. (2002b). Integrating reminiscence and life review techniques with brief, cognitive behavioral therapy. In J.D. Webster, & B.K. Haight (Eds.), *Critical advances in reminiscence work. From theory to applications* (275–288). New York: Springer-Verlag.

Kurokawa, Y. (1998). Couple reminiscence with Japanese dementia patients and their spouses. In P. Schweitzer (Ed.), *Reminiscence in dementia care*. London: Age Exchange.

Larkin, P. (1964). *Love songs in age*. London: Faber & Faber Ltd.

Lederach, J.P. (1997). *Remember and change*. Conference paper, 35–54. Enniskillen, Northern Ireland: Fermanagh District Partnership Board.

Levine, L. (1996). Things were different then. *Social Work in Health Care, 22*(4), 73–88.

Lewis, C.N. (1971). The adaptive value of reminiscing in old age. *Journal of Geriatric Psychiatry, 6*, 117–121.

Lewis, H. (1992). *A time to speak*. Belfast, Northern Ireland: Blackstaff Press.

Lieberman, M.A. and Falk, J.M. (1971). The remembered past as a source of data for research on the life cycle. *International Journal of Aging and Human Development, 14*, 132–141.

Lo Gerfo, M. (1980). Three ways of reminiscence in theory and practice. *International Journal of Aging and Human Development, 12*(1), 39–48.

Lutjeans, P. (1990). Its about questions not answers. *Memories in the making '90*. Orange County, CA: Alzheimer's Association.

Lutz, S., & Haller, J. (1996). *Seniors and children: Building bridges together*. Washington, DC: National Council on Aging.

Lynn, L.E. (2001). A shadow over this day. *Social Service Administration Magazine*. Chicago: University of Chicago Press.

Mace, N.L., Rabins, P.V., Castleton, B.A., McEwen, & Meredith, B. (1999). *The 36-hour day*. Baltimore: The Johns Hopkins University Press.

Manton, K.G., Cornelius, E.S., & Woodbury, E.A. (1995). Nursing home residents: A multivariate analysis of their medical, behavioral, psychosocial and service use characteristics. *Journal of Gerontology, 50A*(5), 242–251.

Martin, R. (1995). *Oral history in social work*. New York: Sage Publications.

Mastoris, S. (2003). In small things remembered: Life laundry, bereavement, and significant artifacts. *Reminiscence, 2*, 11–13.

Matthiesen, V. (1989). Guilt and grief when daughters place mothers in nursing homes. *Journal of Gerontological Nursing, 15*(7), 11–15.

McAdams, D.P. (1993). *Stories we live by: Personal myths and making of the self*. New York: William Morrow.

McCartney, K. (2001). *Technology in the service of reminiscence: The experience of the people's history initiative. Unpublished conference paper, UK Reminiscence Network*. London: Age Exchange.

McConkey, J. (1996). *The anatomy of memory: An anthology*. Oxford, England: Oxford University Press.

McCormack, B. (2003). A conceptual framework for person-centred practice with older people. *International Journal of Nursing Practice, 9*, 202–209.

McCourt, F. (1996). *Angela's ashes: A memoir of childhood*. New York: HarperCollins.

McCourt, F. (1999). *'Tis: A memoir*. New York: Touchstone.

McDonough, A. (1994). *The golden stage*. Portland, OR: ArtAge Publications.

McGowan, T. (1994). Mentoring reminiscence: A conceptual and empirical analysis. *International Journal of Aging and Human Development, 39*(4), 321–336.

McKee, K., Wilson, F., Elford, H., et al. (2003). Evaluating the impact of reminiscence on the quality of life of older people. *ESRC Report.* Sheffield, England: University of Sheffield.

McKinlay, P. (2001). *The spiritual dimension of ageing.* London: Jessica Kingsley Publishers.

McPhillips, J., & McCartney, K. (2002). *People's history: Using COMMA in community education.* Unpublished conference paper. Belfast, Northern Ireland: Northern Ireland Reminiscence Network.

Meacham, J.A. (1995). Reminiscing as a process of social construction. In B.K. Haight & J.H. Webster (Eds.), *The art & science of reminiscing: Theory, research, methods & applications* (37–48). Washington, DC: Taylor & Francis.

Menec, V. (2003). The relation between everyday activities and successful aging: A six year longitudinal study. *Journal of gerontology, 58B*(2), 574–582.

Mental Health Testimony Archive (1998). *National Life Story Collection.* London: British Library Publications.

Mere, R. (1995). Arthos Wales: Working in hospitals. In J. Bornat (Ed.), *Reminiscence reviewed: Perspectives, evaluations and achievements* (126–134). Buckingham, England: Open University Press.

Merriam, S.B. (1980). The concept and function of reminiscence: A review of the research. *Gerontologist, 20,* 604–08.

Merriam, S.B. (1993). Butler's life review: How universal is it? *International Journal of Aging and Human Development, 37*(3), 163–175.

Merriam S., & Cross, L. (1982). Adulthood and reminiscence: A descriptive study. *Educational Gerontology, 8,* 275–290.

Miesen, B. (1992). Attachment theory and dementia. In G. Jones & B.M. Miesen (Eds.), *Care-giving in dementia* (38–56). New York: Routledge.

Miller, B. (2001). Functional correlates of musical and visual ability in fronto-temporal dementia. *British Journal of Psychiatry, 176,* 458–463.

Miller, B., Snyder, L. (2001). *Fragments of genius.* London: British Brodcasting Corporation TV Program, 11 March 2001.

Miller, E.J., & Gwynne, G.V. (1972). *A life apart.* London: Routledge.

Mills, M. (1998). *Narrative identity and dementia.* Brookfield, VT: Ashgate Publishing Co.

Mills, M., & Coleman, P. (1994). Nostalgic memories in dementia: A case study. *International Journal of Aging and Human Development, 38*(3), 203–219.

Mills, M., & Coleman, P. (2002). Using reminiscence & life review interventions with older people: A psychodynamic approach. *Journal of Geriatric Psychiatry, 35*(1), 63–76.

Moberg, D.O. (Ed.). (2001). *Aging and spirituality: Spiritual dimensions of aging theory, research, practice and policy.* Binghamton, NY: The Haworth Press.

Molinari, V., Cully, J.A., & Kendjelic, E.M. (2001). Reminiscence and its relationship to attachment and personality in geropsychiatric patients. *International Journal of Aging and Human Development, 52*(3), 173–184.

Molinari, V., & Reichlin, R. (1985). Life review reminiscence in the elderly: A review of the literature. *International Journal of Aging and Human Development, 20,* 81–92.

Moody, H.R. (1986). The meaning of life and the meaning of old age. In T.R. Cole & S.A. Gadow (Eds.), *What does it mean to grow old* (9–40). Durham, NC: Duke University Press.

Moody, H.R. (1988). Twenty-five years of the life review: Where did we come from? Where are we going. *Journal of Gerontological Social Work, 12*, 7–21.

Moody, H.R. (1995). Mysticism. In M.A. Kimble, S.H. McFadden, J.W. Ellor, & J.J. Seeber (Eds.), *Aging, spirituality and religion: A handbook* (75–120). Minneapolis, MN: Augsburg Fortress Press.

Moody, H.R. (2002). *Concepts and controversies.* Thousand Oaks, CA: Sage Publications.

Moody, H.R., & Carroll. (1997). *The five stages of the soul.* New York: Random House.

Moody, L.E. & Small, B.J. (2002). Advance directives preferences of functionally and cognitively impaired nursing home residents. *Journal of Applied Gerontology, 21*(1), 103–118.

Morrison, T. (1984). Memory, creation and writing. *Thought: A Journal of Culture and Ideas, 59,* 235.

Mosher-Ashley, P.M., & Barrett, P.W. (1997). *A life worth living: Practical strategies for reducing depression in older adults.* Baltimore: Health Professions Press.

Moullas, R., Laforestrie, R., Lizotte, A., & Berthaux, P. (1987). Artistic workshops in a geriatric service: The medical point of view. *Ageing well conference abstract,* No 56, 15. Brighton, England: European Region of International Association of Gerontology.

Nelson-Jones, R. (1993). *Practical counseling and helping skills.* New York: Cassell Publishing.

Nomura, T. (1997). The multidimensional effects of reminiscence and life review groups for persons with dementia. *Widening horizons in dementia care conference proceedings.* 131–132. London: Age Exchange.

Nomura, T. (1998). *Reminiscence and life review: Theory and skill.* Tokyo: Chuuouki.

Nuttall, S., & Coetzee, C. (Eds.). (1998). *Negotiating the past: The making of memory in South Africa.* Oxford: Oxford University Press.

Ohta, Y., & Agari, I. (1999). Japanese reminiscence functions scale for older adults. *Reminiscence and life review conference papers.* Superior, WI: University of Wisconsin—Superior.

Osborn, C. (1994). *The reminiscence handbook.* London: Age Exchange.

Parker, R.G. (1995). Reminiscence: A continuity framework. *Gerontologist, 35,* 515–525.

Parker, R.G. (1999). Reminiscence as continuity: Comparison of young and older adults. *Journal of Clinical Geropsychology, 5*(2), 147–157.

Pear, T.H. (1922). *Remembering and forgetting.* London: Methuen Publishing Ltd.

Perlman, H.H. (1989). *The dancing clock and other childhood memories.* Chicago: Academy Chicago Publishers.

Perlstein, S., & Bliss J. (2003). *Generating community: Intergenerational partnerships through the expressive arts.* New York: Elders Share the Arts.

Petrukowicz, M., & Johnson, M. (1991). Using life histories to individualize nursing home staff attitudes toward residents. *Gerontologist, 31,* 102–106.

Pilkington, D. (1996). *Follow the rabbit-proof fence.* Brisbane, Australia: University of Queensland Press.

Pillemer, K., Hegeman, C.R., Albright, B., & Henderson, C. (1998). Building bridges between families and nursing home staff. *Gerontologist, 38,* 499–503.

Polk, P. (1996). Senile. In M. Goldsmith, *Hearing the voice of people with dementia.* London: Jessica Kingsley Publishers.

Pollock, A. (2001). *Designing gardens for people with dementia.* Stirling, Scotland: University of Stirling Dementia Services Development Centre.

Porter, E. (1998). Gathering our stories, claiming our lives: Seniors' life story books facilitate life review, integration, and celebration. *Journal of Developmental Disabilities, 6*(1), 44–59.

Post, S.G. (1995). *Ethics and dementia: The moral challenge of Alzheimer's disease.* Baltimore: Johns Hopkins University Press.

Post, S.G., & Whitehouse, P.J. (1995) Guidelines on ethics of the care of people with Alzheimer's disease—a clinical summary. *Journal of the American Geriatric Society, 43,* 1423–1429.

Proust, M. (1981). *Remembrance of things past.* New York: Alfred A. Knopf.

Puentes, W. (2000). Using social reminiscence to teach therapeutic communication skills. *Geriatric Nursing, 21*(6), 315–318.

Qualls, S.H. & Abelas, N. (Eds.). (2000). *Psychology & the aging revolution: How we adapt to longer life.* Washington: American Psychological Association.

Rabins, P.V., Blacker, D., Bland, W., et al. (1997). Practice guideline for the treatment of patients with Alzheimer's disease and other dementias of late life. *American Journal of Psychiatry, 154,* 1–39.

Radebaugh, T.S., & Ward-Robinson, J. (2002). Cultural diversity and Alzheimer's disease. *Alzheimer's Disease and Associated Disorders, 16*(Supplement 2), S41–S42.

Randall, W. (1999). Narrative intelligence and the novelty of our lives. *Journal of Aging Studies, 13*(1), 11–28.

Ray, R. (1999). Social influences on the older woman's life story. *Generations, 23*(4), 56–62.

Read, P. (1999). *A rape of the soul so profound: The return of the stolen generation.* London: Allen and Unwin.

Read, P. (2000). *Belonging.* Cambridge, England: Cambridge University Press.

Rentz, C. (2002). Memories in the making: Outcome-based evaluation of an art program for individuals with dementia illnesses. *American Journal of Alzheimer's Disease, 17*(3), 175–181.

Ritchie, D. (1995). *Doing oral history.* New York: Twayne Publishers.

Roberts, J. (2002). Flesh on flesh. In A. Capstick & L. Fox (Eds.), *Each person is special.* Bradford, England: University of Bradford.

Rogers, C.R. (1969). *On becoming a person.* Boston: Houghton Mifflin.

Romaniuk, M., & Romaniuk, J.G. (1981). Looking back: An analysis of reminiscence functions and triggers. *Experimental Aging Research, 7,* 315–336.

Ronch, J.L., & Goldfield, J. (2003). Mental wellness in aging. Baltimore: Health Professions Press.

Rose, L., & Schlingensiepen, S. (2001). Meeting in the dark: A musical journey of discovery. *Journal of Dementia Care, 9*(2), 20–23.

Rose, S. (1992). *The making of memory: From molecules to mind.* New York: Doubleday.

Rose, S. (2001). *Video portrait: Recognizing the whole person.* Stirling, Scotland: University of Stirling Dementia Services Development Centre.

Ross, H. (1990). Lesson of life. *Geriatric Nursing, 11,* 274–275.

Rossetti, C. (1984). Remember. In C.H. Sisson (Ed.), *Christina Rossetti: Selected poems.* Manchester, England: Carcanet Press.

Rubin, D.C. (Ed.). (1986). *Autobiographical memory.* Cambridge, England: Cambridge University Press.

Rubin, D.C. (1996). *Remembering our past: Studies in autobiographical memory.* Cambridge, England: Cambridge University Press.

Rubin, D.C., Wetzler, S.E., & Nebes, R.D. (1986). Autobiographical memory across the lifespan. In D.C. Rubin (Ed.), *Autobiographical memory.* (202–201) Cambridge, England: Cambridge University Press.

Ryan, T., & Walker, R. (1997). *Life story work.* London: British Agencies for Adoption and Fostering.

Sabat, S.R., & Harre, R. (1992). The construction and deconstruction of self in Alzheimer's disease. *Ageing and Society, 12,* 443–61.

Sabat, S.R. (2001a). Surviving manifestations of selfhood in Alzheimer's disease. *Dementia, 1*(1), 25–36.

Sabat, P. (2001b). *The experience of living with Alzheimer's disease: Life through a tangled veil.* Malden, MA: Blackwell Publishers.

Sandford, L.T. (1990). *Strong at the broken places.* London: Virago Press.

Sands, T. (2002). *Song writing with young offenders.* Reno, Nevada: (London: BBC radio program).

Saul, S. (1983). (Ed.). Group work with the elderly. *Social work with groups. 5,2,* New York: Haworth Press.

Schwartz, W. (1971). On the use of groups in social work practice. In T. Berman-Rossi (Ed.), *The collected writings of William Schwartz* (309–323). Itasca, Illinois: F.E. Peacock Publishers Inc.

Schweitzer, P. (Ed.). (1998). *Reminiscence in dementia care.* London: Age Exchange.

Schweitzer, P. (2002). *Age Exchange: The story so far 1982–2002.* London: Age Exchange.

Sherman, E. (1981). *Counseling the aging: An integrative approach.* New York: Free Press.

Sherman, E. (1991a). *Reminiscence and the self in old age.* New York: Springer-Verlag.

Sherman, E. (1991b). Reminiscentia: Cherished objects as memorabilia in late-life reminiscence. *International Journal of Aging and Human Development, 38,* 89–100.

Shopes, L. (2002). *Making sense of oral history.* Retrieved November 14, 2002, from http://www.historymatters.gmu.edu/mse/oral

Shulman, L. (1999). *The skills of helping individuals and groups.* Istaca, Illinois: Peacock.

Sim, R. (1997). *Reminiscence: Social and creative activities with older people in care.* Bicester, England: Winslow Press.

Slim, H., & Thompson, P. (1993). *Listening for a change: Oral testimony and development.* London: Panos Institute.

Smyth, M. (2003). Truth, partial truth and irreconcilable truth: Reflections on the prospects of truth recovery in Northern Ireland. *Smith College Studies in Social Work, 73*(2), 205–225.

Snyder, L. (1999). *Speaking our minds: Personal reflections from individuals with Alzheimer's disease.* New York: Freeman.

Sokolovsky, M. (1996). Case study as a research method to study life histories of elderly people: Some ideas and a case study of a case study. *Journal of Ageing Studies, 10*(4), 281–294. New York: W.H. Freeman and Co.

Soltys, F., & Coats, L. (1994). The Solcos model: Facilitating reminiscence therapy. *Journal of Gerontological Nursing*, 11–16.

Sparks, N. (1996). *The notebook.* New York: Warner Books.

Spector, A., Orrell, M., Davies, S., & Woods, B. (2000). Reminiscence therapy for
dementia: A review of the evidence for its effectiveness. *Cochrane Library*, 4. Oxford, England: Cochrane Library.

Spector, A., Orrell, M., Davies, S., & Woods, B. (2001). Can reality orientation be
rehabilitated? Development and piloting of an evidence-based programme of
cognition-based therapies for people with dementia. *Neuropsychological Rehabilitation, 11,* 377–397.

Spector, A., Thorgrimsen, L., & Orrell, M. (2001). A randomized controlled trial
(RCT) investigating an evidence-based therapy programme for dementia. *International Psychogeriatrics, 13,* 145–148.

Stafford, K.R. (1986). A walk in early May. In K.R. Stafford (Ed.), *Having everything right.* Lewiston: Confluence Press.

Stock Whitaker, D. (2000). *Using groups to help people.* New York: Routledge.

Tabourne, C.E.S. (1995a). The life review program as an intervention for an older
adult newly admitted to a nursing home facility: A case study. *Journal of Therapeutic Recreation, 29*(3), 228–236.

Tabourne, C.E.S. (1995b). The effects of a life review program on disorientation,
social interaction and self-esteem of nursing home residents. *International Journal of Aging and Human Growth and Development, 41*(3), 251–266.

Taft, L.B. & Nehrke, M.F. (1990). Reminiscence, life review and ego integrity in
nursing home residents. *International Journal of Aging and Human Development,
30*(3), 189–200.

Tappen, R.M. (1997). *Interventions for Alzheimer's disease.* Baltimore: Health Professions Press.

Teri, L., & McCurry, S.M. (1994). Psychosocial therapies. In C. Coffey & J. Cum-
mings (Eds.), *Textbook of geriatric neuropsychiatry* (662–682). Washington, DC:
American Psychiatric Press.

Thomas, R.S. (1995). *No truce with the furies.* Newcastle-upon-Tyne, England:
Bloodaxe Books.

Thomson, A. (1997). From memory maps to cyberspace. Report on the annual
conference of the Oral History Society Association, Philadelphia, 10–13 Octo-
ber 1996. *Oral History, 25*(1), 21–24.

Thomson, A. (1998). Anzac memories: Putting popular memory theory into practice in Australia. *The oral history reader* (300–310). London: Routledge.

Thompson, P. (2000). *The voice of the past.* Oxford, England: Oxford University Press.

Thorgrimsen, L., Kennedy, L., Douglas, C., Garcia, C., & Bender, M. (2002). The
group activity form. *Journal of Occupational Therapy, 65* (6), 283–287.

Thorgrimsen, L., Schweitzer, P., & Orrell, M. (2002). Evaluating reminiscence for
people with dementia: A pilot study. *The Arts in Psychotherapy, 29*(2), 93–97.

Thornton, S., & Brotchie, J. (1987). Reminiscence: A critical review of the empirical literature. *British Journal of Clinical Psychology, 26,* 93–111.

Tice, C. (1999). Life review: A celebration of strengths. In International Institute
of Reminiscence and Life Review, *Reminiscence & life review: Selected conference papers and proceedings* (141–143). Superior, Wisconsin: University of Wisconsin.

Tietze, R.B. (1998). Oral history. *Activities, adaptation and aging, 23*(1), 39–59.

Tobin, S. (1999). *Preservation of self in the oldest years.* New York: Springer-Verlag.

Tuokko, P., MacCourt, P., & Heath, Y. (1999). Home alone with dementia. *Aging and Mental Health, 3*(1), 23–27.

Vaughn, S., & Kinnier, R. (1996). Psychological effects of a life review intervention for persons with HIV disease. *Journal of Counseling and Development, 75*(2), 115–123.

Viney, L. (1993). *Life stories: Personal construct therapy with the elderly.* New York: John Wiley & Sons.

Viney, L., Benjamin, Y., & Preston, C. (1995). Mourning and reminiscence: Parallel psychotherapeutic processes for elderly people. In J. Hendrick (Ed.), *The meaning of reminiscence and life review* (205–215). Amityville, NY: Baywood Publishing.

Vorenberg, B.L. (1999). *Senior theatre connections.* Portland, OR: ArtAge Publications.

Waite, T. (1994). *Taken on trust.* London: Coronet.

Walmsley, J. (1995). *Oral History, 23*(1), 71–77.

Warnock, M. (1987). *Memory.* London: Faber & Faber Ltd.

Watt, L.M., & Cappeliez, P. (2000). Integrative and instrumental reminiscence therapy: Theoretical models and intervention strategies. *Aging and Mental Health, 4,* 166–177.

Watt, L.M., & Wong, P.T. (1990). A taxonomy of reminiscence and therapeutic implications. *Journal of Gerontological Social Work, 16,* 37–57.

Webb, N.B. (Ed.). (1993). *Helping bereaved children: A handbook for practitioners.* New York: Guilford Press.

Webster, J.D. (1993). Construction and validation of the reminiscence functions scale. *Journal of Gerontology: Psychological Sciences, 48*(5), 256–262.

Webster, J.D. (1997). The reminiscence functions scale: A replication. *International Journal of Aging and Human Development, 44*(2), 137–148.

Webster, J.D. (1998). Attachment styles, reminiscence functions, and happiness in young and elderly adults. *Journal of Aging Studies, 12*(3), 315–330.

Webster, J.D. (2002). Reminiscence functions in adulthood: Age, race and family dynamics correlates. In J.D. Webster & B.K. Haight (Eds.), *Critical advances in reminiscence work: From theory to applications* (140–152). New York: Springer-Verlag.

Webster, J.D., & Cappeliez, P. (1993). Reminiscence and autobiographical memory: Complementary contexts for cognitive aging research. *Developmental Review, 13,* 54–91.

Webster, J.D., & Haight, B.K. (1995). Memory lane milestones: Progress in reminiscence definition and classification. In B.K. Haight and J.D. Webster (Eds.), *The art and science of reminiscing: Theory, research methods and applications* (273–286). Washington, DC: Taylor and Francis.

Webster, J.D., & Haight, B.K. (Eds.). (2002). *Critical advances in reminiscence work: From theory to applications.* New York: Springer-Verlag.

Webster, J.D., & McCall, M.E. (1999). Reminiscence functions across adulthood: A replication and extension. *Journal of Adult Development, 6,* 73–85.

Weishaar, K. (1999). The visual life review as a therapeutic art framework with the terminally ill. *Arts in Psychotherapy, 26*(3), 173–184.

Weiss, J. (1995). Cognitive therapy and life review therapy: Theoretical and therapeutic implications for mental health counselors. *Journal of Mental Health Counseling, 17*(2), 157–152.

Whitehouse, P.J., Maurer, K., & Ballenger, M.A. (Eds.). (2000). *Concepts of Alzheimer's disease; Biological, clinical and cultural perspectives.* Baltimore: The Johns Hopkins University Press.

Whitfield, C. (1995). *Memory and abuse: Remembering and healing the effects of trauma.* Deerfield Beach, FL: Health Communications Inc.

Wiesel, E. (1992). *The forgotten.* Indianapolis, IN: Summit Publications.

Wink, P., & Schiff, B. (2002). To review or not to review? The role of personality and life events in life review and adaptation to older age. In J.D. Webster and B.K. Haight, (Eds.), *Critical advances in reminiscence work: From theory to application* (44–60). New York: Springer-Verlag.

Wong, P.T., & Watt, L.M. (1991). What types of reminiscence are associated with successful aging? *Psychology and Aging, 6*(2), 272–279.

Woods, R.T. (2002). Reality orientation: A welcome return? *Age and Ageing, 31,* 155–56.

Woods, R.T., & McKiernan, F. (1995). Evaluating the impact of reminiscence on older people with dementia. In B.K. Haight & J. Webster (Eds.), *Art and Science of reminiscing: Theory, research, methods and applications* (233–242). Washington, DC: Taylor and Francis.

Wooly, R.H. (2002). *Psychological information: Protecting the right to privacy.* Madison: Psychological Press.

Worden, J.W. (1996). *Children and grief.* New York: Guilford Press.

World Health Organization. (1992). *International classification of diseases,* 10th edition. Geneva: Author.

Yale, R. (1995). *Developing support groups for individuals with early-stage Alzheimer's disease: Planning, implementation, and evaluation.* Baltimore: Health Professions Press.

Yow, V.R. (1994). *Recording oral history: A practical guide for social scientists.* New York: Sage Publications.

Zarit, S.H., & Zarit, J.M. (1998). Family caregiving. In S.H. Zarit & J.M. Zarit (Eds.), *Mental disorders in older adults: Fundamentals of assessment* (290–390). New York: Guilford Press.

Zeisel, J., Hyde, J. & Shi, L. (1999). Environmental design as a treatment for Alzheimer's disease. In L. Voliar & L. Bloom-Charette (Eds.), *Enhancing the quality of life in advanced dementia* (206–222). Boston: Brunner/Matzel.

Resources

Age Exchange
11 Blackheath Village
London SE3 9LA
United Kingdom
Telephone: +44 (0) 20 8318 9105
Reminiscence projects, training, theatre, exhibitions, and publishing.
The UK Reminiscence Network and the European Reminiscence Network c/o Age
   Exchange
http://www.age-exchange.org.uk

Alzheimer's Association
919 North Michigan Avenue
Suite 100
Chicago, Illinois 60611-1676
Telephone: (800) 272-3900
http://www.alz.org

Alzheimer's Association of Orange County
Various chapter services, annual publication of *Memories in the Making* about art
Project and exhibition
2540 North Santiago Boulevard
Orange, California 92867
Telephone: (714) 283-1111
www.alzoc.org

Alzheimer's Bookshelf
Elder Books
Post Office Box 490
Forest Knolls, California 94933
Telephone: (415) 488-9002
Fax: (415) 488-4720
E-mail: elder@nbn.com

Note: This list of resources is accurate to the best of the author's knowledge. It is unlikely to
be comprehensive and does not suggest any endorsement by the author or publisher.

Alzheimer's Disease Education and Referral Center (ADEAR)
National Institute on Aging
Post Office Box 8250
Silver Spring, Maryland 20907-8250
Telephone: (800) 438-4380
Fax: (301) 587-4352
Information, advice, support, campaigning, training, and publishing
http://www.Alzheimers.org

Alzheimer's Disease International (ADI)
45/46 Lower Marsh Street
London SE1 7RG
United Kingdom
adi@alz.co.uk

Alzheimer's Society Canada
http://www.alzheimer.ca

American Art Therapy Association, Inc.
1212 Allanson Road
Mundelein, Illinois 60060
Telephone: (847) 949-6064
http://www.arttherapy.org

American Association of Homes and Services for the Aging (AAHSA)
2519 Connecticut Avenue NW
Washington, DC 20008
Telephone: (202) 783-2242
Fax: (202) 783-2255
http://www.aahsa.org

American Association of Retired Persons (AARP)
601 E Street NW
Washington, DC 20049
Telephone: (202) 434-2277
http://www.aarp.org

American Dance Therapy Association
2000 Century Plaza
Suite 108
Columbia, Maryland 21044
Telephone: (410) 997-4040
http://www.adta.org

American Music Therapy Association
8455 Colesville Road
Suite 1000
Silver Spring, Maryland 20910
Telephone: (301) 589-3300
http://www.musictherapy.org

American Society on Aging (ASA)
833 Market Street
Suite 511
San Francisco, California 944103
Telephone: (415) 974-9000
http://www.asaging.org

ArtAge Publications
Post Office Box 12271
Portland, Oregon 97212-0271
Telephone: (503) 249-1137
Bonniev@seniortheatre.com
http://www.seniortheatre.com

Association of Personal Historians
1509 S. Raitt Street #C
Santa Ana, California 92704
http://www.personalhistorians.org
An alliance of individuals and organizations that assist people to preserve
    life stories and memories through books, audiotaped interviews, videos, or
    CD-ROMs.

Center for Aging, Religion, and Spirituality
2481 Como Avenue
St. Paul, Minnesota 55108
Telephone: (651) 641-3581
http://www.aging-religion-spirituality.com
An independent graduate institution with an interfaith and multi-disciplinary
    approach to issues related to aging, religion, and spirituality. It undertakes
    education, research, and publication.

Center for Life Stories Preservation
137 Bates Avenue
St. Paul, Minnesota 55106
Telephone: (651) 774-5015
http://www.storypreservation.com

Elders Share the Arts
138 South Oxford Street
Brooklyn, New York 11217
Telephone: (718) 398-3870
http://www.elderssharethearts.org
A community arts organization and National Center for Creative Aging
    Mission and program: "Transforming memories into art" and passing on values
    and history by involving older people in life review, living history arts activities,
    intergenerational projects, story telling, other artistic projects, training in
    intergenerational and life review, arts work, and publishing.

Encore Theatre
Post Office Box 50816
Eugene, Oregon 97405
Telephone: (541) 342-1630
http://www.encoreeugene.net
E-mail: encore.theatre@iname.com

Gerontological Society of America (GSA)
1030 15th Street NW
Suite 250
Washington, DC 20005
Telephone: (202) 842-1275
Fax: (202) 842-0621
http://www.geron.org

International Institute for Reminiscence and Life Review
c/o University of Wisconsin–Superior
Center for Continuing Education/Extension
Belknap and Catlin
Post Office Box 2000
Superior, Wisconsin 54880-4500
Telephone: (715) 394-8170
http://www.reminiscenceandlifereview.org

Life Story Foundation
Post Office Box 1417
Sumas, Washington 98295-1417
Telephone: (800) 661-1141
E-mail: info@lifestory.org

National Adult Day Services Association
772 Grant Street
Suite L
Telephone: (866) 890-7357
http://www.nadsa.org

National Advisory Council on Aging
Address Locator 1908A1
Ottawa, Ontario K1A 1B4
CANADA
Telephone: (613) 957-1968

National Association of Activity Professionals (NAAP)
P.O. Box 5530
Seviervielle, Tennessee 37864
Telephone: (865) 429-0717
http://www.thenaap.com

National Association for Home Care
228 Seventh Street, SE
Washington, DC 20003
Telephone: (202) 547-7424
http://www.nahc.org

National Association of Professional Geriatric Care Managers
1604 North Country Club Road
Tucson, Arizona 85716
Telephone: (520) 881-8008
http://www.caremanagers.org

National Genealogical Society
4527 17th Street North
Arlington, Virginia 22207-2399
Telephone: (703) 525-0050
http://www.ngsgenealogy.org

National Institute on Aging (NIA)
Building 31 Room 5C27
Center Drive
Bethesda, Maryland 20892
Telephone: (800) 222-2225
http://www.nia.nih.gov
Publications on aging

Reminiscence
4 Jacqueline Lane, Rye Brook
New York, New York 10573
Telephone: (914) 937-1972
E mail: familylore@aol.com

SeniorNet
An online membership organization committed to creating and supporting an
    international community of computer-using seniors. Provides a network of local
    centers for instruction and also online tuition and support, chatrooms, advice on
    equipment, and purchasing opportunities.
http://www.seniornet.org

Senior Theatre League of America
Educational Theatre Association
2343 Auburn Avenue
Cincinnati, Ohio 45219
Telephone: (513) 421-3900
http://www.seniortheatreleague.org
E-mail: Jleptak-moreau@edta.org
Undertakes publications, training and development, and an international festival
    and conference

WisdomKeeper
Post Office Box 2135
Clarksville, Georgia 30523
Telephone: (706) 754-2348
E-mail: wsdmkpr@aol.com
Founder: Rosann Kent

Index

Page numbers followed by *f* and *t* indicate figures and tables, respectively.